PUSHED TO THE EDGE

PUSHED TO THE EDGE

Teachers' Stories from the Culture Wars

SUE GRANZELLA

NEW YORK
LONDON

Published in the United States by The New Press, New York, 2026
Distributed by Two Rivers Distribution

ISBN 979-8-89385-014-7 (hc)
ISBN 979-8-89385-041-3 (ebook)

CIP data is available

The New Press publishes books that promote and enrich public discussion and understanding of the issues vital to our democracy and to a more equitable world. These books are made possible by the enthusiasm of our readers; the support of a committed group of donors, large and small; the collaboration of our many partners in the independent media and the not-for-profit sector; booksellers, who often hand-sell New Press books; librarians; and above all by our authors.

www.thenewpress.org

Composition by Westchester Publishing Services
This book was set in Garamond Premier Pro

Printed in the United States of America

10 9 8 7 6 5 4 3 2 1

For Panda Dulce
Keep shining

For my husband, John
Because—everything

CONTENTS

1

UNDER PRESSURE

This trip was off to an ominous start. The narrow road twisting through a storm-darkened canyon was littered with large chunks of rock, which a November deluge had knocked off the granite wall to my right. As I dodged debris and scanned for falling rocks, "Under Pressure" was my mental soundtrack. The song had been my anthem during my final year of teaching, that nightmarish pandemic year when my colleagues and I stared into computer screens and taught lonely children who burrowed under blankets, hugging stuffed animals.

Leaving school in March 2020, we had no idea we wouldn't return. The abrupt separation felt harsh, cruel, as if the cords that connected me to my third-grade students had been hacked through with a machete. Desperate to establish contact with them, I emailed parents in both Spanish and English, unsure which addresses were even valid, sending links to a video platform where I wanted kids to leave a check-in. We'd only used the website once; would eight-year-olds even remember how to log on? Lying in the dark late at night with my laptop, I hit "refresh" over and over, imploring the screen to yield a message. When the video greetings finally started trickling in, I wept, pulling my laptop close and peering through darkness into those young faces. It felt as if we'd each been rocketed to the moon and had found each other wandering around up there.

After months of isolation, the blistering heat of California summer ignited infernos in our forests. The friendly blue sky transformed into our enemy, a suffocating, dark orange blanket pressing down on us, sucking away the air we needed to breathe. For weeks, the air-quality app on our phones screamed, "VERY UNHEALTHY." We rarely ventured outside. In late October 2020, roaring winds toppled trees and crashed Bay Area power and internet, canceling at-home classes for a day. The next morning, my young students' big eyes and nervous chatter told me that the balances had tipped, that taut springs had snapped. Their greetings were tinged with frantic energy.

Armando offered his morning check-in.

"We have the pandemic," he began, counting off on his fingers. "And then the protests about George Floyd. The heat wave. The fires. Then the smoke and the bad air. Now the wind, and the power outage. I feel like I'm trapped in a box that is getting smaller every day."

Distressed nods bobbed across my laptop screen. They all felt trapped. So did I. But it was my job, as their teacher, to tear their box open and help them climb out.

During the spring of 2020 followed by the 2020–21 school year, the tension lodged in my body and squeezed everything it could reach. I worked late into the night, then struggled to sleep. Each day while heating my lunch, I leaned over the kitchen counter and inhaled over the ball of stress that felt like an iron shotput in my chest. I poised on the edge of adrenaline—ready to race to the library parking lot with my laptop when our Wi-Fi failed, ready to scream at my supportive husband, John, if he asked a poorly timed question, ready to Zoom with confused third graders at night when their parents messaged me for help. It was constant pressure that spawned the vigilance: We teachers needed to provide young kids with lifelines to the outside world.

Most late afternoons, I was in contract negotiations, snapping at high-level administrators as they informed us that we didn't need the support we were begging for. What I needed most was a centralized bank of lessons developed by the curriculum specialists who weren't facing students each day on Zoom. During bargaining, I behaved badly, mocking district administrators, interrupting and muttering sarcastic asides, shaking my head and spluttering anger and frustration. Often, when the clock ticked the end of my official work hours, I turned off my camera so administrators wouldn't see me storm to the fridge and gulp plum wine straight from the bottle.

If I finished prepping virtual lessons by 9:00 p.m., I'd watch MSNBC and holler at Nicolle Wallace every time she moaned about how hard it was to be teaching her kid at home.

"YOU'RE not teaching them! WE are! You're just the grown-up in the room! WE'RE DOING *EVERYTHING*!"

Silently, John would change the channel, looking for something to soothe me. Once, it was puppies romping in a field.

Sunday was my (mostly) no-work day. Scrolling through Facebook, I initially saw memes that thanked teachers, calling us heroes for springing into action, for teaching ourselves so much on the fly. But by the summer of 2020, when it was clear that most districts planned to open with distance teaching, teachers had morphed into the enemy. We were accused of selfishly lazing around the house and working short hours, of relaxing at home instead of dragging our unvaccinated selves to unventilated classrooms filled with dozens of young children incapable of keeping masks on their faces. Even John's cousin, who hadn't worked in decades and was safe at home, tweeted her scorn for teachers. She was outraged that most of us weren't eager to risk our lives.

When my school finally reopened to hybrid instruction after more than a year, I blasted "Under Pressure" on a loop every day as I drove to and from school. Lyrics about being crushed by pressure helped, even when Freddie Mercury let loose with a scream in the middle of the song. The music comforted me. At least David Bowie and Queen understood.

* * *

Eventually, I decided I was risking my life simply by staying in teaching and living with the overwhelming stress. Though my school would return to in-person instruction for the upcoming year, things would still be far from the "normal" frenzied activity of teaching and learning. So, with a mostly broken heart, I retired in June 2021 after thirty-two years in the classroom.

I still loved teaching children, but I'd been squeezed too tightly by everything else.

A year later, in June 2022, just as I was becoming capable of speaking about distance teaching without my heart racing and my stomach clenching, my school community made national news. During Pride Month, a group of Proud Boys stormed Drag Story Hour at the San Lorenzo Library, just a short walk from the Title I elementary school where I'd taught for decades.

San Lorenzo is in California's Bay Area, a region thought of nationwide as a liberal haven. I'd lived there long enough to know the political spectrum was wider than just the left, but the event left me shaken.

Aghast at the thought that some of my former students could have been in the library when the invaders struck, I felt compelled to counter the Proud Boys' message of hate. I made two large signs adorned with rainbows and glitter and sat outside the San Lorenzo Library all afternoon, where a traumatized lesbian librarian embraced me upon seeing my message of support. Local TV reporters covering the aftermath interviewed me, and I ended up on the evening news. The *San Francisco Chronicle* published an op-ed I wrote about the incident.

But I couldn't relax. There was more that needed to be said. This was bigger than one day in one library.

Curled up on the couch late at night, I read long chains of comments about the event on the sheriff department's Facebook page. Most commenters expressed support for LGBTQ+ people and were upset about the bigotry shown by the intruders. But some people kept using the words "protect children." Protecting kids is essential, but the underlying message from those commenters was that kids need to be "protected" from exposure to anyone not in the majority. They really only wanted to "protect" straight, white, cisgender children.

I knew about Florida's "Don't Say Gay" law that had passed early in 2022, prohibiting classroom discussion of sexual orientation and gender identity for many students in public schools. Governor Ron DeSantis said teaching kindergarten-age kids that "they can be whatever they want to be" was "inappropriate" for children.[1] It was pretty routine to hear scary education news from Texas, too, like the passage of Senate Bill 3, the "Classroom Censorship Law." That 2021 legislation prohibited specific concepts from being taught or incorporated into courses, including those related to race, gender, and systemic oppression.[2]

I'd also been reading about bans of something called Critical Race Theory (CRT) in states where leaders were unwilling to acknowledge our country's racist history. Closer to home, I read about two California teachers who were harassed by people from around the United States over their leadership of an LGBTQ+ student club. They were eventually cleared of any wrongdoing, but by then they had already quit, done in by the abuse.

And this was in California. In 2022, many people likely were aware of education culture wars in Florida and Texas, and viewed those battlegrounds as outliers. But was it possible that "Don't Say Gay" and bans on CRT were also on their way here? It would mean something very different if the attack on public education was happening in the state long considered the refuge of liberals, the pinnacle of acceptance and tolerance.

And it certainly was possible; California is definitely not uniformly liberal. In parts of the Sierra Nevada mountain range and in remote forestland near the Oregon border, there are billboards welcoming visitors to the "State of Jefferson," the utopian dream of ultraconservatives who want to secede from the Golden State. It was California that gave us Ronald Reagan and Richard Nixon. In 2016, a modern-day Ku Klux Klan rally resulted in a counterprotester being stabbed with a flagpole topped by an American eagle. It happened in Anaheim, the home of Disneyland, known as "the happiest place on earth."

But California is also where striking student activists ignited the ethnic studies movement in 1968. It's where over ten thousand people joined Cesar Chavez in marching for farmworkers' rights, and where Oakland's Black Panther Party challenged police brutality and distributed free food. It was the Golden State that gave rise to 1969's Summer of Love.

So if Florida was the canary in the coal mine of nascent culture wars, California would be the disaster siren, screaming a state of emergency.

If it was happening here, people needed to know. So I decided to find out. Though I'm retired, I'll forever be a teacher, and teachers are wired to stand up for kids. If educators are harassed for supporting the broad spectrum of young people who fill our public schools, kids are the ones who will be most harmed.

So I made a plan. I would embark on a road trip in my home state of California and see if there were public school teachers and librarians who were early casualties of the education culture wars. I'd listen to them and then write their stories, so others would know what was happening to the very same educators who'd been heralded as heroes only months earlier. Some on the far right were now bludgeoning teachers after everything we'd been through during pandemic teaching, and if more people understood that, maybe they'd rise up to stop the scapegoating. And maybe teachers under fire would gain strength from knowing that others understand the injustice of how they're being treated. Maybe fewer teachers would end up leaving the classroom.

It would be my own way of protecting kids.

* * *

I arrived at the isolated motel after dark on that first long day of driving. When I opened the door in the morning, I gasped.

The whole world had cracked open. Clean blue above, soft golden valley before me, and fresh white snow capping the stark desert hills behind the motel. Gone were the granite cliffs and massive boulders, and in their place, only wide-open space and a strange, harsh beauty stretching in all directions.

There was so much room to breathe.

During the year of distance teaching, that iron shotput in my chest made me forget to expand my lungs fully as I took in air. But a year and a half later, in that desert near the canyon of rock and the river of boulders, it wasn't hard to breathe deeply. I inhaled the endless space. I thrilled to the barren landscape, absorbing it all. It excited me to be on this journey to meet fellow educators who were still in the thick of it. I wasn't the only one who'd been squeezed. Some of them were still feeling it every day.

The pandemic yanked culture wars into public education, with parents and others feeling entitled to dictate what should and shouldn't be addressed in public schools. Teachers are on the front lines of the war—some already in battle, while others have yet to be attacked. But the culture wars have affected all educators, whether they feel it yet or not. The work of a public school teacher has fundamentally changed. And unless we change how we view and treat teachers, we're on the path to destroying public education.

I wanted to learn about the pressures on teachers, about the struggles of their students, about the increasing ways that our society squeezes both of them, all of them, until they don't know how to continue. What is it like to be ordered to stop teaching real history? What's it like for Black kids to hear that their district has forbidden the teaching of CRT in an official effort to dispute the kids' lived reality? What about banned books? What information are we withholding from students, from those who will lead society in the near future? Are there districts in California telling educators, "Don't say gay," while outside the schoolroom doors, hatred and intolerance slaughter LGBTQ+ people?

I wanted to learn what teachers fear, and if they ever think of leaving education. As a thirty-two-year veteran of teaching low-income students in California public schools, I know that teaching is hard. Would I be able to stay for thirty-two years if I were just starting now?

If today's teachers can't stay for thirty-two years because they're squeezed too dry, that's a problem for all of us. If teachers don't stay in the classroom long enough to become skilled in this difficult profession, what kind of education will students get? Who will mentor new teachers if everyone else flees after just a few years? Who will teach children to expand their view of this diverse world?

So, I would set out and listen to educators' stories. Maybe by writing them down, I could help more people understand how crucial it is that we enable teachers to remain in education, so that we give students the support and the education they deserve.

On that morning in the desert, I couldn't know all that I'd learn along the way. But in the wide-open space, everything felt hopeful. So I just breathed it all in, and steered my Prius toward the snowy pass.

2

THE OTHERS

A month before waking up in the desert motel, I was in my recliner with my laptop, staring at a blank spreadsheet. I had the seedling idea for this road trip project, and plenty of time and motivation. But how would I find California educators willing to talk to me? I knew they were out there. Where were the ones with a story to tell?

I'd already written to several journalists who had published stories about California teachers and harassment from the far right. Hoping the people they had interviewed might be willing to speak with me, a fellow educator, I asked the writers to share my contact information with their sources. One journalist wrote back, promising to pass the message on. I heard nothing more.

Facebook wouldn't help much; it would connect me with people I already knew, but I wasn't interviewing friends for this project. I'd never posted on Instagram; I only had the account so I could see the artwork of a friend, the one person I followed. And establishing a following on TikTok felt impossible. Besides, having to learn to make the short videos reminded me of distance teaching.

So I decided to go old school and find people via email. After a few clicks on the California State Department of Education website, my spreadsheet was filled with links to each of the nearly one thousand school districts in the state. Then I chose scattered cities and towns on a map of California and started clicking on the corresponding school districts.

At the beginning, my actions were largely arbitrary. I'd click on a random school in some district and send emails to random teachers at that school. Depending on my mood, I sometimes contacted just one person at a site, while for other schools, I emailed every educator on the staff. I wrote to people at massive schools, smaller ones, and a few tiny ones with only four or five teachers. If I noticed that a school had a kindness club, an empathy club, a Black student union, a Muslim student union, or a GSA (gender-sexuality alliance) or rainbow club, I'd email the teacher-adviser for that club, figuring that the person might not be opposed to my message. I tried to sound personal in order to convey that I was an actual human, but I assumed that most recipients would still figure it was junk mail and delete it without reading it. That's what I used to do. A friendly sounding work email from a stranger was almost always someone trying to sell something. No, *thank* you!

In my emails, I introduced myself as a retired California teacher, naming the two districts where I'd taught. I told them I was also a writer, and then I laid it all out, explaining my project about far-right extremism and the current reality of teaching in California public schools. I spoke of the Proud Boys incident at the library near my worksite, providing links to the TV news coverage where I was featured and the op-ed I wrote for the *San Francisco Chronicle*. People would need to be certain where I stood.

I told these invisible strangers that the far right's effort to whitewash history and silence any mention of LGBTQ+ people not only was wrong but also made an already difficult job nearly impossible. To ease fears, I promised anonymity to anyone who spoke with me, and pledged to answer any question they asked me. I provided my phone number, as well as a link to my website to show I really was a writer. There was no reason to obscure my agenda going in. I wasn't a journalist striving for neutral, equal coverage of both sides; I wanted to give voice to those who couldn't speak out because they're still teaching. Besides, if I weren't clear, I might end up driving nine hours to meet someone whose mission was to inform me that white people are the afflicted ones and that queer people are going to hell.

My old college roommate was also a teacher, and she was excited about the project but unhappy that I planned to do most of the interview trips by myself.

"Does John even know where you'll be? At some house in the middle of nowhere, with someone you've never even *met*?"

Sheepish, I shrugged. "I'll be fine. I get a sense of people from how they sound in the email."

She rolled her eyes and insisted that I download the what3words app on my phone, so that if I ended up locked in the trunk of someone's car, I could text my location to loved ones.

* * *

The email process was laborious and, at first, unproductive. Some school websites let me email a large group at once, but most systems forced me to send just one at a time, often after completing four or five captchas. It was a process that I'd continue for many months after I began interviewing people.

I became obsessed with checking my email, and I repeatedly expressed uncertainty to John and to my writer buddy, Sarah.

"What if nobody answers? Or what if only one person answers? Or what if . . . ?"

Astonishingly, out of the many hundreds of emails I sent, only two people responded to tell me that they disagreed with what I was doing. Both were firm but polite, and I wrote back to each, thanking them for reading and apologizing for wasting their time. A few others wrote to me intimating they'd been targeted, before fading away after we exchanged multiple emails. With those people, it mostly seemed that they were afraid.

Not long after I sent the first round of emails, replies of willingness began trickling in.

It was time to fill in my calendar and hit the road.

* * *

Choreographing visits with all interested teachers in one massive road trip was never part of my plan. Between my months-long querying process, the variation in teachers' availability, the overwhelming size of California, and my unwillingness to be away from my husband for months, I'd known from the start that I'd be taking multiple moderate-length trips.

Before my first long road trip that would take me over the Sierras and into the desert, I scheduled a single-day meet-up. It was with Liliana, a fellow third-grade teacher in the Central Valley, not terribly far from my Bay Area home and doable in a long day. Another teacher I'd contacted had steered Liliana and me toward each other. She knew that Liliana had talked about gender with her students, and that there had been complaints. She also knew that Liliana was not backing down.

The best way to understand the geography of California's enormous Central Valley is to watch the 1970s commercial for Home Pride Butter Top Bread. In the ad, a long knife slices along the length of a raw loaf, and melted butter is poured along the trough. The butter bakes into the crust, which forms two high ridges along the long outer edges of the loaf—akin to the Sierra Nevada to the east and the Coast Ranges to the west—and a deep valley all the way down the center, rich and soft and buttery-gold. In California, the buttery part—the valley floor, with its carpet of dried summer grasses—is over 450 miles long.

Anyone who's traveled the Central Valley knows the basics: sweltering heat for half the year, dried golden hills overlooking orchards of nut trees in military formation, lush fields of bush crops, and a network of canals that carry water to Southern California. In my childhood, our rare trips south through the valley were punctuated by pungent aromas: the eight-hundred-acre cattle feedlot and my dad's favorite vacation treat, sardine sandwiches.

But as an adult driving through the Central Valley, I noticed different things. Long after Barack Obama was elected president, billboards on I-5 heading north still demanded that he produce his birth certificate. To the south, migrant farmworkers wore broad-brimmed hats and stooped low, plucking strawberries and cutting lettuce. On this journey to interview Liliana, I spotted signs posted alongside shriveled orchards, expanses of brittle trees and swirling dust from the scorched, drought-cracked earth.

The angry printed messages were consistent:

"Make America Great Again: Build more dams"
"Newsom, stop stealing our dam water!"

"Congress created this dust bowl"
"Stop dumping our water into ocean!"

During California's historic droughts in 2012–16 and 2020–22, agricultural giants pumped excessive amounts of water, and residents suffered. In some small towns, faucets spouted sand instead of water. Hundreds of Central Valley wells went dry in 2022, affecting many farmworkers who harvest the crops. Those who sweat in the sun to pick the produce I eat for lunch—there wasn't enough water for them to drink.

* * *

Eventually, I arrived at the Central Valley coffeehouse that third-grade teacher Liliana had suggested. Inside, I glimpsed a curly haired middle-aged woman watching me as I scanned the room. She was the only person there wearing a mask. Putting mine back on, I waved at her. We carried our orders to a large table away from the clinking cups and the whoosh and whine of the espresso machine.

As I nibbled on a blueberry muffin, Liliana spoke of empathy.

"When I read your writing, you talked about concern for your former students and for other kids. That's why I said yes to meeting with you. When people only stand up for something that directly affects them, it doesn't show the empathy that I think we need. We need to be concerned about others."

And with that, Liliana spun the story of her background, explaining that she was born in Mexico and came here as a toddler. Her family was very Catholic, very Mexican, and very Eurocentric.

"My mom still thinks that anything white is much better. I grew up hearing, 'Don't go out in the sun, because you'll get darker.' There was always that 'otherness.'"

I winced.

Adding to her feeling of "otherness," Liliana was one of just two Mexican farmworker kids in her school, which was mostly populated by ranchers' children. She excelled as a student but always felt like she wasn't part of the group, despite her mom's encouragement that Liliana could be "as good as the white people." She thought of herself as "the smart Mexican" but figured out, even as a child, that things weren't set up for people like her. "I realized it's *who* you know, not so much *what* you know," she told me. Since her parents were farmworkers, she felt further separated by economics and class.

"My parents are still on a very limited income. My dad is seventy-nine and still works in the fields."

I felt my eyes pop wide. When driving past Central Valley farmworkers, I had *never* imagined that one of the people I saw picking tomatoes and sweating underneath a broad-brimmed hat could be seventy-nine years old.

Liliana eventually married and had kids, following the path that a good Catholic, Mexican American woman should follow. But when she was around forty, her perspective shifted. Weary of the constraints that had squeezed her forever, she resolved to stop trying to please others. She would refuse to remain within the boundaries she no longer respected.

"I didn't really believe that white people are better than the rest of us. I don't believe in this system that says if you work hard, you're going to get where others might. My family was racist toward people darker than they are, and they were homophobic, because the Catholic Church tells you that gays are wrong."

The conviction and confidence of the woman across from me made her seem taller, more powerful, as if she were giving a speech to a crowd.

"This system makes us see everybody in different groups, and it tells us, 'Everybody is out to get you, except us.' I think 'otherness' is what makes us less empathetic."

Otherness. Empathy. A memory flashed, of a long-ago child from Yemen who came midyear into my fourth-grade class. Though the students hovered over Zayd, I felt sorry for him. He couldn't understand any of us, and we couldn't understand him. He must've felt so lost and lonely.

One day, I heard whispering during the supposedly silent reading time. I traced it to the cramped reading corner, where I found Zayd pressed up next to Dominic, their heads on the floor, jammed together under a tiny table. Their four hands clutched the cover of a book called *Zoo Animals*.

Dominic pointed to a page and said, "Giraffe."

Zayd giggled. "Zhuh-*duf*."

Then Zayd pointed to the same page. "Za-ra-fa."

Dominic repeated in a whisper. The two boys grinned and flipped the page.

Liliana is right that "otherness" quashes empathy. It works the other way, too. Empathy is the bridge from otherness to community.

* * *

The morning after Donald Trump was elected president in 2016, I faced my class of distraught third graders, almost all of them children of color, many from immigrant families. During the campaign, they'd heard Trump speak of Mexicans as criminals and rapists. They knew that his wall was supposed to keep white America safe from their parents and cousins, their *tias* and their elderly *abuelitos*.

That postelection morning, Antonio said, "I know why he wants the wall. He probably doesn't like Mexicans."

From Gabriela: "I think a lot of Americans voted for Donald Trump because they don't like Mexican people."

Then Carlos spoke.

"I know why Donald Trump won. Because all the white people don't like Mexicans."

"Otherness" is powerful, and kids absorb it whether it's spoken aloud or not. They know when they're being seen as "other," and they learn that to be "other" is to be the enemy.

* * *

In 2016, Liliana, too, had students frantic that their parents would be deported and their families would be separated. Despite the terror her students surely felt, her presence must have been a comforting one. Listening to her speak, it was impossible not to notice how much she cares about children. Again and again, she pointed out the parallels between her third-grade students and the messages she received as a child.

"I teach a bilingual class, and my students are like me. They only see a little bit of their world, because of socioeconomic factors, and even the

English language. So they have a very small worldview. I try to expand it, to build empathy."

To bring the bigger world into her classroom, she plays American Indigenous music, mariachi, and Peruvian music. During art, she'll put on instrumental music or sometimes BTS, with their upbeat messages of hope for youth and opposition to anti-Asian hate crimes. She scrutinizes the lyrics first even though most of the songs are in Korean. Sometimes Liliana won't play music at all, and they'll have conversations about how everyone's preferences are different, and why it's important to respect differences.

She explains Black Lives Matter to her Latinx students by opening with a look at "environmental equity." A video depicting different neighborhoods with varied access to resources leads to a discussion of differences her students notice between their own neighborhood and the ones in the video. They'll talk about things like proximity to grocery stores, shopping areas, and nice schools. Once her students understand the concept of inequities between environments, she explains that it's not just Latinos who often experience inequities. She talks about the country's long history of oppression of Black people by white people, and the critical struggle for civil rights.

Her students read books about Dr. Martin Luther King Jr. and Harriet Tubman. They're stunned when they learn that Ruby Bridges is still alive, and that the landmark *Loving v. Virginia* Supreme Court decision in 1967 struck down state laws banning interracial marriage in the United States.

"Just a few years ago," Liliana tells her students, "I couldn't have married my husband, because we're different."

Her diverse collection of books covers a wide range of topics, including queer people.

"One of my favorite books is called *Red: A Crayon's Story*. It's about a crayon who's blue, but he believes he's red, and he doesn't know why people call him blue when he doesn't feel that way."

Though the gentle book simply conveys that people can be their truest selves and never mentions anything about being LGBTQ+, it sparked a classroom moment in which a third grader said, "I have an uncle who dresses like a girl."

Liliana asked the child if the relative did fun things with him, and if he loved the relative. He affirmed that he did, and his classmates took the conversation in stride.

Liliana also tells her students that just as they have loved ones who are gay, she does, too, and that it's fine. To me she said, "There are Latino gay and trans people, and Black gay and trans people. It's universal. At least 8 percent of people identify as LGBTQ, and those are just the ones who feel safe self-reporting. So if 8 percent of my class is sitting there hearing the message that they are safe, that they are seen, then I'm going to keep doing it even if it's just for them."

But we both know the truth. It isn't just for them. That's not the way it works.

* * *

I often wish I could have do-overs as a teacher.

Over a wide swath of my career, my classroom approach toward mentions of orientation and identity mostly consisted of scolding children after they used "gay" as an insult. It's not that I decided *not* to raise LGBTQ+ topics with the entire class. It was simply easier to praise acts of empathy and kindness, and to teach students to be allies of anyone being bullied. I just didn't list what the focuses of the bullying might be.

For many years, whole-group discussions of same-sex partnerships and of gender identity occasionally took place in my classroom, but those conversations were not preplanned. A kid would pop out with a seemingly random question and I'd answer it, deal with a few startled yelps, and then move on before things got too uncomfortable.

Then my former students grew up.

I began seeing a few of them out and proud, on social media and in person. And while I was happy to see young people openly living who they were, I began thinking about how I'd failed them. Not that I'd done anything intentionally harmful or ever allowed hurtful comments or bullying behaviors to go uncontested. But other than putting out fires, I'd been largely silent.

And silence doesn't openly embrace the breadth of human experience. It doesn't emphasize to children that they can safely emerge from the shadows, that they are not strange or wrong, that they matter and they belong. Silence is the auditory equivalent of making things invisible.

We can't expect to raise a generation that transcends the bullying of others if we're afraid to tell kids that the others have the right to exist.

* * *

Several years ago, I was heading down the hallway to meet my third graders on the yard after recess. Running up to intercept me came Kesha and James, breathless in that unmistakable way of the victims of recess aggression.

"Diego hit James!" cried Kesha, outraged on behalf of the boy who had been her nemesis earlier in the year.

Diego approached, and I heard the three testimonies. All parties agreed on these facts:

Kesha accidentally bumped into Diego during a spirited game of four-square. Though she apologized, Diego pushed her, so she pushed him back.

Just as Diego rushed at Kesha to do more damage, James stepped between them, his hand upraised like a traffic cop's.

Facing Diego, he said, "Stop. Chill."

So Diego punched James instead.

Then Diego turned to Kesha and hollered, "You're GAY!"

At this part of the story, Kesha turned to me, indignant. "I told him I'm *not* gay, but even if I was, it wouldn't matter because I have the right to be who I want to be in this country!"

I nodded approvingly at Kesha, then glared at Diego. Once again, he had been impulsively violent with kids over *nothing*, and this time he'd added some homophobia for good measure. He spent the next recess with the principal, who called Diego's mother.

The following morning, I phoned Diego's mom and asked her to bring in the overdue permission slip for our upcoming field trip to ride the ferry to San Francisco. When she popped her head in the door, I knew right away who it was although I'd never met her. She had Diego's chubby cheeks, round hazel eyes, and placid expression. Standing close to her was a compact young woman with a short spiky haircut. I now saw Diego's "GAY!" of the previous day in a whole different light.

Later, after I'd deposited my class in the music room at the far end of the recess yard, I asked Diego to hang back with me. We sat on the ground near the playground's red plastic slide. The morning sun warmed my back as Diego pushed chunks of tanbark with his shoe.

"Hey, your mom signed the permission slip! Now you can go on the trip!"

His face lit up. "I'm so excited!"

I continued. "I'm glad I finally got to meet her. And the person with her was so nice! Who was that?"

He leaned toward me, dropping his voice.

"Promise you won't tell?"

I winced inside but molded my expression to neutral.

"I'm not going to tell your business to the kids."

Though we were the only two on the yard, Diego's voice was a whisper. "That's my mom's *girlfriend*." His eyes searched my face.

"That's great!" I said. "I'm glad they both came! Do you like her? Are you comfortable with her?"

Now a smile grabbed hold, and he nodded. "Yeah. She's really nice!"

Two weeks later, a local author came to read to my students. Her book, *One of a Kind, Like Me*, was the true story of her son, who realized his dream of being a purple princess in his kindergarten Halloween parade. After finishing the book, she opened a general discussion of diversity.

"People all look different. My mom was white, and my dad was Japanese, so I'm biracial," she explained. "And people don't all speak the same language either. My husband only spoke Spanish, and my first language was English."

"That's like *me*!" exclaimed Diego. "My mom only speaks Spanish, and her girlfriend speaks English!"

He didn't even seem to notice that he'd revealed two things at once.

It took two weeks, two conversations, and one children's book for Diego to go from whispering his scary secret to exclaiming in unselfconscious delight. I'm glad that in my later years as an educator, I talked about LGBTQ+ people more directly and intentionally.

But in those earlier years, how many children hunched in silent shame, averting their eyes, guarding either themselves or a family member?

Is any adult's comfort level worth that cost?

* * *

After I finished licking every last muffin crumb off my fingers, I pulled my mask back up and leaned forward to catch every word, which wasn't easy with all the banging and grinding noises of a crowded morning coffeehouse.

"At the start of the year, I tell my class, 'My name is Ms. Ortega, and my pronouns are "she," "her," "hers." And this is because, when I was born, the doctor said I was a girl, and on the inside, I feel like I'm a girl, so those are the pronouns I use.'"

At Back-to-School Night, Liliana openly tells the parents about the topics she has raised and will raise with their children. She tells parents she wants each child to know that they can talk about whatever they like in class, that they can be safe, and that they can be whoever they are.

"I also want parents to see that their children can be more open to the world than they were. I tell them, 'I don't want to step on you. I won't ever go into religion or tell children that what you say is wrong. But I am going to discuss with the children that there are those who are people just like they are, and there's nothing wrong with them.' I tell the parents that there's no one who should be seen as less than, just like their own children should not be seen as less than other kids."

"And with you being Mexican," I said, "the parents can't write you off as, *Oh, she just doesn't understand our world.*"

"Right. I speak their language in more ways than one."

Speaking the same language helps to smooth communication. But despite a commonality in language, the path between two people can still be a bumpy one.

When you work with children who are still learning English, you must teach them the structures of the language. As a step toward learning words used for comparing and contrasting, Liliana paired kids up and told them to interview each other with seven questions. Later, they'd draw themselves in a circle of a Venn diagram and would make up short sentences to practice the language of comparing and contrasting.

"Ask your partner what their favorite kind of pizza is," she instructed. "And tell them what your gender is—if you're a boy, a girl, or if you're nonbinary. Also, ask them their favorite color."

Predictably, a child asked, "What's nonbinary?"

So Liliana gave a brief, basic explanation, ending with, "And it's okay."

It didn't take long for a parent to lodge a formal complaint against Liliana, even though the parent hadn't first requested a meeting. When the mother finally met with her, she told Liliana that it was inappropriate for her son to be learning the word "nonbinary."

I felt nervous just hearing the story. But Liliana knew she stood on solid ground.

"The reason I talk about it is that I want my students to be aware that there are a lot of people on the gender spectrum. I want kids to be aware so that they are kind and empathetic and respectful when it comes. That is what we teach them in school."

When Liliana's principal called her in to tell her that, regretfully, she'd be putting the parent's letter of complaint in Liliana's personnel file, Liliana's response was polite but steely strong.

"No. I'm sorry that the mother is offended by me teaching it, and I'm sorry that she doesn't believe in it. But I have a right to talk about it. And actually, it's not so much a 'right.' It's my *duty*."

She's right, and she wasn't just talking about an ethical duty. California's FAIR Education Act of 2011 requires that social studies teaching in California K–12 public schools provide "fair, accurate, inclusive, and respectful" representations of our diverse ethnic and cultural populations. LGBTQ+ people are among the cultural populations included.

"I know that many teachers are uncomfortable with it, and parents are even *more* uncomfortable with it. But I'm *supposed* to be teaching this."

I'd noticed how often the words "comfortable" and "uncomfortable" had filtered into our conversation, and my mind floated back to decades earlier, when I was in my credential program, studying to be a teacher. We'd read an article about creating the conditions for learning.

"It seems like so many adults want to remain *comfortable*," I said, "but learning *isn't* comfortable! I don't feel 'comfortable' when I go to a museum or art exhibit that teaches me ways that white people wield power over Black people. But I need to learn that. And when you're feeling uncomfortable, when you're struggling to figure something out and to incorporate new ideas, that's where the learning is happening."

Liliana nodded and told me about a teacher she knows who says she respects everyone; the teacher bolsters her claim by touting the fact that her sons have gay friends. Her belief, though, is that it's inappropriate to bring up gender and orientation in the classroom.

Liliana's response to her was, "And that's why some kids won't learn it, and why some will grow up to be homophobes—because *you* don't feel comfortable. But it's not about *you*. It's not our job to teach kids what they already know so that they can remain *comfortable*. It's to teach them how big the world is. Knowing that will help them to live in it."

* * *

It can be nerve-racking to deal with parents, occasionally downright frightening. I got along well with most parents during my decades of teaching, but the few difficult relationships are forever lodged in my memory. It's the same for other teachers I know. Though most experiences with parents are positive, there's usually a whisper of worry when a parent unexpectedly requests a meeting or picks up the phone.

Liliana received a surprise call from a mother one day, shortly after she'd had the talk with her students about which pronouns she uses.

"I'd like to talk with you about something," said the mother. "My son said that you were talking about pronouns and telling the kids what they can be."

Liliana felt the familiar-to-any-teacher thud in the stomach and repeated to the woman what she'd said to her students.

"I want the kids to feel comfortable," she told the mother. "We had a great conversation. A couple of the kids brought up situations with family members, like one child said, 'Oh, my uncle dresses like a girl-girl and we just call him Uncle Chris,' and someone else said that their mom's friend was gay, and . . ."

"Oh, no," said the mom. "That's not it. I just wanted to thank you. Because I don't know what Alejandro is going to be when he grows up. But I want him to be free."

I don't know what he will be.

But I want him to be free.

* * *

As we bused our table, Liliana told me about the conversation she'd had with her husband when she decided at age forty that she was doubling down on her intentional classroom talk.

"I told him I might get fired. He just told me, 'Go for it.'"

"He's a keeper!" I laughed.

But we both knew being fired was a real possibility. A white Tennessee teacher was fired for teaching white students about white privilege. A Florida teacher lost her job for hanging a Black Lives Matter flag over her classroom door and rewarding student activism. A *Washington Post* analysis of news reports found more than 160 educators who resigned under pressure or were fired from their jobs from 2020 to 2022 due to education culture wars. The *Post* says the tally "is probably a significant undercount, as scores of firings and resignations go unreported in local media, and the reasoning behind them remains unclear."[1] California tied with four other states for the greatest number of these types of job losses among educators.

Then Liliana told me about a parent who'd come into her classroom and complained about the small Pride flag that she had hanging on the wall.

"I don't think that's appropriate," said the mom.

"Thank you for sharing your thoughts with me," said Liliana.

Then she went out and bought an extra-large Pride flag and hung it up over the little one.

* * *

I reconnected with Liliana in early 2025, just a few months after Trump's second inauguration. She compared students' reactions after the 2016 election to what is being seen eight years later.

"The last time, I had some kids telling me they were worried that their family would get separated. But it's nowhere near what I've heard this year."

She told me of colleagues' widespread reports of frightened children, of students in tears because they were terrified a parent would be taken away. She spoke of students withdrawing from schools in her district.

"We just can't risk it," is what parents have told school staff.

There is a group working to get legal help for parents afraid of being picked up off the street, and Liliana is part of that group. If parents can designate alternative guardians for their children, the young ones can stay here with someone trusted if their parents are deported. Teachers work hard to support their students, but I'm betting Liliana never imagined that supporting her students would take that form.

The director of library services for Liliana's district says they're "toning down" some of their language about books in 2025, since some terms—likely concerning race, gender, and orientation—might be flagged by the Department of Government Efficiency. Their school board has slanted to the right, and courses on ethnic studies have undergone significant scrutiny. Increasing numbers of parents have spoken at school board meetings—not overtly about banning books, but about concerns over what books their children can choose.

"And I'm okay with that," said Liliana. "I make sure to make that point with any parent, at any time. 'It's YOU who is responsible for your child. You're just not responsible for what OTHER people's children read, and they're not responsible for what YOUR child reads.'"

Despite her district's increasingly guarded approach, Liliana is not censoring her own. Her 2025 job title is teacher-librarian, and she gives presentations to colleagues on diversity and the importance of access to literature.

She told me of a school display that included a book called *I Am Muslim*.

"This little girl came in, and her eyes got *big*. She grabbed the book and hugged it. 'I am Muslim!' she said. 'And you have a book about that!'"

"*That* is the dream," Liliana told me.

For children to see themselves represented in books—that, indeed, is the dream.

* * *

Back at the café in late 2022, I handed Liliana a thank-you gift. It was a box of Poop Bingo, a game that teaches kids about various types of animal excrement, each corresponding to a different species. An odd choice, perhaps, but I knew it would be great for third graders stuck indoors for rainy-day recess. We embraced in farewell, and I floated back to my car in a daze. I had to sit for a few moments to ground myself before starting the engine.

On the road back home, all I saw out the window were the monotonous fields of the Central Valley. Just bright blue above and buttery-gold all around.

But in my mind, I kept replaying our conversation: Liliana's description of her classroom music that reflected a big world, her lessons for Mexican kids on Black Lives Matter, her commitment to welcoming every student into the fold, and her refusal to remain silent and risk leaving marginalized children to feel "other." I envisioned Liliana's extra-large rainbow flag hanging high on her classroom wall, defiantly shouting support.

On the long drive home, the world looked a little brighter.

3

A LOW BAR

Lynn doesn't hide the fact that she's a lesbian, and when she told friends a few years ago that she was going to teach in a remote rural region of California, she heard the same thing from almost everyone.

"How do you think it's going to be for you out there?"

Her friends were concerned she might not find as much acceptance as in a larger city.

"I told them it would probably be just like it is every other place I go. I just meet people like I always do, with an open heart and a smile."

I had already encountered that open heart. Lynn had welcomed me into her home.

Many of the friends she has made in the sparsely populated region are conservative, and Lynn has learned that some conservative people there perceive a liberal elitism.

"People here feel like if you're an educated liberal, you probably think you're better than them." Lynn doesn't see herself as better than her fellow townsfolk and has carved out a place for herself there in the high desert.

But even though people have mostly been accepting, Lynn sometimes feels the sting of being viewed with suspicion. In her tiny school, one student was upset when Lynn got on him for not following directions, so he went to the principal.

“The student said he didn’t respect me because I’m gay, and in his family, that’s not okay,” she said. “He had a hard time working with me because of that.”

Then she told me about a student whose single-parent mother was overbearing and overprotective, and seemed to have it out for Lynn, perhaps because of Lynn’s orientation. When the girl—very beautiful—complained about her looks during class and the mom heard that Lynn didn’t stop teaching just to assure the girl of her beauty, the mom became very upset. Then she challenged Lynn about a simple journal prompt that Lynn had chosen for her students from a long list of routine prompts. Eventually, the mother pulled her daughter from Lynn’s class. This was no easy feat; the entire school had only a handful of students.

At holiday time, the school did Secret Santa, and the student Lynn was supposed to give presents to was the daughter. In addition to the gifts, Lynn wrote her an encouraging note, since the girl was known to have struggles at home.

“I basically said, ‘Right now, you’re not really in charge of yourself. But one day you’ll go to college, and you’ll be at the helm of your own ship. Just hang in there.’

“Then I made the mistake of saying, ‘It gets better.’”

It gets better.

The three innocuous words were intended to uplift, but they also named the nonprofit cofounded by Dan Savage, journalist and LGBTQ+ activist. The organization supports queer youth, and the mother decided that Lynn was trying to indoctrinate her daughter into being a lesbian.

“Her mother and another student’s mother went to the school board,” said Lynn, “and said I was trying to make the girls gay.” Lynn was certain that if she’d been straight, the mother would not have lodged a complaint over “It gets better.”

Even though neither the principal nor the school board gave any credence to the mothers’ accusation, it affected Lynn. When a different parent with a queer child asked Lynn if she’d start a rainbow club, Lynn said no.

"Those two moms already thought I was trying to recruit. I wasn't going to start a gay club at school. It would have been good to have something like that. But I wasn't going to be the one to do it."

Because two adults blamed Lynn for something she hadn't done, a queer young person had to pay the price and continue to feel isolated. It's a shame, but I didn't blame Lynn. If I were gay and teaching in that remote region, I probably wouldn't have started a rainbow club either. Even with friends and support, it's not easy to be an LGBTQ+ teacher in a rural area.

* * *

Upon undertaking this road trip project, I quickly saw that my path to meet interviewees kept branching out. Teachers and librarians would steer me toward other educators and, a couple of times, to a young-adult student. One teacher in Southern California had received death threats after making public comments about the need to support queer kids. That teacher was too fearful to talk with me but urged me to connect with former student Cece, an eighteen-year-old gay and gender-fluid person attending community college. Cece was eager to talk with me, the teacher said, and could give me an idea of what a queer student in a rural area goes through.

I reached out to the student, and we made a date. Heading out of the coastal town where my last interview had been, I chose a route that would take me on roads I'd never traveled. The contrast between the densely populated areas in California and the open expanses of remote locales continued to amaze me as I crisscrossed my home state. On that clear winter morning, I took county roads that ribboned for miles over soft green hills, where I saw so few cars that the soothing landscape felt like my happy little secret. Eventually, the road led me through fields of oil drills like the ones that had frightened me as a child, with their eerie pump heads bobbing up and down.

Once seated in the wide-open student center of Cece's college, I gazed at the variety of students passing through and realized I didn't know what Cece looked like. Then my phone lit up with a notification:

I think you're sitting diagonally from me.

I looked up and saw Cece, wearing a blue flannel shirt and a big, friendly smile. We sat near a floor-to-ceiling window and began.

Cece attended a school forty miles away from their hometown, because the thought of attending the one college near the high school where they had been bullied so much was intolerable.

"I've always been a feminine boy per se, and it's never really gone well," Cece told me. "I've always had the bullying issue."

In sixth grade, Cece came out to a few friends as gay. Raised in a heavily religious home, Cece also opened up to a youth pastor at church.

"I was struggling with the religious conflicts of being gay and Christian," Cece told me. "So I put my trust in my youth pastor. I shouldn't have."

The youth pastor spilled Cece's secret to the head pastor. At church one day, Cece was summoned by name to the altar, and in front of the entire congregation, the pastor said God had told him that Cece was questioning their gender and sexuality.

"A whole prayer team came up and prayed for me to wash the gay away. It was the most traumatic experience I've had in any religious forum. My faith in Christ is very little because of mistreatment I've had from Christian people."

Cece explained what the bullying of a "feminine boy" looks like at school.

"In eighth grade, word started trickling around that I was dating a boy. . . . They were just like, 'Oh, okay. They're gay.'"

But in high school, Cece began wearing feminine clothing, wearing "different things that maybe other guys wouldn't wear." That's when the bullying and harassment became physical and sexual.

"There were guys who would touch me for no reason. They would come and poke at me, and it was in a provocative way. It was just to make fun of me, like . . . 'Oh, you like it. Why are you uncomfortable?'"

One day, Cece was cornered in a restroom by a large group of boys. Cece didn't elaborate, except to say that it was frightening. A few weeks later, the same group of boys came up from behind, grabbed Cece's waist, pulled them into the bathroom, and said things that were "very uncomfortable."

By junior year, Cece had changed their name and gender in the school system, and the restroom became a big problem. After what had happened before, Cece was terrified to enter the boys' restroom. The staff reserved the only single-stall restrooms for teachers.

"I looked behind my back every time I went into a restroom, because I was scared someone was following me," said Cece. The high school eventually gave Cece a complicated schedule of when they could use locked bathrooms, a schedule that changed with each class period.

"I'd only use the restroom during sixth period, when teachers were all in their classrooms," they said. "That was safest, and I wouldn't get questioned."

Teachers who didn't know why Cece was using a restroom key would ask, "What are you doing? Why are you going there?"

Cece's tired response would be, "If you'd like to go talk to the dean, go ahead. I have approval."

* * *

Cece said the high school bullying worsened after COVID-19, bringing Cece to a crossroads. There still had been no known consequences for those involved in the incidents in the bathroom.

"The school system failed me, stating they had no evidence to punish the boys. I realized there needs to be a change. So I got really heavy into the GSA, and started working with [the club adviser] on being able to share my story."

GSAs, which have existed since the 1980s, are student-led clubs for queer students and allies. California's Education Code provides that if a school allows any noncurricular student clubs, a GSA must also be allowed if students want one. One teacher told me she'd taught at a school that disallowed *all* student clubs because they didn't want to risk being mandated to institute a GSA.

Per Ed Code, schools don't have to divulge GSA membership rosters, so parents won't know if their child belongs to a GSA unless the child tells them. GSAs can serve multiple functions: promoting awareness of LGBTQ+ identities, histories, and current issues and fostering community and solidarity while providing an affirming space. Simply having a GSA demonstrates to everyone that queer people are worthy of inclusion. In GSAs, students can build confidence and work toward equity and protection for all. About 44 percent of U.S. middle schools and high schools have a GSA.[1]

Becoming active in their high school GSA helped Cece blossom. By the time we met in February 2023, they were a full-on college activist, serving on a committee to improve conditions for oppressed minority groups attending community colleges.

"I'm trying to achieve it not only here but at all community colleges. It's still a big deal for LGBTQ people. They don't feel comfortable going to a place where it is supposed to be comfortable. And it's not just a problem for *me*. It's a problem for the Black community, the Muslim community, the Arabic community, and the gay community."

I learned that Cece was the driving force behind an upcoming meeting, one that would be attended by many professors who wanted to hear Cece's story: In a month, Cece was to speak before the board of trustees for the county's entire community college district.

"When a person speaks who's had firsthand experience with these things, it makes it way better," said Cece.

I had to tell myself to close my gaping mouth. After years of harassment that has continued into their college years, Cece has still been able to dig deep for hope and use it to fight for a better world. When we communicated again about a year after we'd met, Cece was traveling to Northern California as part of a delegate assembly for Southern California Community Colleges, where everyone would vote on new bills being released to the Senate. Cece was also moving to a state university to complete a degree in social work.

At a crossroads, people choose a path. The path Cece is on is to channel the energy from painful experiences into a force for change. They do it for themself, but also for those whose trauma forces them to retreat as a means of survival.

The terror endured by Cece in high school bathrooms haunts me, as does the fact that Cece's most supportive teacher in high school was threatened with death because of being vocal about that support. Educators can't separate out students' orientation and identity from the rest of who they are, just as it's impossible to place a student's race, temperament, or physical and

mental ability into distinct personality compartments, like individual sections of a plastic lunchbox. Educators must address the needs of the *whole* child, because supporting a student's academic growth means supporting the entirety of who they are.

Since meeting Cece, I've often wondered where they would be without the adamant, visible, unquestioning backing of their high school teacher. Because of that support, Cece's college activism will help many other marginalized students in the future. But when teachers are targeted for voicing the need to support students on the edges, is it any wonder that some may decide to skip the death threats and leave the profession?

* * *

It was eighteen degrees when I stepped onto the frozen sidewalk, my breath puffing out in little clouds. Before my lunchtime appointment with middle school teacher Alicia, I needed to find a computer repair place in Truckee, a small town in the High Sierra. Turns out that a seven-hour train ride with an open water bottle and a laptop in the same bag isn't good for the laptop after all. Who knew?

Following my phone's directions, I wandered under a freeway, past fresh bear poop, up a snowy path in the woods, back down the same snowy path, up a steep hill, and into a tangle of icy roads. When Siri announced my supposed arrival, all I saw on that hilltop was the spectacular view. It was still very cold, but I didn't have a scarf; I'd given away all of mine to my third graders when we had returned to school in April 2021, to the ready-for-COVID freezing-cold classroom, with its fans on high and doors yawning wide.

Grateful that Alicia had been willing to drive far enough to meet me in Truckee, I strolled into the pub two hours later. The smiling greeter led me to a high-top table, directly under the speaker spewing 1970s hits. Most everyone there was within a few years of thirty, fit-looking people wearing leggings and cargo pants, layered shirts and knit caps, clomping around in heavy shoes. I represented a different demographic. I'd instructed Alicia to look for someone with a light-blue coat, disheveled gray hair, and a

lime-green fanny pack. Still, I felt slightly smug in this young, cool crowd. The music was from *my* era. I belonged here, too.

When a woman with long dark hair and a cozy-looking green pullover showed up, the greeter led her over. Alicia and I busied ourselves with the menu. I ordered the garden pizza. She, a pretzel and tea.

We dove in.

When I asked Alicia why she had agreed to talk with me, her brow crinkled and she tilted her head in thought. Then her eyes met mine directly.

"Because . . . it's hard being a queer teacher in a rural place. And it's hard watching queer kids not get their needs met in rural places. So, let's have a conversation about that and see what could happen."

She continued, saying how hard it is for kids to get through high school without knowing that other gay kids exist.

So I told her about my friend, whose teenage trans son had experienced extreme isolation.

"After he came out to her, he said that for many years of his young childhood, he'd thought that *everyone* felt bad when they got dressed for the day."

Alicia nodded. She already knew.

She told me how queer kids know she's a safe person to be around.

"I never made that invitation—it was never like, 'Hey, anyone who wants to can come in at lunch.'"

She pointed to a small rainbow tattoo on the inside of her forearm.

"The kids who need to see my rainbow notice it. I say things like, 'If you grow up and decide to date people, your partners will be . . .' I use the word 'partner' to show I don't assume that kids will want to get married. Kids figure out there's some flexibility in thinking. Sometimes they just need to know that there's a person who *sees* them."

Again, I thought of my friend's trans son. I'd asked him once if he had advice for me about what a third-grade teacher could do to help kids who might feel different and alone. His suggestion was simple: Invite a high school student from the GSA to come volunteer.

Not to talk about anything, he'd said. *Just to help in class. Because when you feel different and you're not sure* how *you're different, you're always looking at other people and wondering, "Are you like me? What about you? Are you like me?"*

I remembered the pain of my thirties into my early forties, when so many of my friends partnered up and had kids. Even though I had a life rich with people, opportunity, and work, the ache of feeling different—alone—was awful. *I don't matter . . . I don't matter . . .* It was a constant refrain in my head when I was thirty-four. I floundered in the worst depression of my life.

I told Alicia about that, adding, "As an educated adult, I felt it so strongly, the pain of societal 'difference.' So for a child who's feeling alone? How do they even walk in the world every day?"

Alicia nodded soberly, then continued.

"I've always had that group of nerdy kids who hang out at lunch, whatever they're nerdy about. They just seem to understand that when they can't be themselves in the cafeteria, being nerdy in my room at lunch is okay. In recent years, that's led to quite a few gay kids hanging out. They need a safe place to be."

Safe. I'd never experienced not feeling safe at school. When I was a teenager, I wondered if my rose-colored slacks looked like old-lady pants, and if I looked fat in my PE uniform. Could Brendan tell I had a crush on him? Did my Wallabee shoes look as cool as I thought they did? Was I good enough to make the softball team? Those were my concerns.

I reached back in my memory, thinking of classmates who might have felt unsafe. Had I ever helped them feel connected? Or had I left them to feel all alone?

As we ate, Alicia talked about the fears that burden LGBTQ+ kids. Through her role as club adviser for her school's GSA, students share the worries that consume them.

Some of the things Alicia hears:

Are you sure you don't have to tell my mom if she asks?

How did it go when you told your mom?

How can I ever tell my parents about me when every time they see "gay" on TV, they make gagging noises?

She assures them that California doesn't require teachers to tell parents about their membership in a GSA. She tells them that her mom was fine with the news of her orientation, and that it would *not* have been fine with her father, if he had lived long enough. When kids say, "It won't be fine at my house, so I don't think I'll tell," she reminds them that there's no imperative to come out.

"It sounds like you're keeping yourself safe," she tells them. "There's no pressure to come out. You'll be living in your parents' house for years. So if it doesn't feel safe for you to tell, then keep yourself safe."

To me, she said, "I have a lot of Latino kids from Catholic families. Being gay and Latino is hard. The Catholic Church isn't real big on homosexuality."

I couldn't stop my muttered response. "Yeah, they're not big on sex period. But I guess some priests never got that message."

Alicia then said, "I want high schoolers to make it to adulthood."

It's a shockingly low bar. I think back on years of excruciating staff meetings where we spent hours crafting meticulous mission, vision, and goal statements. All of it used to make me want to scream. If, after endless conversations and debates over word choice, we decided on "elevate" instead of "advance," would that *really* change what we did with students each day? Maybe the mission, vision, and goal tasks would have felt more relevant if, instead of obsessing over words, we'd just been blunt:

"We will allocate more money to classrooms so that kids in poverty get extra support."

"Students will all learn to read because we'll help teachers more."

"High schoolers will make it to adulthood."

* * *

Alicia wasn't being melodramatic; she's had a queer student attempt suicide at school. That's not surprising. Suicide is the second leading cause of death for all young people aged ten to fourteen and the third leading cause among fifteen-to-twenty-four-year-olds. But LGBTQ+ young people are at a much higher risk. They are more than four times as likely to attempt suicide as

their peers. The Trevor Project's 2023 national survey found that 41 percent of LGBTQ+ young people seriously considered attempting suicide in the previous year, including about half of transgender and nonbinary youth. As affirmed by the Trevor Project, the sobering reality is that queer kids "are not inherently prone to suicide risk because of their sexual orientation or gender identity but rather placed at higher risk because of how they are mistreated and stigmatized in society."[2]

When Alicia's student attempted suicide at school, another student found the troubled young person and raced to get Alicia. The student survived.

Alicia's position in that district did not.

"Yeah, attempted suicide made a statement that no one wanted to hear. There was a meeting the next morning with all the county people, counselors, and supervisors. They all came to help our school deal with it.

"At the meeting, I spoke up and asked if this was the part where we would finally start supporting our queer students. I wasn't tenured at the time, and that pretty much signed my death warrant. It was right before the March 15 pink-slip deadline, and my job went away."

After decades of union activism, I understood the power of March 15. Some districts cry poor in early March, asserting that they don't have the funding to pay for as many teachers as are employed. In my district, it was usually a tactical move; if administrators claimed there wasn't money to employ all the teachers, they had an excuse for denying us a pay increase in our contract negotiations. Once negotiations were wrapped up, they'd contact most of the teachers they had cut loose. The ones who hadn't yet accepted jobs in other districts were usually offered their jobs back for the next school year.

But other strategies are also behind the handing out of pink slips, and I didn't doubt Alicia's suspicion that her outspokenness had marked her as "expendable." I'd many times marched in protest of my school district's excessive distribution of March 15 pink slips. I wondered if anyone had marched in support of Alicia.

Two questions lingered for me.

"How did your principal respond when you mentioned the lack of support in front of the whole group?"

"He just said, 'But we don't have any queer kids here.' So I said, 'Oh, okay. Because I have eight of them in my room every day at lunch.'"

"You've got guts," I observed.

Alicia shook her head in silent disgust.

"His answer was, 'Why are you prying into your students' lives?'"

I sighed and asked my second question.

"What would 'support' for LGBTQ kids look like?"

Alicia said that there had been no GSA at that school, and no acknowledgment of the need for one. The year prior, she'd taught her first transgender student. The principal, instead of listing all the ways teachers could support that student, merely said, "This is what our lawyers say to do."

"We didn't do anything about having binary bathrooms," said Alicia. "We just gave the kid a key to the staff bathroom so they could be the weirdo who walks into the other room. It was all about, 'Here's how we don't get sued.'"

I felt my shoulders slump. Though I hadn't faced that situation in my district, the "let's not get in trouble" response sounded depressingly familiar.

Alicia continued.

"Can't we just focus on what's right for this kid, and have them worry about the legal part without us? Can't we just do our jobs and teach?"

* * *

There were more examples of the lack of LGBTQ+ support. Alicia told of a teaching colleague who would openly gay-bash during staff meetings. This would happen in front of the principal, who was also the superintendent of the small district. He never stopped it or even acknowledged that it was a problem, not even after three teachers wrote letters to the school board and enlisted union support. The same principal once outed a student to the child's parents. It didn't matter that both the California and U.S. Constitutions grant students a protected right to privacy, preventing school staff from speaking about a student's sexual orientation and gender identity with anyone—including the kid's parents—without the student's permission.

Support for LGBTQ+ people in Alicia's current school, small and rural, is visible in the Pride flags that are up in classrooms. Teachers come down hard on kids who bully anyone, especially if the target is an LGBTQ+ student. And Alicia goes further.

On the first day of school, she gives kids a sheet that asks them to write both what their name is listed as on her roll sheet and what name they like to be called.

"If there's anything else, like pronouns or maybe something going on at home, just tell me whatever you need me to know," she says.

She also recognizes that it's not easy for some teachers.

"Even though the 'Don't Say Gay' bill isn't in California, teachers wonder, 'Will I get in trouble if I say this?' It's not that hard to use new words for things, but I think teachers feel that they need permission to speak that way in a classroom."

Just a few words can make a life-changing difference to kids, and Alicia ensures that they hear those words.

"I make sure they know it's okay to not come out. It's okay if they think it's for now, and then they change. It's all okay. I tell them, 'You're fine just how you are.'"

Another way to support queer kids and other children is by doing what Alicia's current school has done: employ a full-time counselor.

"Kids can't learn if they're dealing with stress and trauma," said Alicia, "so her entire job is to be a counselor."

I was floored. In my experience, psychologists are employed by districts, but they usually aren't people who talk with children about their problems. They are split among multiple school sites and spend much of their time administering tests to assess whether children have learning disabilities. A full-time counselor whose sole responsibility is to meet with kids? What a difference that could make for all students who feel isolated and alone.

Alicia told of a long-ago student who was obviously gay, a young man who wrote a haunting poem about a teen who couldn't be himself. *The church hates me, / My mom is terrified for me,* the boy wrote, then continued the list of all the ways people in this hypothetical kid's life were not supportive.

"So I chatted with him," said Alicia, "and he said, 'Oh, it's not about me.' And I said, 'Well, if I was talking to the kid from the poem, here are some of the things I'd say.'"

Then she told the "fictional" child that she knew four years sounded like forever. But she also wanted him to know that when he left for college in four years, he'd be surrounded by people who look like him and talk like him. He'd meet people who think the way he thinks.

"That's so much of being a middle school teacher—just telling kids, 'Hang on a little bit longer. You can do this,'" she said. "But why does this institution require kids to hold on by the bloody stumps?"

* * *

Some of my colleagues referred to me as "the Field Trip Queen." I loved taking nine-year-olds on hikes into redwood forests, on ferries that splashed across the San Francisco Bay, into tide pools at the edge of the Pacific, and up to Gold Rush towns in the Sierra foothills. All the grant-writing, fundraising, and applications were worth it. Watching students experience the world as their classroom was one of my great joys as a teacher.

Alicia knows that joy, too. When she taught high school last year, she secured funding from the local arts council and brought her U.S. History students to Reno to see *Hamilton*. Her students loved it and talked about it all year. Alicia began following a few of the actors on Instagram and noticed that one frequently posted photos of himself and his husband, with messages about pride and standing up for what's right.

"I always put up bulletin boards for Latinx History Month, Native American History Month, and things like that. We definitely put one up for Pride Month," she said. "So I messaged him and said, 'My class came and saw you, and I think you're amazing.'"

She told him she assumed that many members of the *Hamilton* cast might be gay, and asked if he might give her some names of cast members who were publicly out, so that she could add their photos to her Pride Month board.

His enthusiastic response was gratifying, but it was also hard for her to hear.

"You are actively saving lives with this," he said.

He went on to explain that while some lesbian women often aren't visibly identifiable as gay, the story is different for many gay men. He described the significant trauma experienced by himself, his husband, and their friends, even though they lived in New York City.

"We can't look at it as 'It would sure be nice IF we supported LGBTQ kids,'" he told her. "It has to be 'It is critical THAT we support them.'"

Teen suicide rates among LGBTQ+ youth are real. Bullying and anti-LGBTQ+ legislation—they can have lethal effects.

Alicia said simply, "We need to find ways to keep our kids alive."

For once, I had no words. I nodded heavily and dug out the credit card from my lime-green fanny pack.

* * *

It was a weird feeling, saying goodbye to someone who'd been a stranger just an hour and a half earlier, someone who'd shared so much and whom I might not ever see again. We hugged outside on the icy sidewalk, and as she drove away, I realized I'd forgotten to give her the book I'd just promised her.

The next morning, before my train left, I met up with my young cousin and her fiancé. We strolled alongside the Truckee River. The sky was brilliant blue, the air was crisp, and their big black dog was goofy, bounding across wide expanses of glittering snow. They left me at the train station, and I leaned back on the bench in a state of perfect contentment.

Once settled on the train home, I took out my phone and began scrolling. On Facebook, I noticed post after post reading "Colorado Springs," covered with broken-heart emojis and cartoon faces streaming tears. Googling, I read with horror about the massacre at Club Q barely twelve hours earlier.

Five people at the LGBTQ+ nightclub had been killed. Twenty-two other people were injured. An unknowable number of lives—changed forever.

Spectacular scenery streamed past outside the window. I barely noticed a thing.

4

THE HOLE THAT REMAINS

Sister Mary de Chantal was my third-grade teacher. I adored her warm Irish brogue, the green eyes dancing behind her cat-eye glasses, and her smile shining bright against the long black veil of the habit that encircled her face.

Sister de Chantal spent most recesses teaching Irish jigs to us girls. Our scuffed white oxfords tapped and thumped the asphalt as our scratchy blue plaid jumpers swayed with our hops and skips. *One-two-three, one-two-three, kick-your-heel-and-one-two-three.* She was patient, frequently gracing us with her hearty laugh. With her, learning seemed easy. I watched her with boundless love and decided that I, too, would one day become a teacher.

And then I had Sister de Chantal again in seventh grade. This time, she seemed impatient, her green eyes flashing sparks and her frustrated voice snapping at us throughout the day. My adoration shriveled, and I wondered if I was the only student who felt betrayed by the perceived about-face. I couldn't know then that adolescents are notoriously self-absorbed and rebellious, and that those who teach them are deserving of medals. I decided I would *never* be a teacher. Why choose a job where dozens of kids might dislike me each year?

* * *

After college, I spent four years as a live-in volunteer in Portland and Oakland, working with low-income seniors, undocumented immigrants, refugees from Central American wars, and unhoused people. Eventually, the tales of loss, the desperation for legal and medical resources, and the midnight calls about women and children needing shelter drained me dry. I slumped through the days, flinching when there was a knock on the door or a ring of the phone. Previously, I had run toward those sounds, but now I yearned to escape and go hiking in the hills.

Exhausted and heavyhearted, I moved into an East Oakland apartment, patching together odd jobs to pay the paltry rent. My expenses were minimal; I made my own yogurt and bread, ate fruits and vegetables from the shared yard, and rode my bike everywhere. I hoped that I'd eventually be able to return to "helping" work; in the meantime, I chose jobs that required nothing of me emotionally. Most mornings, I dictated legal transcripts for budding court reporters, and in the afternoons, I biked up into the Oakland hills to clean fancy houses. During breaks in my light work schedule, I hid out in the bookstacks of the downtown library and napped on the grass alongside Lake Merritt.

By 1988, I was twenty-nine and floundering. I knew I didn't want to retreat from people-work forever, but I felt stuck. My mind flickered back to my youthful desire to be a teacher, but a voice inside kept telling me why I would fail.

You're not creative. Teachers need to create EVERYTHING.

You'll make too much money. It will corrupt you. (Yes, I see the humor in that now.)

You couldn't handle it if kids were mad at you all day.

My college roommate had become a high school science teacher, and while visiting her near Los Angeles, I asked about the Ranger Rick booklets on her end table.

"Oh, those have hands-on activities for whatever science unit I'm covering. I use them constantly."

"You don't think up everything yourself?"

"I get *all* of my ideas from books. And teachers share ideas with each other. Nobody does it all by themselves!"

I felt a wave slowly lift me.

The next afternoon, while I waited aboard a Greyhound in the LA bus terminal, I thought about our conversation.

A Greyhound bus is probably not the site of most epiphanies, but that's where mine happened. I tried pretending that I could conquer the mental obstacles blocking me from teaching; immediately, my breath quickened, my heart raced, and I knew. From that moment, I never wavered in my resolve. I couldn't wait to get home and research how to get a teaching credential. It was already early July, but maybe it wouldn't be too late to find a college with openings in its education program.

By early August, I was still riding my bike high into the Oakland hills, but this time it was to attend classes in a credential program. By the next summer, I was setting up my own classroom. I took a day off from classroom prep to go to Dave Dravecky's postcancer pitching comeback for the Giants, and brought markers and index cards with me. As the weekday crowd cheered in rare sunshine at San Francisco's Candlestick Park, I scrawled sets of math gamecards in my seat in the outfield.

The happiness was as profound as I'd ever felt in my life.

* * *

Everything was shockingly difficult that first year. I worked until 10:00 p.m. most nights, and all day Sunday. There were thirty-four fourth graders crammed into my classroom that would've felt crowded with twenty-five. A number of the kids lived with ongoing trauma and often erupted in anger. Every day, I was faced with routine dilemmas I had no idea how to solve.

When Anthony stood up in class and hollered, "This is all a bunch of BULLSHIT!" I knew I needed to do *something* but didn't know what. There was the day that Jackson and William got into a full-blown, rolling-around-on-the-ground fight while we were on a field trip to see a play at UC Berkeley. Then there was the day that Glen's mom showed up drunk to chaperone another trip. And the day that I broke up a fight between Troy and Agustin. I'd grabbed each boy's arm, but they kept leaping and kicking at each other with me in the middle like the hub of a human wagon wheel. None of those scenarios had been covered in my teacher training.

Some challenges were heartbreaking. There was the sweltering day when Alberto wouldn't take off his knit cap—until he finally did, revealing bruised lumps and cuts all over his shaved scalp. While taking lunch count for the cafeteria one morning, the numbers weren't adding up, so I asked Agustin if he'd brought his own lunch. He stood, grabbed the legs of his single-person desk, and with the powerful thrusts of an Olympic weight lifter, flipped the desk over his head before heaving it toward the cloudy plastic windows.

"I DIDN'T BRING NO GODDAMNED LUNCH!"

The class was stunned into silence, until George cried, "Dang! He's a *barbarian*!"

My mind exploded in panicky bursts: *So strong . . . What the hell? . . . What do I do? . . . How does George know the word "barbarian"?*

Later, the assistant principal told me that Agustin's grandmother hadn't had time to get food for him that morning. The kid was hungry.

That first year was overwhelming and exhausting, but not even the bitter teacher on the other side of my classroom's accordion wall could crush my spirit. I knew I was where I was meant to be. And I was right. Myriad memories from my teaching career still sparkle, whether tiny or something grand.

* * *

On a field trip to a science museum in San Francisco, we took BART. My group of twenty-nine third graders and six chaperones pressed into the densely packed crush of morning commuters, and Alejandra began to hyperventilate in a panic. A kind man gave up his seat, and after Alejandra's lightheadedness passed, I told silly jokes to distract her until we reached San Francisco.

The next month found us on the commuter train again, heading to the Oakland Museum. This time, most kids got a seat. I glanced around the car, searching for Alejandra, and spotted her near the door. I made my way over.

"How are you feeling? Better this time?" I asked.

Alejandra nodded with a silent smile. Then I noticed her hand contracting in rhythmic motions.

"What are you doing?"

Nathalia, sitting next to her, answered for Alejandra.

"I remembered she got scared last time, so I brought a little squishy ball for her to squeeze. It calms her down. I think it's helping."

It was a great field trip. But my favorite moment was on public transportation.

* * *

In my third year teaching, I wrote a grant to take my fourth-grade class of city kids on an overnight trip, camping at an environmental education farm on a bluff above the Pacific. Our first day had been full: serial episodes of carsickness on the bus, kids running with baby goats through sweet-smelling grass, pelican sightings, allergy attacks, collaborative tent setup, group meal prep, and a night hike. The activity and the weight of responsibility had exhausted me, and I was ready for sleep. I zipped myself into the solitude of my solo tent.

Then a zipper hummed and footsteps rustled right behind my head. I had expected nighttime silliness. Torrance, Kao, and Jahvon were skittering their fingers against one of the girls' tents. I crept out of my enclosure. Captured in the beam of my flashlight, their eyes popped wide.

"Okay, kids, time for bed. Get in your tents and stay there." My tone was good-natured.

The boys retreated, giggling. I zipped myself back inside.

This scenario played out a few more times with new bands of merrymakers. After each occurrence, my directive became less cheerful and more "I mean business."

Then I heard a chorus of wailing and traced it to a tent of homesick girls. After I reassured them and left them with their chaperone, I zipped them in and peered into the night, on the lookout for mischief. Spotting no flashlights, I headed back to my tent. But just as I flopped down with a sigh, I heard footsteps, and the quietest of whispers. Then more footsteps.

It had been a long day, and tomorrow promised even more activity. Any disturbance could set the girls off again. I'd already tolerated a generous amount of after-hours playfulness. Didn't the offenders realize that most teachers don't take kids camping? Didn't they know how lucky they were? The least they could do was follow directions.

I yanked on my tennis shoes and flung open my tent, scanning for the troublemakers. There they were—five kids perched on a bench, ten feet back from where the hillside dived down to the sea.

I marched over. "I told you to stay in your tents! What are you doing out here?"

After a moment of silence, Kimberlee whispered, "Looking at the stars."

There the five sat, a Mien child with Black, Cambodian, and Tongan kids, all staring up at the midnight sky speckled with millions of stars they'd never seen in Oakland's ever-lit night.

"Scoot over," I whispered.

* * *

Kengkla lived in an apartment across the street from school. One morning, he showed up an hour early, sobbing in the dark hallway outside because his sick kitten had just died. When I asked where he'd buried her, he said that his building had no dirt, so he'd put her in a milk carton and placed it in the dumpster out front. When the rest of the class came, I allowed him to sit in the quiet indoor hallway between our room and the unoccupied library. He asked if his friend could join him. Every time I poked my head out to check on them, Kengkla and Hai were sitting side by side against the wall, quiet in companionship.

At recess time, I asked Kengkla if he'd like us to retrieve the kitten so that he could give it a proper burial after school, perhaps with a few friends. He brightened, and the two of us speed-walked to the office, darting past the open door. We crossed the street with alarm bells clanging in my head; leaving campus during work hours was forbidden, especially with a student in tow.

Nervously aware that I was in plain sight of my principal if he looked out his office window, I acted quickly, pulling myself up and over the edge of the dumpster.

"Hey, what size carton is she in?" I tossed a few knotted plastic bags out of the way, trying to put my paralyzing fear of all things rodent out of my mind.

"It's skinny, but bigger than the ones in the cafeteria," he said.

Okay, so a quart-sized container. I spied one and peeked inside. There she was, looking just as forlorn as I'd imagined a tiny dead kitten in a milk carton in a dumpster would look. Back in the classroom, we stashed the carton in the cabinet with the construction paper. Kengkla whispered invitations to a few friends; all four returned to the classroom at 3:30, forgoing after-school playtime. By now breaking rules right and left, I asked no one's permission to take five students to the park. Off we went.

On the ten-minute walk past homes with barred windows and black metal security doors, there was no talk of Katie the kitten, and there were no tears. They were just a little band of boys heading to the park.

The park was small but had plenty of dirt. We headed to an out-of-the-way corner, where I hoped no one would catch us burying a pet. Then we grabbed a few sticks and started scraping the ground near the base of a towering redwood. It took no time to dig the tiny grave.

One of the kids laid a large leaf in the hole. Kengkla gently placed Katie on top of the leaf, and before we covered her up, those children murmured the simple words they somehow knew to say.

"Katie was a good cat."

"We'll miss you, Katie."

"Rest in peace, Katie."

Curtis placed his hand on Kengkla's shoulder. We all put a little dirt over the kitten, and then it was done.

The heartache was still fresh. Kengkla had still lost his beloved kitten. But one of the most beautiful sights I've ever seen is the image of those five fourth-grade boys heading down the little hill all in a row, a tangle of arms hooked over shoulders, Kengkla in the middle.

* * *

Oscar was a large third grader who faced his world with narrowed eyes and a sullenness that warned people away. His rare smiles were guarded. He'd had great difficulty getting along with peers in younger grades and began third grade by intimidating others with physical aggression and cruel, cutting words. When Oscar's victims voiced their hurt to him, he would roll his eyes before muttering, "Sorry," appearing anything but remorseful.

The structure of our twice-weekly restorative circles was to check in, discuss problems, express healing and hurts, and share compliments with each other. Tiny cracks were detectable in Oscar's hardened exterior during circle time. He seemed particularly attentive during conversations involving feelings and rarely said "pass" when the talking piece reached him. I found myself growing increasingly fond of his prickly self, joking around with him and tallying tiny victories if he revealed a fleeting smile.

Over time, his aggression toward others became less frequent. When we handed out compliments at the end of each circle meeting, kids began praising Oscar for being funny, and I'd watch a smile flicker at the corners of his mouth as he mumbled, "Thank you."

In a circle meeting late in the year, I invited the students to finish the sentence "I wish more people knew . . ." Many said, "I pass," and a few said something brief and superficial. I was about to end the meeting when Oscar announced, "I have something to say."

To prevent the chaos of multiple kids chattering at once during class meetings, the rule was that the only person allowed to speak was whoever was holding the talking piece. So someone tossed our talking piece—a fuzzy brown stuffed hippo—to Oscar, and he began.

"I wish more people knew I'm not a bully anymore. A long time ago, I used to be a bully. Some people think I still am, but I'm not. That's what I wanted to say."

There was a hush in the circle. I said, "You're really brave for telling us that. What made you not act like a bully anymore?"

He stared straight ahead, his jutting chin taking on the world.

"I don't know. I just didn't want to do it anymore."

A few more kids spoke, but I barely heard a thing. In that moment, all I saw was a little boy, as soft as the squishy stuffed hippo he held in his hands.

* * *

I'm not unique; nearly all teachers have stories of the sweetness of young people, of their inspiration and strength, of hope amid tragedy, of courage and growth. For many teachers, it's what fuels them to continue when they're feeling battered.

Many teachers are vocal about loving their job. For thirty-two years, I was, too. (I was also vocal about the aspects of it that need to be changed, but that's another book.) That's why leaving the profession is especially heartbreaking for teachers: For most, it's more than just a job. They love working with kids and helping them grow. That's why they chose education.

And it's why some feel so betrayed and broken when they decide they have to leave.

* * *

A 2022 study found overwhelmingly that "teachers' primary motivations for entering and staying in the profession are to help students, and to make a positive difference in our world today," and it showed that many teachers still find their work rewarding.[1] But among the 4,600 California public school educators who were polled in 2022, about 1 in 5 was considering leaving teaching within the next three years, including more than one-third of teachers younger than age fifty-five. The majority of responding teachers reported feeling exhausted and stressed, with burnout cited as the top reason for leaving.

Can anyone blame them?

Teachers enter education to help students and to make a positive difference in our world. When we condemn them for teaching about racism, when we denounce them as pedophiles for supporting LGBTQ+ students, and when we publicly shame them and make their lives a living hell, the miracle is that more of them have not already left the profession. When we threaten them with death for doing the essential work of being an educator, we are chasing them out at a dead run.

And as each one leaves, do we realize all that we've lost?

* * *

To address their shortage of teachers, some states are recruiting first responders, subject-matter professionals, or retired military personnel. It's not a terrible idea; some of those people might discover they're well suited to a second career in education. But being a teacher requires skills beyond proficiency in combat or understanding of a subject area. To educate a classroom of children in a public school, a teacher has to be much more than simply the adult in the room. A true "teacher" can't be swapped out for just anyone who needs a new job. Can military personnel and first responders simply fall in line to fill that empty space?

A common maxim in education is the reminder that we don't teach *math*, say, or *social studies*—we teach *children*. And to teach children is to understand that they bring their entire beings into the classroom, their vulnerable selves, each with a home life and a history, with personality, quirks, sensitivities, and scars. A teacher must address the needs of the whole child and the whole classroom community, not just instruct kids how to place punctuation and solve equations.

Any given day or lesson can range from frustration to perfection. Moments can be excruciating or joyous. Every child, every day, is different.

To choreograph learning for a roomful of human beings requires an abundance of skill, knowledge, passion, and energy. When a teacher leaves, the vacant spot can't simply be filled by the next automaton in line.

* * *

Aaron is a high school teacher. A straight, white, cisgender man, he is the adviser of his school's rainbow club. When a student wrote a homophobic slur in chalk on the sidewalk, the club president raised the concern to the administration, who took no real action.

So the club president found the kid who'd written the slur and confronted him. The two had a productive conversation, and the offending student apologized and erased the slur. Then he posted online about it, taking responsibility for his actions and saying he shouldn't have done it.

"You try to give them little tools," Aaron told me. "It was the best possible outcome I can imagine. I told [the club president], 'You took control. You took agency. You talked to this person.' It was the happiest ending."

Aaron helped a teenager develop the courage to express his hurt to another. Someone else taught the other teen to listen to another's hurt, and to own his responsibility in causing it. The offender apologized, educating other teens in the process.

A tiny bit of healing in the world, fostered tenderly by a high school math teacher.

* * *

A kindergarten teacher learned that the father of one of her students had been diagnosed with late-stage cancer. So the teacher bought a huge teddy bear and had all the child's classmates sign the bear's T-shirt. She also asked each kindergartener to hug the teddy bear after signing the shirt, explaining that the love in their hugs would be carried by the bear to the ill father. The simple ritual empowered the class to express care and concern for the small child and his suffering family. The symbolic yet tangible expression of love not only touched the child and his father but provided tremendous comfort to the entire extended family. And the teacher's students absorbed a lifelong lesson in empathy.

Marie was a high school science teacher for nearly forty years. For her, everything boiled down to relationships. By asking questions and keeping current with music, artists, and anime characters, Marie learned about her students' lives.

She learned that while one student's mother was working, the student—from a big family—had to take care of the younger kids and help the school-age siblings with homework. In their tiny home, the only place where the older girl could be alone when she finally had time to study was in the laundry room, on top of the washer. Marie, her colleagues, and the girl's mom figured out a way for the girl to stay late at school twice a week, abandoning the washer for uninterrupted time at a desk.

Noticing when capable students' homework was hastily done led Marie to learn about their after-school jobs, home responsibilities, and transportation issues. Her school was in a poor community, low on resources. She learned which kids had no money for prom and worked with colleagues to sign kids up with organizations that cover most prom costs.

Building relationships helped Marie know when students in foster care were about to be turned out at age eighteen, and she'd help them find housing. She enlightened kids about myriad scholarship opportunities, leading one student to show up at Marie's room at 7:00 a.m. for months. While

Marie worked in the early-morning stillness, the girl sat in the quiet classroom and applied for money for college.

One consequence of building strong relationships with her students was that Marie spent hundreds of unpaid hours over the decades writing letters of recommendation for college admission, summer programs, and work experience opportunities. She didn't copy-paste the letters; instead, she had each student fill out a "brag sheet" of facts and accomplishments, and she scheduled lengthy one-on-one conversations to learn specifics of each student's background. She'd take another forty-five minutes to write each letter.

Contemplating the total time spent writing letters over nearly forty years of teaching makes my head hurt.

"I had to think about what makes each person different," Marie told me. "It might be, 'Oh! *Three families* living in your home?' It gives perspective. Kids do great things in school, even with so much going on outside."

She did it all because she wanted kids to love learning. Helping her students get to where they wanted to be in life was, for her, a labor of love.

Could a person who's hired mostly to be the adult in the room routinely pull this off?

* * *

On the last day of the 2022–23 school year, the teachers and staff at my old school had a surprise for hundreds of elementary students. When the 7:55 bell rang and kids lined up awaiting their teachers, they began screaming as the staff came into view. Why?

Because most of those entrusted with educating children were clad in ridiculous, bright, bouncy inflatable costumes. Instead of smiling teachers in sneakers and jeans, or energetic educators wearing T-shirts and shorts for the traditional staff-versus-fifth-graders kickball game, a parade of colorful nylon-clad goofballs swarmed the yard. Unicorns, bananas, flamingos, dragons, and dinosaurs greeted their young charges. The principal rode in on the back of an inflatable bear. My pal Jen was saddled up on a neon-green alien. Children's joyful shrieks filled the air.

"The whole playground was screaming," Jen recalled, laughing. "It was hilarious! It was like we were a nineties boyband!"

Clearly, the blow-up attire was a huge hit, even though the dinosaur's tail took out a fifth grader rounding first base during the kickball game.

Why did the teachers do it?

Because they knew that laughter is restorative, and that the kids would never forget it. Because more than a year of distance learning had sucked so much joy from lonely kids' lives that nearly two years later, the teachers were still trying to pour some back in. Because they love working with kids and helping them grow.

It's why teachers teach.

We can't just grab people off the street and think they can plug the hole that remains when teachers quit. Despite how the dinosaur, banana, and unicorn costumes make it seem, teaching is not a one-size-fits-all profession.

* * *

Educators don't tend to advertise it when they go above and beyond for their students or their students' families. So we often don't know what happens before 8:00 and after 3:00, what takes place beyond the classroom door. Curious to learn about extra things that teachers do to "make a positive difference in our world today," I did a quick survey of my Facebook friends who are educators. I asked them to share anything extra they'd done themselves, whether something grand or tiny.

Here's a bit of what I learned.

When one student's family became unhoused, Melissa organized donations of money and Christmas presents. Shirley told me of a young child who wrote about grandparents being "sad" because food was low. The teacher arranged for grocery donations and hauled the bags to the school gate at dismissal. The shocked grandparents fought to hold back tears.

Tracy's student was in the foster care system but lived on her own and was in the last weeks of pregnancy. While shopping for groceries for the girl, Tracy got the call that contractions had started. In a panic, she forgot the already-paid-for groceries at the store and raced to the girl's apartment, empty-handed. Tracy then dashed back for the groceries, unpacked them at the apartment, and drove the girl to the hospital; on the way, she stopped to satisfy the teen mom's last pregnancy craving, a Slurpee from 7-Eleven. Tracy felt like the dad in a 1950s sitcom, clueless and frantic. The only thing missing was the celebratory cigar.

During the pandemic, Ashley gathered donated stuffed animals and children's books. Then she distributed them to her homebound kindergarteners, introducing each stuffed animal as a "reading buddy" with whom the five-year-olds could share their books.

When Lori's second-grade student was crying in class because his dad's tools—the family's livelihood—had been stolen from their truck, Lori spread the word and raised funds to replace the tools.

Early in the pandemic's distance learning, one of Angela's kindergarteners was desperate for conversation, and one day she remained online after the other five-year-olds had logged off. For the rest of the year, for ten minutes or sixty, Angela let the lonely child stay on after each day's online class. They'd chat the whole time, despite the child's mother in the background repeatedly urging her daughter to let her teacher go.

* * *

Each May, my district embraced Teacher Appreciation Week by giving us gifts. One year, we each received an apple in our office mailbox. In recognition of our hard work, the district over the years gifted me a pen, a notepad, a pin, and a cup, among other items. Often, a large tray of cafeteria cookies for us to share was delivered, sometimes after the official five days of appreciation had passed. We could usually count on a mass-produced certificate, most of which piled up in the recycling bin underneath the office mailboxes. Grandiose thank-you emails, presumably composed by assistants with better writing skills than the superintendent, arrived in our inboxes.

Delete.

But at school board meetings, the talk was less appreciative. A high-level district administrator once stated that there was no need to reduce class size, because "when you teachers had lower size before, you still failed." At the bargaining table, to illustrate why we needed basic first-aid kits, I pantomimed for the administrators how I'd leapt over a classroom puddle left by a child streaming blood. The district negotiators' response was to refuse our request, because "Band-Aids for every classroom would be too expensive." The head of HR scoffed at teachers' claims of job stress, declaring—backed by no data—that teachers just have "a culture of absenteeism." Secret sources revealed to me that a past superintendent had expressed his goal of breaking the teachers' union. Years after we narrowly averted a strike, I learned that our board members were incredulous that teachers continued to accept the district's pitiful "last best offers," year after year. This, when the board members themselves dictated what district negotiators could offer.

Teachers aren't asking for jewels or shiny appliances for Teacher Appreciation Week. But demeaning us for most of the other weeks—it sure makes a sweet apple taste sour.

Even during the worst of the pandemic, my district administrators seemed oblivious to our crushing workload. With no lead time, we were suddenly developing endless hours of digital educational content, using tools utterly foreign to us. An assistant superintendent appeared puzzled during negotiations.

"Why don't you just tell the kids to read a book and write about it? Done!"

I saw my gaping mouth on the Zoom screen. How did she not know that most of our low-income district's elementary students didn't own books? Or that many young or struggling kids didn't know how to read a physical book, much less a digital facsimile of a book on a laptop screen? Or that telling kids to "just read and write about it" every day is the *opposite* of engaging students, and engaging kids is what was desperately needed during those awful months of isolation?

For month after pandemic month, my K–12 district refused to negotiate the conditions for our eventual return to on-site instruction; their only interest was discussing how to get teachers to use a new digital platform designed for college level. Not only was this enraging, but it further exhausted us on the bargaining team. It wasted time we didn't have. Each day of bargaining into the early evening meant that we teachers on the team couldn't start our prep work for the next day's instruction until after dinner. On bargaining days—sometimes two to five days per week—I might not finish the next day's prep work until 10:00 p.m. I'd stagger into the TV room to join my husband, play video solitaire for ten minutes of mindlessness, and then shuffle off to bed to rest up for teaching, lesson planning, and more bargaining the next day. The schedule and workload broke me. It's a big part of why I decided to retire.

But the biggest reason was that I could no longer contain the tidal wave of rage in my body, the disbelief over being forced to do the most difficult work I'd ever done, but with no district support beyond the abundant assistance of my principal. My blood pressure skyrocketed. My hands trembled, rebounding from continual bursts of adrenaline. I wept during Zoom bargaining sessions, in my principal's office, while reading books to my third graders.

And all of that was before the fiery culture wars zeroed in on teachers as the enemy.

When teachers are slammed on popular podcasts, or doxed for insisting that they teach the truth about Black history—*American* history—how do they stay?

When teachers and school librarians are called out on Fox News for reading inclusive books with students that reflect the bigness of the world, how do they stay?

When LGBTQ+ teachers are targeted and threatened by strangers until they're afraid for their families, how do they stay?

When teachers receive death threats for upholding California law and respecting frightened students' requests to keep personal information private, how do they stay?

Increasingly, they don't. Increasingly, they are fleeing the job that is so essential to society.

Teachers enter education to help students and to make a positive difference in our world. Can the same be said of the computers that will replace them unless we stop villainizing teachers for doing the job we hired them to do?

5

UNCOMFORTABLE TRUTH

There once was a little girl named Lori who grew up with what today would be called food scarcity. Lori and her two sisters were raised by their mother, whose income was below the poverty level.

From a very young age, Lori loved the library. She felt comfortable there, because she knew she was welcome. The library was the great equalizer, available to anyone, regardless of income, age, or status. The library was for everyone. The library was for *her*.

When Lori was nine, she needed information. She had crushes on women on TV; she didn't know what that meant and didn't have the vocabulary to describe her feelings. Lori had never heard the word "lesbian," and though she'd vaguely heard the word "homosexual," she didn't know its meaning.

So she got brave, headed to the library, and asked the reference librarian how she could learn about the word.

The librarian placed the big, heavy *World Book Encyclopedia* on the table, and Lori started reading, poring over words in search of understanding. Every time she came upon a word to cross-reference, the librarian would lug the next *World Book* over, and Lori would keep reading.

Hours later, she rose, tired and satisfied. She had learned enough to understand herself better.

Lori's love of the library remains alive decades later. Her experience at age nine led her to her life's work. There's no way to calculate the power of feeling seen, but Lori has one measure of that power, which she keeps in a file folder. It's the diploma for her master's in library and information science.

Lori is a librarian.

* * *

The most magical building in the old section of my hometown was the Napa Children's Library, built from blocks of local fieldstone. When we were little, Mom hauled the four of us kids there each week, and I'd hurry through the alleyway to gaze at the library's cornerstone, which proclaimed the year of the building's birth in 1901. Then I'd clomp up the echoey stairwell, lugging the previous week's pile of books. I was breathless. New treasures awaited.

That library is where I discovered the fourteen books about the Land of Oz, which kick-started my imagination and filtered through into nighttime dreams. The eight volumes of Anne of Green Gables ignited me with its adventures of a girl who was brilliant, hotheaded, brave, and kind all at once. The wall of mystery novels taught me to analyze clues, look beyond the obvious, and be tenacious. From the shelf of baseball biographies, I learned about Lou Gehrig's ALS, the Negro Leagues, the racist treatment of Willie Mays, and Jackie Robinson's courage.

The general biography section included dozens of books from a single series, each giving a tidy 180-page synopsis of the life of a U.S. historical figure. Though the stories were whitewashed of nuance and minimized perspectives that should have been magnified, I still learned about massacres of Native people and how the United States repeatedly broke treaties. I learned about the enslavement of Black people and the oppression of women. I learned of rebellions and triumphs, of horrors and heroes. I learned that books could make me cry.

My Catholic elementary school had no real library, other than the Bookmobile that came and parked each month between the church and the fifth-grade classroom. The teachers—Sisters of Mercy from Ireland—each kept a classroom bookshelf full of worn hardcovers without pictures, raggedy paperbacks with dog-eared corners, and old-fashioned titles with brittle pages that would flake off on my fingertips in papery bits. I read them all.

On Saturday mornings, I'd hole up in the garage with my book, hoping Mom wouldn't find me and make me do chores. When I'd fight with a sibling and be sent to my room, I'd read on my bed and forget I was being punished. Over breakfast, I'd keep reading until long after the last bite of cinnamon toast, so absorbed that I'd be late getting ready for school. Gripping my scuffed white Oxford shoes and a bag lunch, I'd run in my stockinged feet out to the car, where my siblings and Mom waited.

Reading opened the world to me, and me to the world. I could never get enough.

* * *

In my teen years, there were library books that shocked, enlightened, horrified, and enthralled me. I read about racism in *Yes I Can*, the autobiography of Sammy Davis Jr., and I still feel queasy when I hear his name; the book opens with his description of the car crash that cost him his eye, and I can't unsee the images he created with words. Reading about racism felt like following a trail of clues to a mystery; *Yes I Can* led to *Black Like Me*, which pointed me to *Nigger: An Autobiography*, by comedian–political activist Dick Gregory.

In high school, we studied the New Testament and comparative religions; then I came home and read about murder. The notorious Zodiac killer had struck near Napa a few years prior, in an event so well known that my visiting cousin was afraid to sleep near our bedroom window. I became engrossed in reading true stories of grisly mass killings—Truman Capote's *In Cold Blood*, and *Helter Skelter*, the story of the Manson Family murders.

Did my parents know that I read these books of cruelty and slaughter? Or that I stayed up until 3:30 on a school night to finish *The Exorcist* and then was too frightened to fall asleep? Probably not—I don't remember questions about content or boundaries placed around my book choices. They were happy I was reading.

One of my nonmurder book choices was a novel; I've forgotten the title, but I remember that the main characters were gay men, including one who was a prostitute. Almost every page detailed aspects of a life I'd never known to exist, and all of it fascinated me. At home, there never would have been discussions of people having sex; until a ridiculous age, my hazy hypothesis was that to have sex, a man and woman did something mysterious while standing naked together in a closet.

The sexually explicit novel did not damage me; it was *The Exorcist* that kept me awake at night for weeks. Reading about gay sex didn't frighten or appall me. It just colored in one more section of the road map of life and opened my mind to have sympathy for a fictional gay man named Vito.

* * *

Drag Story Hour (formerly Drag *Queen* Story Hour) is a nonprofit with a global network of local organizations, in which storytellers use the art of drag to read books to kids in libraries, schools, and bookstores. To build empathy, programs celebrate gender diversity and all forms of difference, with the hope that as kids see someone defying gender restrictions, they'll "imagine a world where everyone can be their authentic selves."[1] New York City's Drag Story Hour website declares that the atmosphere of acceptance created at their events helps to stave off teasing and bullying. A testimonial asserts, "It's important kids know that it's okay to be different."[2]

Before the 2022 event at the San Lorenzo Library, staff members were already on alert. Strangers had been calling, fretting over what children would be taught, and Libs of TikTok learned of the upcoming story hour and spread the word online. The library communications team was monitoring the situation, and staff members knew to call the cops if trouble brewed. Still—they didn't really expect trouble. This was a *library.*

Advance sign-ups were required for the story hour, and all children needed to be accompanied by an adult. The "queen" was dressed in San Francisco Giants garb, and the twenty-five in attendance were mostly preschoolers and their parents. Panda Dulce, the storyteller, read the first book and led the children in song.

Then four men entered and headed directly to the room where the kids were. The library manager told me, "My heart dropped, and I just knew." She and her boss dashed to the children.

The men loomed over the preschoolers, screaming at the parents and at Panda, calling her a groomer, a pedophile, a tranny, and an "it." A few more men arrived, several wearing shirts emblazoned with pictures of an AK-47. At least one man's rifle shirt also bore the words, "Kill your local pedophile." They yelled at parents, "Why are you bringing your kids to this?" A staff member at the front desk called 911, expecting to hear gunshots at any moment. A little boy said, "Mommy, why was that man calling us sick? We all had our masks on and he didn't."

Staffers pushed a crafting table into the children's section of the library, so the families who hadn't left could busy their kids with coloring. A security guard grabbed Panda by the hand and whisked her away to safety. One staff member was attending as a parent, but when the hostility erupted, she set up her three-year-old in a cozy corner under a table and rushed to help her colleagues protect the public.

The library manager had trained in de-escalation techniques, telling me, "This is not a safe job. You have everybody and their brother in there on their best and their worst day." So she knew what to do: ask questions, keep the room quiet, separate the angry people, don't argue, keep an eye on exits, and use "calming hands."

When law enforcement finally got them to leave, the men brought their protest to the sidewalk, shouting into a bullhorn. More protesters showed up, urging passersby to join them. Some pressed up against the library windows, looking for rooms where Panda might be hiding. Others videoed the children through the front window, until a dad stormed outside, ordering them to stop recording footage of his child.

Someone who lived nearby told a library staffer, "Those are the KKK right there. I moved away from the South to get away from this. And now I'm seeing it out my bedroom."

* * *

A few days after the event, as I sat outside the library with signboards of glitter and rainbows, a stranger strode across the parking lot, heading straight toward me. Her whole face was a smile and her arms were outstretched, like a conductor before the orchestra.

"You're *here*!" she cried.

Spontaneously, we embraced.

"My name is Lori," she said. "I work here."

After she told me about the reference librarian who'd helped her when she was nine, more stories flew between us.

"Straight and cisgender people never have to think about if they see themselves in the world, because they're *everywhere*," said Lori. "That's *all* they see. But when you're gay, you're always searching, always looking to find a reflection of yourself out there."

Lori and I didn't pose theories as to why the Proud Boys had chosen San Lorenzo to show their disdain for queer people. There's no explanation that could have justified it to us anyway.

* * *

The fallout of the whole experience was extreme. A California state senator decried the event and received a death threat the next day. For weeks, the library phone rang nonstop with people calling from around the country. Most of them were "raging homophobes," screaming at whichever unfortunate staffer picked up the phone. The library had to monitor its social media for threats. Staff members were jumpy and fearful, obsessively wondering, "Who's out there? Who's looking at my car? Should we be parking somewhere else?" Counselors were brought in to help.

The library manager flinched at every sound when out in public, convinced someone was watching her. She wasn't wrong; people tried to break into her bank account and stood outside her house.

She told me, "I was targeted because I work at a library and decided it was important to have a representative program for my community, for people who are underserved and underrepresented."

And yet—

The San Lorenzo Library also received homemade cards and letters of support from around the world. Allies dropped off homemade goodies and flowers. The library and the county supervisor's office funded twelve months of supportive LGBTQ+ programming, calling it "Every Month Is Pride Month." In late 2024, Transgender Day of Remembrance was hosted by the San Lorenzo Library, in the same room where such terror had transpired.

"It was one of the most beautiful evenings I've ever had," Lori told me recently. "It was a show of resiliency and everything came full circle. We had so many beautiful people there. That was the day we fully reclaimed our space.

"The whole thing was such a contrast with my childhood experience. If I had been little when that happened, my whole sense of safety in libraries would have ended."

I completed the thought silently. Lori would never have become a librarian.

* * *

Here's the ironic postscript to Drag Story Hour in June 2022:

Once the Proud Boys had been cleared out, Panda—incredibly—decided to finish story hour. Though the vibe in the room had transformed from joyful to sober, Panda began reading *Families, Families, Families!*, by Suzanne Lang.

The book begins, "Some children have many siblings, and some children have none. Some children live with two dads, and some live with one mom. Some children have many pets, and some just have a plant."

The accompanying illustrations show goofy animal families—pigs wearing ties, a lion draped in a string of pearls, and a gorilla in a pink T-shirt reading "Doug."

When Panda read the words, "Some children live with their grandparents," one child called out, "Hey! That's what my family looks like!"

The anger, the fear, the disruption—none of it deterred a young child from seeing his own family being validated.

He didn't see how Panda was dressed.

He saw himself in the pages of a book.

* * *

Kids need to see people like themselves doing important work so they can be inspired to dream big. When students of various identities—racial, ethnic, language, gender, ability, sexual orientation, and so on—see themselves reflected in the leaders, books, and curriculum at school, they can begin to realize that they have something valuable to contribute. Representation matters.

Lori was only one of many librarians and teachers who spoke to me about the importance of representation. Another was Theresa, a teacher-librarian in a Central Valley school district.

Theresa and I convened in her backyard, where I began nibbling homemade candied almonds as she talked about information literacy. Her speech was fast and dense, peppered with Education Code statutes. My mind strained to keep up. I grabbed a whole handful of almonds.

Before this teacher-librarian launched into the topic of book battles, she spoke of her firm belief that a movement has been alive for years, and its overarching goal is to shut down public education. It was a refrain that I would hear many times over the next year-plus of interviews.

"The radical right keeps picking different topics to focus on," she said, "but the movement is still the same. Every little thing is being nibbled away all around us."

She listed the most recent targets: CRT, Black history, books mentioning sex, and LGBTQ+ topics.

There are many prongs in the pitchfork that is stabbing public education in the heart. Back in 2011, a Tea Party leader stated that "public schools should go away" and that the party's ultimate goal was to "shut down public schools and have private schools only."[3] Some conservatives want privatization because it would weaken teacher unions, a stronghold of Democrats, and could be "used to woo African American and Latino voters to the Republican Party."[4] The far-right Moms for Liberty is linked with the Council for National Policy; according to professor Maurice Cunningham, author of *Dark Money and the Politics of School Privatization*, the council aspires to "destroy public education and privatize schooling . . . in order to reorient education toward Christian nationalism and transform the culture of the nation."[5]

But all that is a blip compared with what's happening under Donald Trump's second administration. The Departments of Defense and of the Interior are developing plans to divert their public school funds to private schools. Trump directed cabinet secretaries to plan on eliminating funding for schools that "directly or indirectly support" "discriminatory equity ideology."[6] Grants that support teacher preparation have been canceled, and portals have been set up so that parents, teachers, and others can report diversity, equity, and inclusion practices in public schools. Trump's education secretary is crafting plans to close the Department of Education, and there are budget proposals to eliminate funding for Head Start, the early-childhood education program for children in poverty.

Although Trump's assault on public education is unprecedented, the punitive nature of it is not. The No Child Left Behind Act (NCLB) of 2002 was severely underfunded, with a central flaw identified by Stanford professor Linda Darling-Hammond: "NCLB seeks to improve the schools poor students attend through threats and sanctions rather than the serious investments in education and welfare such an effort truly requires."[7]

Teacher-librarian Theresa believes the current movement against public schools took root with NCLB and high-stakes testing.

* * *

Around twenty-five years ago, in the early days of high-stakes testing, everyone at my school received a bonus of several hundred dollars. A short-lived California program rewarded employees at schools where students' test scores hit the growth target, and ours had. Outraged, I refused the check; a system that used children's test scores to determine my excellence would denounce me as unfit as soon as my kids' scores failed to reach the ever-rising goal. Many colleagues agreed; we forwarded our checks to a neighboring school that had been chastised for its low test scores.

A few months after the bonus, my coworkers and I learned that our students' most recent scores had not reached the *new* state target, and that we were therefore now on the state's list of "bad" schools. After class one day, I pulled a slick color pamphlet from my mailbox in the office. The district's quarterly newsletter belatedly congratulated schools for awards won the previous spring. Our school was on the list. Apparently, the district office hadn't yet realized that we were now officially bad teachers.

During the NCLB years, there were top students who bombed the springtime test because they were sick, unable to stay home since their parents couldn't afford to skip work. I remember when one of the best readers in the class—whose first language was Spanish—tanked the reading test; he scribbled random bubbles on the scantron so he could finish quickly and get back to his book. Countless students over the years were too hyperactive, too new to English, or too troubled, unmotivated, or emotionally fragile to pour energy into a test that didn't matter to them. I watched them haphazardly fill in wrong answers when I *knew* they knew the correct ones, but we weren't allowed to suggest they try particular problems again. They were eight and nine years old, far too young to understand why we were desperate for them to do their best.

During the test, I patrolled the room in state-mandated silence, trying to exude serenity so that any nervous kids would absorb my artificial calm and achieve their maximum potential. In the lunchroom afterward, we teachers were not allowed to speak about any test questions. We'd just shake our heads, close our eyes, and sigh.

After our school's scores missed the ever-rising target for several consecutive years, sanctions were leveled on us. We had a choice: either restructure our entire reading program, or be split up and sent to teach at different sites. (Apparently, terrible teachers damage fewer children when they're scattered.) We reluctantly overhauled our reading program to mirror one that the district was pushing. The following year, the district quietly abandoned that program, and we returned to the methodology we'd used before. But by then, NCLB had succeeded on one front anyway: In-fighting among us over the best methods for teaching reading had led several teachers to transfer from our school voluntarily. For some of us who stayed, the months of arguments left a hurt that lingered for years.

In the early days of NCLB, I was too idealistic to believe the wild idea that anyone might want to eliminate publicly funded education. Like my young students, I still had a lot to learn.

* * *

When Theresa became a teacher-librarian after years of teaching history, she dove into her new position like a Labrador chasing tennis balls at the beach. She purchased books that would excite kids and stimulate learning, and trained library staff to do the same. Passionate about representation and about developing students' information and digital literacy, Theresa pushed successfully for her district to hire more teacher-librarians, and to approve her requests for money to update library collections sorely in need of diverse titles.

Lack of representation in books conveys powerful messages to all children, to the ones who see themselves on the page and to those who remain invisible. A math teacher near Sacramento told me about the time his textbook had a word problem in which one character's name was clearly African American. There happened to be a boy in his class with the same name.

"That kid pulled me aside and said, 'I've never seen that name in a problem. Did you do that?' I told him no, and that it was just part of the problem. But seeing it in his face . . . you know? He asked me if it was fate. I told him it was just part of the book. He was saying, 'I've never seen my name, like, ANYWHERE.'

"People don't realize how powerful that is. That's one of the beauties of being a teacher. You get to see these moments, where kids can relate and connect. You could make a difference that builds a connection to a student that could hopefully be very powerful in their lives."

* * *

Years ago, Theresa introduced the game "Book Face Friday" to her high schoolers. In order to play, each kid had to begin by finding a book with a person on the cover who somewhat resembled them.

"So one day, this girl decides she wants to play," said Theresa. "She was African American. And you know what? We couldn't find a book with a Black face on it in my whole library. There was one book with Zora Neale Hurston, but it was the full body, so it wouldn't work."

Theresa got busy. This powerhouse wrote grants, connected with people eager to infuse school libraries with inclusive books, and ordered hundreds of new titles, including ones centered on Indigenous groups and Black, Latinx, and LGBTQ+ people.

"We have a very diverse student body," she says, "in ways you can see, and in ways you can't. We want books for ALL of them."

* * *

As a teacher, I understand wanting to keep things comfortable. Even when lessons run smoothly and kids are peaceful, classroom chaos silently lurks, ready to erupt. At any moment, there can be a spider invasion (with accompanying screams), projectile vomiting, heater breakdowns, bloody noses, or birds unable to escape after flying in through the open window. One day I brought my class in from lunch to find our entire room under two inches of water. A coworker once had a goose come waddling in the back classroom door, and another found a squirrel staring at her from atop a cabinet. I once sliced off a sliver of my index finger with an ancient paper cutter. Loath to disturb my students, who were—miraculously—working quietly, I whispered to two kids, asking them to fold a large wad of paper towels and grab the packing tape off my desk. Despite the mess in the sink and my temporary lack of availability, most of the others never noticed a thing. A coworker once led a PE activity that stirred up an underground hornet nest. One minute, her thirty-one students were frolicking in the sunshine. The next, they were screaming, back in the classroom and whacking each other with clipboards and notebooks, beating hornets out of T-shirts and braids.

Maintaining classroom calm is essential. It's survival.

I also understand wanting to hide certain books rather than deal with potential disruption. In my personal classroom library of many hundreds of titles, there were twenty-one from a series of artist biographies. The books included hilarious cartoons to accompany the perfect-for-third-grade text and the color reproductions of famous works.

"This is *inappropriate*!" squealed more than one nine-year-old during the month after I bought the Michelangelo book. They'd stand before me waving it, opened to the page showing the Sistine Chapel's painting of God and Adam, complete with genitalia.

Tired of the shrieks and of explaining that the world-famous treasure depicted a normal part of the human body, I eventually stashed the book in my file cabinet. Though I felt a little guilty doing it, the number of disruptive kids that year made me long for classroom tranquility.

But where I feel more than a little guilty is in noting that, until the last third of my career, I didn't initiate conversations explaining that some people are queer. There was no intentionality on my part. As I mentioned previously, my "methodology" of discussing the existence of spectrums and variations in orientation was to become angry whenever one upset child would hurl "gay" at another to win an argument. I'd sternly order children to *never* use that word as an insult, but I didn't try hard enough to communicate to young kids that not everyone walks a straight line through orientation and gender identity. Awkward, uncertain, and leery of parents' reactions, I skirted uncomfortable conversations and hoped my students would pick up on my generalized acceptance of each one of them.

Finally, while at an awards luncheon for union leaders, an elementary school teacher showed me that introducing children to the breadth of diversity didn't have to be as complicated as I was making it.

"Just read a book," he said, "and ask the kids to write about it. Or talk about it. Or both."

Read, write, talk. It was so much easier than what I'd built up in my head.

I resolved to head to the bookstore.

* * *

A few days after the luncheon but before the bookstore, my class was on a field trip in San Francisco, and I ended up next to Gaby's mother at lunchtime. Gaby was new to the school. She was bright-eyed and shy, with long black hair that fell over her face when she ducked her chin with a smile. Her bubbly mom was outgoing, overflowing with warmth and a ready laugh.

For the first few months of school, I hadn't heard mention of a dad in Gaby's life, but I heard the name Karla quite a bit. I figured she was a coparent with Gaby's mom, Elena, but Elena was the only one who ever contacted me. That day on the trip, Elena and I sat on the cold concrete steps outside the science museum, watching kids climb on the play structure. As we munched on our sandwiches and basked in the spring sunshine, Elena talked about Karla.

"I don't know if you knew that Karla is Gaby's other parent."

"I wasn't sure," I said. "I just know Gaby mentions her a lot."

Elena nodded. "Actually, Karla wasn't always a woman. We got together a long time ago, before she transitioned."

She trusted me. I put down my sandwich.

"Will I get to meet her? Does Karla ever come pick Gaby up?"

Now Elena's words poured out. "Not very often. She had a terrible experience at Gaby's old school. Someone who worked in the office ridiculed her in front of the children and adults. We pulled Gaby out the next day. That's why she's here."

Back at school late that afternoon, I thought about what I didn't know—whether Gaby remembered Karla before her transition, whether all three still lived together, or whether I would ever meet Karla.

But there was one thing I definitely knew. I'd head to the bookstore before going home.

The next day in class, I read *And Tango Makes Three*. It's the true story of a couple of male penguins at New York's Central Park Zoo who became partners, hatched an abandoned egg, and raised a penguin chick together. Two adorably awkward birds who just wanted a baby to care for? It was a no-brainer; third graders would love it.

The text described how the two males ignored females, instead spending their time with each other. When I read, "Their keeper noticed the two [boy] penguins, and thought to himself, 'They must be in love,'" there were a few gasps, and a couple of giggles. But by the end, with the successful hatching of the new chick, the kids were unanimous, with cheers that came to rest in happy sighs.

"What was in your mind during the story?" I asked them. "Did you think about anything new?"

As a flurry of eager hands shot into the air, the words exploded from Gaby.

"I have two moms!"

Her wide-eyed urgency pierced me. How long had she been silent and secretive, feeling alone, waiting for permission to speak of her family?

It was just a simple story about *penguins*.

It only took one book.

A book that is one of many titles that people across the United States want to ban.

* * *

More than fifty years ago, the Supreme Court affirmed that students "don't shed their constitutional rights to freedom of speech or expression at the schoolhouse gate."[8] The Court has also determined that freedom of speech is not only the freedom to produce and disseminate information; it also protects the right to *receive* information and ideas.

In June 2023, California's governor, attorney general, and superintendent of public instruction collaborated on a strongly worded letter conveying these points. They sent it to superintendents and principals throughout the state. It reminded school leaders that "access to books—including books that reflect the diverse experiences and perspectives of Californians, and especially those that may challenge us to grapple with uncomfortable truths—is a profound freedom we all must protect and cultivate."[9]

Though her district is supportive of having well-stocked libraries, teacher-librarian Theresa still must educate adults daily on what it means to protect and cultivate the freedom to receive information.

"Principals will say, 'What's this book doing here? You need to get this out.' Teachers sometimes grab a book out of a kid's hand and march into the library, saying, 'Did you know this was on the shelves?'"

She told me of a couple of district employees setting up a library one summer. They found two off-kilter desks jammed together, with edges overlapping. When they pulled the desks apart, down tumbled all the sex books that had been wedged between them. No child had put them there. It was the library tech.

When teachers and principals confiscate a book from a student, explaining to Theresa that the content made them uncomfortable, her response is always unflinching.

"I'm sorry you feel uncomfortable," she tells them. "You have that right. But we don't buy books to make YOU feel comfortable or uncomfortable. It's about the kids' right to have this info. Give it back to the kid."

One teacher who had taken a sex-related book from a student assured Theresa, "Oh, no, I'm *totally* comfortable."

Theresa asked, "Then why did you take it out of his hands?"

"I just told him he has to tell me *why* he wants to check it out."

"When he checks out *Harry Potter*, does he have to tell you why? When he checks out *Captain Underpants*, does he have to tell you why?"

Theresa continued naming books that a teacher would never ask a student to justify, then underscored her point.

"So why should he *ever* have to tell you why he's checking out any book? He's checking it out because he wants to read it."

* * *

At a training for site and district administrators, Theresa distributed the district's policy on students and book choice. Each attendee had a copy. Using familiar books that some might consider controversial for language or content but not for sex-related concerns—books like *Harry Potter*, *Captain Underpants*, *The Giver*, and *Maus*—she presented four hypothetical situations that could arise in a school library. Each time she asked, "What if this happened?" the attendees all knew the answer.

"Oh, no, you can't take that book away," they repeated over and over. "Kids have the right to read. Our district uses the approved resources to determine which age gets to read which books."

Then, for the fifth practice case, Theresa used *Sex Is a Funny Word*, a comic book for eight-to-ten-year-olds that has won awards in the United States and Canada, and received high praise in the *School Library Journal* and on well-regarded review sites.

Commotion broke out.

Theresa observed, "Well, that's interesting, because you understood the rules for the other four cases. But this one makes you uncomfortable."

She reminded the squirming school leaders of what they already knew.

"The point is that whether you're uncomfortable or not, the kid has a right to read whatever book is in the library for them.

"Nobody HAS to read this book. It's not in the curriculum, which would be a different selection process. But *these* books? We buy them with the approval of our library director and our 'prevention services' social worker. These were deemed to be the best books for kids at these ages. We *need* these books."

* * *

It's not just school employees who sometimes get uncomfortable around books. Kids absorb shame and secrecy, and they feel the discomfort, too. Theresa spoke of a book for high schoolers about male puberty.

"Whenever there's a group of ninth-grade boys gathered, it's always around that book," she said. "I just go ask them if they want to check it out."

Invariably, the embarrassed boys pass the book around (*YOU take it! No, YOU!*) until it's in Theresa's hand. The kids fidget and avoid eye contact, but Theresa plays it cool.

"We bought this book on purpose," she tells them, "so that you can have this information if you want it. If not, just go ahead and put it back on the shelf." Apparently, though, ninth-grade boys are too self-conscious to actually check it out. It sits on the shelf until the next group of giggling boys heads over.

A librarian in Theresa's district told her of a middle school student who consistently checked out all six of his school library's books on physical maturation. When they'd come due, he'd return them and immediately check them back out.

The librarian asked the counselor to casually check in with the boy and say, "Hey, how's everything going?" in case he had any concerns he wanted to talk about. The librarian's only concern was that no other kids had a chance to read those six books. The counselor agreed, asking the librarian to pop in when they met up.

When the three convened, the librarian and the boy struck a deal: He could check out any two of those books, and when he returned them, he could take two more. The kid had no worries he wanted to discuss. Everything was fine until the counselor asked one last question.

"Do we maybe need to call your mom and see what she says?"

Here, Theresa faced me, hands upraised.

"WHY? Why would she *say* that to him?!"

After that day, the boy returned all six books and stopped checking them out.

But he spoke to a buddy. The buddy now checks out two at a time and passes them straight to his friend.

* * *

Theresa conducts role-plays with library staff to prepare them for awkward situations. She instructs them to remain calm when kids get too disruptive around a book, and to ask if anyone wants to check it out.

To teachers, she says, "If a kid is creating a scene, that's a teachable moment. Just say, 'Oh, I see you're not quite ready for this book. I'll put it back in case someone else wants it. But I'll make sure the librarian knows that when you're ready and mature enough, you can check it out.'"

A group of fifth-grade girls at one school enjoyed helping their librarian reshelve books during lunchtime. *Sex Is a Funny Word* (along with a few similar books) was often lying around, pulled off the shelf by curious students. After the girls would finish reshelving, the librarian kept finding it tucked into hidden nooks.

When the librarian asked the girls about it, they told her the book made them uncomfortable. She asked them to just leave it where they found it, but they continued hiding the book. They wanted to "protect" other students from something "naughty."

Finally, Theresa met with them.

"If any book, or anything, or any*one* ever makes you uncomfortable, you're *exactly right* to get away from it. So don't check that book out. Don't even take it off the shelf.

"But here's the thing—it has really good information. Your parents might have great conversations with you. But some kids don't have parents who talk to them or help them. We need to have that book for *those* kids. That's why we buy books. This book isn't for every kid. It's for the one or two kids in this whole school who might need it."

Over time, a kind of détente was reached. The girls never ended up *liking* that the book was there. But they came to accept that for some kids, the book would be helpful. They extended their thinking to consider others' needs. They stopped hiding the book.

It's an impressive feat for fifth graders—to allow conflicting feelings to coexist for the sake of the greater good.

Maybe some of us missed that part of fifth grade.

* * *

Sometimes, teachers are simply uncomfortable with a book's content. But sometimes, they want to eliminate specific titles because they're thinking, "I'll be blamed if the parent sees this book. So I'll take care of it."

Theresa's district has built-in safeguards to prevent children from checking out books with subject matter too mature for them. The computer system won't check out titles if the child's grade is lower than the recommended grades in the database. Even if students are old enough, parents can request that their child not be allowed to check out materials on any given topic. Parents can also specify which books they don't want their child to read, and if the child tries to pull a fast one, a pop-up will block the librarian from proceeding.

The fear educators feel is real. She's heard library staff say, "I just won't buy books like that. I think I'll just order more books about animals and motorcycles and cars."

Rather than argue, Theresa tells teachers, "If you get parent complaints, just refer them to the library. We'll take all the blame. I'll take it all myself."

When she defends book selections, Theresa arms herself with her school board's policy, along with documents like the American Library Association's "Freedom to Read" statement, updated in 2004. In part, it reads, "*It is not in the public interest to force a reader to accept the prejudgment of a label characterizing any expression or its author as subversive or dangerous.* The ideal of labeling presupposes the existence of individuals or groups with wisdom to determine by authority what is good or bad for others. It presupposes that individuals must be directed in making up their minds about the ideas they examine. But Americans do not need others to do their thinking for them."[10]

Theresa knows her stuff. After she used board policy and documents like the "Freedom to Read" statement to justify the purchase of *Sex Is a Funny Word* to a principal nervous about the book, he said, "Ah, *shit*. There's no way we can win this one. The documentation is too strong."

He wanted to dodge parent complaints. I get it. I'm a sneaky Michelangelo hider. But when student rights are upheld, complaints can't be avoided. Theresa hears more book-complaint stories now than ever before.

In late 2022, a parent strode into a library in Theresa's district, demanding, "I want a list of every book in this library."

The library tech answered, "I don't know how to get that, but I can show you how to use the catalog."

Fuming, the woman slapped down a piece of paper and scribbled down her contact information.

"I expect you to call me back with an answer to this!"

The tech was frightened, knowing the woman would eventually return. Theresa reassured her.

"Don't worry, you're done with her. When she comes back, she'll go to your principal, and he'll send her to me."

Theresa knows how it will go. When the woman returns, Theresa will follow directives and present the woman with a printed list of every book, even though the district has a public-facing catalog that anyone can use to search for books.

She also knows that parents who analyze the catalog will find new listings of "social-emotional learning" (SEL) books, and that many parents will be upset by that discovery. Storylines of SEL books allow students to learn empathy, resilience, and problem-solving in a natural, relatable way. Studies of classrooms using SEL strategies show that students' attendance and grades improve, along with their ability to solve problems, cope with emotional stress, and avoid peer pressure to join in harmful activities.

"But parents won't like it that we're talking about kids' feelings," says Theresa.

It boggles the mind.

How can *anyone* think it's possible to spend even a day teaching and not talk with kids about their feelings? We comfort them when grandparents die, and we celebrate with them when siblings are born. When a student at my school died suddenly, the teacher had to help her young charges navigate through grief all year, even as she was struggling with it herself. We teach them to stop hitting others, and how to better handle their frustration. We show them how to be patient with those who lack understanding, and to invite others to join in when someone feels left out. We encourage children to describe how it feels to be bullied, in hope that the harmful behaviors will cease. We help kids celebrate their strengths gracefully, and ask others for forgiveness.

Of *course* we talk about feelings. And race. And queer people. And inclusion. We speak about life, because life happens within the classroom walls, and it continues happening when they leave that safe space. We speak in words, and we read words in books. It's not always comfortable, but learning *isn't* comfortable. It can't be. We teach students that discomfort happens when what we know is challenged. Sitting in discomfort can jump-start self-reflection, stimulate problem-solving, and spawn new ideas.

It's how we change and grow, which is our goal for students in school.

At least, that's what educators try so hard to do.

We help them change and grow.

* * *

In addition to everything else it was, distance teaching during the pandemic was simply bizarre. I introduced multiplication concepts to eight-year-olds as they curled up in pajamas, nuzzling stuffed unicorns. Through their unmuted laptops, microwaves beeped and vacuum cleaners roared, while babies occasionally screamed in the background. TVs blared until it was all I could do not to start screaming myself.

Your child is trying so hard to learn! Can't you at least turn off the TV?!

Keeley slurped ramen all morning, without ever losing focus on her work. When I read chapters aloud from *The Miraculous Journey of Edward Tulane*, Anton bounced nonstop on a yoga ball, back and forth across his living room. Nayeli logged in from a large daycare center; whenever she unmuted to ask a question, the ambient hubbub sounded like a tiny-person frat party. One day, I heard myself say, "Kayvon, *you CAN'T keep unmuting yourself when you talk to your chicken*!" (The squawking chicken's name? Noodle.) Two kids regularly set up shop in their respective bathrooms, the only place where they had relative peace. Maybe it sounded quiet to them, but when they spoke, we'd hear distant echoes and a mysterious gurgling as if the children were speaking underwater.

Another weird thing about distance teaching was that parents who were home could hear every word if they wanted to. I wasn't self-conscious; proud of how much I had learned and of how hard I was working, I *hoped* parents would pay attention. Did they realize I had adapted for virtual learning the raucous, whole-class online dice games we played, and aligned them perfectly with each day's math lesson? Had they noticed that kids were so absorbed in the chapter book I read to them that they unmuted themselves to whisper things like, 'Hey, are you crying, too?' Did they watch my homemade video showing kids how to blend pastels, the ones I'd purchased myself and delivered to each kid's home? What about the video that guided them to create replicas of Black artists' works from the Harlem Renaissance? Did they notice that during writing time, their children wrote beautiful poetry, more moving than anything I'd read in my previous thirty-one years of teaching?

The parents I worked with that year noticed my efforts and consistently voiced their appreciation. They asked questions, too, and a big one came during Back-to-School Night, on Zoom. That same day, I had read the book about the two bonded male penguins. In the (online) presence of all of the parents, one mother spoke up.

"I heard the book you read today, and I have some questions. I'm not saying I'm upset. I just worry that maybe these kids are too young to think about the topic of being gay. Can you talk about why you read it?"

Even as I was marveling at how genuinely and bravely she had expressed her concern, my heart was racing. There I was in the hot seat, alone in our guest room, staring at the little squares of faces I was just beginning to recognize.

I dove in, explaining to parents and a few grandparents that kids need to see themselves in books, to hear their lived experience spoken aloud. My job as a teacher was not to present the experience of only the majority; it was to teach about the world, in all its rich diversity. All children need to feel a sense of belonging, to understand that they fit somewhere. I told the parents that children of color have for generations felt—and been—excluded when children's books were filled only with pictures of little white kids. Children with physical disabilities feel shut out when characters in books all climb trees and run.

When kids don't see themselves represented, they receive the message that they don't matter. When kids don't see *others* represented, they receive the message that *others* don't matter as much as they do. And when adults pretend that men only love women and that everyone's physiology matches what their mind is telling them, children who might one day realize they are queer can feel like freaks, like outcasts. Kids with LGBTQ+ family members can absorb the message that their family is not acceptable.

Silence not only conveys stigma to LGBTQ+ kids, but it teaches straight cisgender kids that everyone different from them is wrong, is less-than. *All* children need the message that *everyone* matters, that we all belong. Compassion, empathy, and inclusiveness make us better. That's part of what a teacher is supposed to teach.

I thanked the mom for asking her question, and then I repeated the whole thing in my imperfect Spanish for the parents who wouldn't have understood me the first time. By the time I was done, I was sweating, already trying to replay in my head the words that had poured from my mouth. Had I said it all? Did I sound defensive? Did I invite feedback? Had I made sense, or did it come out all jumbled?

I decided it was good enough. It was impossible for me to undo my years of near silence regarding LGBTQ+ people, but I wasn't silent that night. I'd seen some nodding heads as I spoke, and no one had asked any follow-up questions. Were they in complete agreement? Or were they simply reluctant to challenge my confidence? I don't know, but at least that final group of parents I worked with before my retirement knew exactly why I read that book, and why I'd go on to read others like it that year.

And more importantly, their children heard those books, those mind-broadening ideas, those words that can plant seeds of understanding, hope, and kindness.

When I was teaching, it could be nerve-racking when a parent asked a potentially controversial question I wasn't expecting. Tricky questions could be about race, student behavior, or disciplinary measures taken against other people's children. Though I hadn't anticipated that question on Back-to-School Night, I'm grateful to the mother who posed it, showing me what it can look like to disagree without attacking. She probably wasn't comfortable asking it, and I was kind of nervous hearing it.

But it wasn't our comfort that mattered. We were all there for the kids, so together, we waded through the discomfort. And we all emerged on the other side. Maybe a little changed. Just like we hope for students.

I think we did the kids proud.

6

ROOT FOR THE KINGS

Straight teachers reveal their orientation to students all the time, without ever being reported or sparking outrage. Their work websites introduce smiling opposite-sex spouses. Teacher desks and bulletin boards display pictures of those same beloved partners. Husbands drop off flowers for wives in the school office on Valentine's Day and on birthdays.

Many times, my own husband came to my classroom to bring a coat or lunch I'd forgotten at home. After he retired, John drove a carload of kids whenever I was short a driver for field trips. Each year, when teaching descriptive writing to my third-grade students, I'd tell the story of when John and I picked up our rescue dog and she ran away. Sometimes, when I was sick at home, John went to my classroom and grabbed books I needed so that I could write lesson plans for the next day's substitute teacher. Every student in every class from 2006 on knew that I, a woman, was married to a man.

But it's different for educators who are LGBTQ+. Some gay or gender-nonconforming teachers aren't out at school; fear of repercussions from parents leads some to keep themselves muzzled. One young teacher contacted me after seeing my social media post announcing this interview project and explained that she'd been recorded while telling her middle school students that she and her girlfriend were going on a road trip over break. The recording was shared, and soon, strangers from the alt-right were spreading her private information on social media. She began receiving death threats. Her message to me was tinged with a frantic energy, and though I promised anonymity and tried to make my responses nonthreatening and reassuring, she eventually stopped answering me. I think about her often.

Openly discussing gender and sexual orientation can be scary for many teachers, regardless of their own orientation or identity. A first-year teacher who was the adviser for her school's GSA sent an enthusiastic response to my query. We messaged back and forth; she said she had lots to discuss and was very eager to be interviewed. Then—nothing. Maybe she shared her excitement with a seasoned colleague who counseled her to keep her untenured self quiet. Maybe she was already learning that speaking up about LGBTQ+ issues can catapult a teacher into a hostile national spotlight.

In Chico, California, a mother sued the school district, alleging that her child's school "socially transitioned" the student by allowing the child to use male pronouns and a new male name while hiding the change from the parent. Though the district adhered to California law in not informing the parent of the child's gender identity or expression without the student's consent, the mother referred to that practice as the "Parental Secrecy Policy." The suit went on to say that "schools in the district are prompting students to question their sexuality and gender."[1] It all started when the fifth grader told a school counselor that she felt like a boy.

Barely two weeks after the Chico lawsuit was filed, hundreds of people showed up for a school board meeting in Bakersfield, nearly four hundred miles to the south. A Bakersfield teacher had been quoted in *The New York Times* affirming the importance of respecting students' preferred names and pronouns before adding, "Sometimes, [kids] need protection from their own parents."[2] While some in attendance voiced support for the teacher, many others erupted in applause when the pastor of a local church called for the teacher to be investigated and perhaps fired.

The educator did not attend the board meeting, having already received multiple death threats after the article in the *Times*.

It's safe to say that most people who enter teaching don't imagine that strangers will one day threaten their lives because of the job they do. When I started, my greatest fear was that I would run out of planned lessons and the kids would get wild. Every year while I was teaching, my back-to-school summer anxiety dream was some variation on the theme: I'd show up for the first day of school without lesson plans, and bedlam would ensue.

Today's teachers certainly still have back-to-school anxiety dreams disrupting their summer sleep. But in the current teaching climate, death threats are featured in the nightmares of some.

* * *

When I saw the turn-off for Yuba City on my way to Sarah's school farther north, I remembered a recent news story. In the fall of 2022, the local high school football team had staged a mock slave auction in the locker room and then posted on TikTok the video of Black players on the "auction block." It wasn't even that far from diverse Sacramento. Though the participating players faced serious consequences, it was still chilling to realize that kids had considered such a blatantly racist activity a "prank."

I passed the turn-off and continued north, thinking about Sarah's reply to my email query. She'd responded with just one word: "ABSOLUTELY." Momentarily forgetting that Sarah was the GSA adviser for her school, I wondered if I should have verified what "ABSOLUTELY" meant. What if she was a right-winger who wanted me to drive three hours so she could tell me how depraved I was for doing this project?

I finally reached her school. Entering the main building, I donned my mask and waded through the crowded hallway in search of the office. Spying two boys who weren't part of the herd, I asked brightly, "Can you tell me where the office is?"

The shorter of the two pointed to the door to my right. The women's restroom. As they laughed, I tried to hide my exasperated eye-roll. How did secondary teachers do this every day?

When I reached Sarah's room, she was conferring with a student in the otherwise unoccupied space. She motioned me in with a wave, and the first thing I saw was a large rainbow flag on her wall, including shades for transgender people and people of color. The meaning of "ABSOLUTELY" was clear.

The student was challenging Sarah about the solution to a math problem. The girl was assertive and logical in supporting her reasoning, and Sarah was firm, yet patient. Finally, the girl agreed that Sarah was right and then fretted over having to miss the next week of school and turn in assignments late.

Sarah smiled. "You're an excellent student. Just go with your family and be excellent. I'll see you when you get back."

The girl sighed with obvious relief. Tossing her long black hair, she thanked Sarah and headed out. I was impressed by how persistent yet warm they'd been with each other, and the teacher in me thrilled to see a student so invested in learning advanced math. Then Sarah turned her perky energy and bright eyes toward me.

She explained that she'd taught at a number of schools over her twenty-six-year career and had served as the GSA adviser at several.

"It's part of my life's work," she said. "My husband and I were as gender-neutral and open-hearted with our two kids as we could be, to the point where, when they were teenagers, they 'came out' to us as heterosexual. Ha! I just told them that it was fine, and that I still loved them."

I grinned.

She continued, telling me about a small alternative high school where she'd previously taught, a charter that attracted kids who needed a safe place to be themselves.

"I try to make sure all my students feel included and not judged. I celebrate who they are. At that school, a trans student stood up once in my algebra class and announced, 'This school saved my life. YOU saved my life.'"

Sarah's expression grew serious as she talked about her current school.

She spoke of a gay colleague who had worked with her at the alternative place, and who'd also transferred with Sarah. "At that small school, he was out, but here, he's back in the closet. It's all fear, fear, fear. This place is *very* different."

As adviser of the school's GSA, Sarah hears a lot.

"Kids talk to me about bullying, or about how they can't be who they are with their parents. Some kids want to transition, but their parents aren't supportive. For kids here, more than any kids I've ever known, their community makes it so hard to be LGBTQ."

She told me about what had happened during Club Rush Week of 2021, when information tables were set up at lunchtime. With teachers supervising and older students staffing tables for each club, freshmen were milling around, asking questions and gathering info. Club Rush is normally a happy time, when ninth graders learn about high school, and older students enjoy being peer leaders.

But that year, kids with Donald Trump flags and American flags surrounded the GSA table, harassing club members and hurling slurs before a teacher rushed over to rescue them. The students at the table were deeply shaken, frightened by their peers.

After Club Rush, the harassment kicked into high gear. On social media, a student posted a threat to kill all the gay kids at the school. GSA students told Sarah that as they crossed campus, others would approach them and mutter, "I hope you die." They'd be bullied while in class, and teachers either wouldn't hear it or wouldn't address it.

During homecoming week, clubs make floats for the lunchtime parade past the nearby elementary and middle schools. In the back of a teacher's rainbow-decorated pickup, GSA members sat atop a hay bale and rode along the route, blaring music and waving Pride flags. After lunch, with kids back in class, that teacher was cleaning his truck and putting away the sound system when a student leaned out of a classroom window, yelling at the teacher, "You fucking fag! Get out of here, you fucking fag!"

When the GSA next gathered, kids waving American flags stood outside Sarah's open classroom door as club members nervously trickled in. Even after the meeting started, one flag-bearing student remained outside, blocking the doorway.

"So I went to him and said, 'That's cool. You can have your flag. But we're having a meeting right now, so just move one way or the other.' He stood there and said, 'No. I can stand wherever I want.'"

Sarah went back and forth with him. The incident so disturbed her and the club members that she composed an email to all staff. It was the only time in seven years she'd ever sent a school-wide email.

Even when a topic seems innocuous, composing a whole-group email requires political savvy and precise word choice. I once sent a short schoolwide email to thank a hardworking PTA president who felt unappreciated. My principal then chastised me, declaring that I was contributing to staff divisiveness. He said I should've considered that the rivals of the PTA president would be offended, thinking I was taking sides.

But when Sarah shared her email with me, I was confused as to why anyone found fault with it. After all, she was adviser of the GSA. It opened,

> Dear Colleagues,
>
> Our students need your help. They need your leadership and role modeling. Homophobia and sexual harassment incidents are on the rise on our campus. Here is a list of what has happened during the past few weeks.

Then, in words that were supportive and student-centered, she listed the episodes of harassment she'd shared with me, all of which she'd either observed herself or been informed of by the GSA kids. Next, she listed positive developments:

> Some support and help that I've noticed so far: There is currently an investigation being conducted by the District Office, by Mr. R. And Ms. H. has asked how she can support the GSA. Security was buzzing around outside of my classroom during our GSA meeting yesterday.
>
> This is what I am asking of you. Please be aware. Please be diligent. Please stand up to bullies by having a zero-tolerance policy. Be our students' role models. Lead and educate these children so that they can learn to be kind. Thank you for your time. I appreciate everything that you are currently doing for our students.

I think my former principal would have loved it.

But not Sarah's principal. She was summoned to the office and berated for "causing problems [since] we're working on it from our end." Sarah's email garnered only two replies; each was from someone complaining that Trump-flag-waving students were not being allowed the freedom of speech that rainbow-flag-waving students had. One respondent was upset that Trump was "still being bashed for everything that goes wrong." She said it set up a hostile school environment.

Sarah was demoralized. All she could think was, "Where the heck am I working?"

* * *

Tiny things can help a child feel supported. When one of my former third graders was in middle school and came out as a lesbian, questions raced through my mind. *What did I say that year? Which books did I read? Was I supportive enough?*

I realized I shouldn't have to *wonder*; I should make more of a conscious effort to be supportive. So, on social media, I asked LGBTQ+ friends to tell me what they wish their grade-school teachers had said. The first respondent was the mom of my now-out former student.

"I want her to talk to you," she said. "She told me that something you said made her feel easier about it all."

So a few weeks later, Allie dropped by my classroom after school. We sat at the big semicircular table where she used to read with me as I'd hunch close to hear her whispered words. Now she was the teacher.

I'd always admired Allie's even temperament; in third grade, she didn't argue, tattle, or pout over little things. Back then, her composure presented as serenity. Now that she was a seventh grader, I saw it as quiet confidence, as wisdom. She knew who she was.

I felt myself choking up as she told me about her family's wholehearted support. Then I asked her if she remembered what I'd said to that year's third graders that had helped her. I expected her to bring up some shining moment I'd forgotten, perhaps something about embracing beautiful diversity. Maybe something about the bigness of the world, and the spectrum of people who all share this planet.

Her forehead crinkled over her large dark eyes. "I think we were doing research."

"Research?" That was unexpected.

"Yeah. Maybe something about jobs when we grow up."

"Really? That doesn't even *sound* like me." Maybe she was thinking of the wrong teacher.

"It was something about what jobs we might have in our future. And when someone asked you a question, you just said, 'Anybody can do anything. You get to be who you want to be.'"

"Wait. We were researching *jobs*?"

Her voice was strong.

"I remember it felt good to hear that. You were saying, 'Just be who you are.' The next year, I started questioning everything, and that helped me. I could just be who I am."

Grabbing a pen, I began scribbling down her words.

People don't realize that just four little words can change a life: "Be who you are."

Kids absorb the tiniest clues signaling support, which means that the unkind whispers, the fleeting expressions of distaste, the narrowing of eyes—those speak clearly, too.

Either way—it really doesn't take much.

* * *

Not all queer kids at Sarah's school attend GSA meetings; some make themselves known in quiet ways. Sometimes, kids just pop their heads through the doorway and tell her, "I love when I see that flag there. Thank you." Then they move on.

The year following the Club Rush harassment, there was a complete overhaul of administrators at her school, and the new administrators came to the first GSA meeting, just to communicate, "We support you." Sometimes, fellow teachers visited GSA meetings for a few minutes, which Sarah encourages.

"It lets the students see that adults support who they are. That means a *lot* to them."

Her school has taken other steps to address bullying and bigotry. The administration brought in consultants to lead a portion of students and staff members through a daylong event. Through guided activities, students shared their experiences with each other. The belief is that it's hard to hate someone whose story you know. Results were promising.

And teachers began approaching Sarah, asking for advice.

"I'm just this straight, white, cisgender woman who happens to be the GSA adviser, but I've become the de facto person for answering the most basic questions, like 'My student is asking me to use "she." What do I do?' Then use 'she'! Why do we need to talk about this?"

Though I understood Sarah's exasperation, I felt heartened as she told me of the positive movement at her school. That's why I was shocked when she slipped in that she was planning to leave teaching after June.

This person had just spent her prep period talking to me about teaching instead of tackling myriad tasks on her Friday to-do list. The walls of her classroom bore reminders to be kind and were papered with student-sketched posters of graphs and equations. While we spoke, three students had wandered in to ask questions—again, during the time that was supposed to be "free"—and she greeted each with friendliness, patience, and full engagement. After decades in education, I recognized it easily. Sarah was a born teacher.

So why was she quitting?

"I root for the Sacramento Kings," she said. "And before my own kids could put two sentences together, they were rooting for the Kings, too, just because I was their parent. They didn't even know what the Kings were, but they knew to do what I did.

"It's the same thing—these kids here learn it from their parents. They hear stuff at home, and then they repeat it. Some people think, 'Oh, they're repeating it but they don't know what they're saying.' But they're fifteen, sixteen, seventeen, eighteen. They know what they're saying. I think people have pulled the wool over their eyes."

She talked about how unsafe she feels at work. In addition to the bullying of students, there have been bomb threats, bullets, and guns on campus.

"And the fights . . . oh, the amount of fighting. It doesn't feel like a safe place."

It felt like an understatement. Sarah had told me about opening her work email on a Saturday morning and finding a message for her sent via the school website:

"I HATE ALL FAGGOTS. DIE."

She immediately contacted the district administration, telling them she was afraid for her safety. She was assured that messages like this would not be tolerated. When Sarah asked on Sunday night whether it was safe for her to show up for work on Monday morning, she was told to wait for IT to chime in. But when the IT guy replied that similar messages sent in the past were likely to have been pranks, Sarah was not comforted. Assuming that it was a prank sounded an awful lot like "tolerating."

Plus, as Sarah told me, "I don't feel like the IT guy is the person to do a threat assessment." I couldn't argue.

So she called the police. They were dismissive and wondered why she'd waited for two days before calling. She said, "The school was going to do it, but I don't know if they have."

Finally, on the advice of a friend who works in embassy security, she called the FBI. They, along with local police, decided that the message wouldn't qualify as a direct threat, because it didn't say, "I WILL KILL YOU." It only said, "DIE." The message would have to be more explicit to count as a direct threat.

* * *

Sarah said she used to be a lot more forgiving, understanding that kids are young, still growing up. But since she started at her current school in 2016, she's noticed increasing numbers of students acting on their intolerant beliefs, and she's tired of working amid cruelty. For a while, she thought maybe she simply needed an antidepressant.

"I love what I do, and I love the kids. But then I realized it's not me. It's that *the kids are different*. So I'm going to leave before it gets worse."

It's hard to know if what Sarah noticed in the students was more about "who" or more about "when." Maybe it was simply the difference between the culture of her previous school—a smaller school with a liberal culture—and that of her current, larger one in a more conservative region. But it also could be related to *when* she began working at her current school. Remember—it was in 2016.

Widely reported results of a survey administered by the Southern Poverty Law Center after the 2016 election revealed the election's "profoundly negative impact" on schools and students.[3] Ninety percent of the more than ten thousand educators responding reported a negative effect on school climate. They described many thousands of incidents of racist and misogynist harassment, assaults on students and teachers, property damage, slurs and derogatory language, fights and threats of violence, and incidents involving swastikas, Nazi salutes, and Confederate flags. Respondents told stories of boys cornering girls against lockers, tossing around the word "pussy," and yelling things like, "Trump that bitch!" Educators emphasized that the severity and frequency of the incidents were new, and that many students instigating the harassment referenced Trump.

In 2024, *The Washington Post* analyzed FBI data and reported that "school hate crimes targeting LGBTQ+ people have sharply risen in recent years, climbing fastest in states that have passed laws restricting LGBTQ+ student rights and education." The data reveal that in states with restrictive laws, "the number of hate crimes on K–12 campuses has more than quadrupled since the onset of a divisive culture war that has often centered on the rights of LGBTQ+ youth."[4]

Of course, the majority of students still do not target marginalized people. I'm too enmeshed in the world of education and schools to believe that *all* students succumb to whatever pressure compels some to attack others. The relationship between the 2016 election and the subsequent changes in school culture is certainly complex. Maybe some students are more likely to act on their impulses if they sense a permissiveness among adults with views similar to theirs. Perhaps they're echoing sentiments and statements they hear at home. Maybe some kids feel powerless and cave in to peer pressure in order to grab power wherever they can find it.

But even if the source of the acts of bigotry could be pinpointed, it wouldn't make it any easier for educators to manage. I looked around Sarah's room, at her colorful signs reminding students to be kind. I can recognize joy in a classroom, and it was clear that Sarah was a teacher who knows that joy, the joy of helping kids grow.

Her students tell her that they've never learned math like they do with her. Some teens tell her that they love her. She gets thank-you notes about how much she has helped them.

And she's leaving because she doesn't feel safe in the place where students come to learn. The actions of some of those very students have pushed her out.

* * *

But what forces have acted on the students? And is there anything powerful enough to rein them back in, to help them abandon the intolerance they've recently felt entitled to express?

I looked around her bright room, realizing that someone else would occupy it not long in the future. I couldn't blame her for leaving.

Which made me wonder about the thousands of California teachers who haven't left yet.

Not *yet.*

Because don't we all just assume that teachers will forever be there to teach kids to read, to write poetry, to learn music, to explore science, to create art, to open doors to the wonders of our world, to the wonders of learning itself? No matter how much we increasingly demand of teachers, no matter how little we pay them, and no matter how much we blame them for society's ills, aren't we all banking on the one thing everyone knows about teachers, the one thing that fuels them each day?

That one thing we all know: Teachers will do *anything* for their students.

It's for the kids.

In contract negotiations, I once sat at the table while a colleague in special education explained to administrators why SpEd teachers needed a few more sick days than general ed teachers. She described common behaviors of children with severe emotional needs, telling the administrators that the children often express their frustration physically. She described how SpEd teachers are commonly bitten, kicked, and punched. The physical demands of lifting are extreme and often result in wrenched limbs. She was not complaining; she was explaining why those teachers need a few extra days to allow them to recover from injuries received on the job.

We were hoping to gain a bit of relief for all of the district's SpEd teachers. The administrators dismissed our appeal.

"Teachers who get into special education know what they're in for," said one district administrator. "We can't give them more sick days."

So teachers need to just wipe off the blood, slap on an ACE bandage, and get back to work.

It's for the kids.

In the world of education, that four-word sentence is powerful enough to silence conversation, to halt debate. Sometimes it's a bludgeon used on teachers, one that blames, inspires guilt, and shouts its underlying message: "If you care *anything* about students, you'll do whatever it takes and you won't complain. *That's* what a *real* teacher does."

For decades, I heard it from the administration, from coworkers, at the bargaining table, and in staff meetings. Even when no one is speaking it aloud, teachers hear it on their own, that mantra that hums inside with a steady beat.

It drummed inside me, too. It's why I spent many thousands of dollars of my own money on classroom furniture, carpeting, curtains, myriad books, appliances, art supplies, and field trip entrance fees. It's why I worked every Sunday for thirty-two years, and why I spent weeks of my summer vacation taking nonrequired courses and prepping my classroom for the new group. It's why, in the early days of the pandemic, I lay in bed in the dark, unable to sleep, haunted by the faces of my young students whom I couldn't yet reach online.

Trusting that teachers will never stop caring because "it's for the kids" enables us to see schools as a steady fixture, a given, an institution that will always be there no matter what. It's what enables the system to keep going.

Until it doesn't.

Until it *can't.*

Until "for the kids" is no longer enough.

7

KINDERGARTEN DREAM

I was accustomed to the traffic of the Bay Area, but the freeways surrounding Los Angeles are a different animal. The GPS screen looked like a tangle of spaghetti noodles. By the time I finally located the coffeehouse where I would meet this stranger, I was frazzled and cursing.

A young woman stood and waved me over toward the boxy cushioned furniture outside. Cassandra's response to my email query had been direct:

"I'm a young, queer, woman of color teaching in Orange County. I would love to talk with you."

I was eager to meet her.

I hadn't even taken a bite of my avocado toast when Cassandra started.

"Isn't it a shitty dichotomy? We need teachers, but we also don't want just *any* teacher. We want teachers who are going to fall in line and not cause any issues. We want *silent* teachers."

And so began my time with this not-so-silent teacher.

When we met in late 2022, Cassandra was only twenty-seven years old and held four degrees. Her first official year of teaching came just in time for the pandemic, but that didn't slow her down. Despite her youth, the Orange County Department of Education invited her to be a guest speaker on student wellness, and the LA Clippers honored her as Rookie Teacher of the Year. I felt hopeful, knowing that such an accomplished educator was teaching young people.

Though some high schools in California have been offering ethnic studies for years, the course wasn't to be required by state law until the 2025–26 school year, and it was to become a graduation requirement with the class of 2030. However, just three months before the start of the 2025–26 school year, Governor Gavin Newsom's proposed budget withheld the funding for ethnic studies. The law specifies that school districts aren't required to teach the course if state funding is not allocated for it, and between a shaky California economy, Donald Trump's bias against "wokeness," and a governor who likely has presidential aspirations, the ethnic studies mandate is now deep in limbo.

Cassandra was passionate about ethnic studies, so in the early 2020s, she represented her school on the district committee developing the prospective course. The committee spent a year on the project, and members were ready to present their completed work to the school board.

Then a neighboring school district debuted its own ethnic studies course.

By then, the term "Critical Race Theory" had caught fire in places where people—overwhelmingly, white people—were upset by how race is handled in classrooms. CRT is "an academic and legal framework denoting that systemic racism is part of American society—from education and housing to employment and healthcare." Around since the 1970s, CRT holds that "racism goes far beyond just individually held prejudices, and is in fact a systemic phenomenon woven into the laws and institutions of this nation."[1] Do K–12 educators teach it? Scholars attest that CRT is written in academic language or published in journals not easily accessible to K–12 teachers.

"Their parents revolted, and said their kids were being taught Critical Race Theory and the idea that white kids are bad," Cassandra explained. "So our district pulled the plug on our already-created course. Instead of saying, 'Wow, for the first time, our students will be represented in a course!' they said, 'No, we don't want to deal with the parents.'"

* * *

Parents.

Working with parents is inseparable from being a teacher. When the partnership between parent and teacher is strong, it can facilitate student progress. But tension and distrust in the teacher-parent relationship can exhaust both parties, with the child paying the price.

I've worked with maybe two thousand parents over the years. A few have become good friends, and many have inspired me. Some "parents" were grandparents who'd thought they were done raising children. They attended conferences and Open House, chaperoned field trips while limping on arthritic knees, and volunteered to come back in August to help me set up the classroom for my new group of students. A single father who worked the graveyard shift once drove straight from work to meet us on our field trip in the redwood forest. He hadn't yet slept, but his child had a broken leg, and the exhausted dad didn't want me to have to push the wheelchair through the woods.

I've known soft-spoken parents who fight with steely strength for the rights of their children with special needs. Immigrant parents have sat with me on plastic chairs built for eight-year-olds, teary with pride as their child reads words foreign to their ear. When a labor strike loomed and teachers picketed in front of my school, parents swarmed in support, marching with us to the school district office. At a late-evening board meeting, the Spanish-speaking mother of one of my students stood at the mic, declaring her fierce support of the teachers. She held two young children, one on each hip.

A Mien grandmother who had lived in a Thai refugee camp before immigrating came on our class camping trip. Without knowing a word of English, she immersed herself in every activity. A faded photograph shows her and her granddaughter spinning wool at the seaside farm where we camped, the grandmother in her traditional headwear. A few years ago, a mother handed me a flat package, though it had been more than a decade since I'd taught her daughters. Inside was a brilliant floral blouse, embroidered by hand in satiny stitches of blue and green. She had brought it back from her home village in Mexico, where her mother had made it specially for me.

Parents have educated me, too. A Black mother helped me understand that my impatience with her son's outspokenness had racial roots. From a fiercely protective mother who respected my teaching but disliked me personally, I learned to open difficult conversations by affirming parents' primary devotion to their child. Thanks to parents, I improved in admitting uncertainty, recognizing my mistakes, and apologizing when wrong.

Teaming with parents—when it works, it unleashes a powerful force that can maximize learning for the child. And when it fails, it can lead to overwhelming stress, anger, and fear. It can make a teacher want to quit.

For much of my teaching career, I was older than the parents of my elementary school students, but I still sometimes felt nervous dealing with them. Not all parents behave well, and field trips often showcase bad behavior. I've had parents show up drunk or strung out to chaperone a trip. Once I asked a dad to toss out the beer he'd started drinking while supervising my third graders; he glared at me for the rest of the trip. Another time, a student leaped into a small, fetid pond with a rusty metal pipe sticking out of it. When I hollered at him to get out, his mom—who'd laughed as she watched him jump in—yelled, "How *dare* you order my son around when I'm *right here*!" A dad once opted not to use the toilet during a scheduled bathroom break, but as soon as our bus headed up the long, narrow road into the mountains, he told me to direct the bus driver to stop so he could urinate in the dirt. When I told him that the bus driver refused because it wasn't safe, the dad yelled at me.

"What do you want me to do? Hang it out the *window*?"

While these instances were aggravating, they weren't frightening, as some parents' expressions of rage can be. A student once gave our vice principal a black eye. Later, when I called his father to discuss another episode of the boy's aggression, the man blasted me with threatening curses until I finally hung up. A mom picking up her son at the classroom door once yelled at me, "You're a *bitch*!" It was the first day of school. That parent eventually lodged a formal complaint against me, claiming I had avoided her. When I attended the hearing at the school district office, I defended myself in front of administrators and my union rep, humiliated as I explained that I'd cut short a conversation with her because I had a bladder infection and only seven minutes to use the restroom. One parent's harassment of me was so unceasing that the district ordered her to stay a hundred feet away from the school. The last straw had come when she shouted curses at me in front of a kindergarten class on their way to lunch.

It can be scary to start conversations that might end with a parent's anger. Once I called a mom because her eight-year-old child had written a note telling other kids what a "shithead" I am. The next morning, the enraged mother stormed into the classroom while I was teaching, exclaiming that her child *couldn't* have written the note, because the child had denied doing so. As my shocked third graders listened, she demanded that I hand over the paper so that she could conduct a handwriting analysis. That same student was terribly violent, which necessitated many calls home. When the mother eventually demanded a meeting, she brought three adult family members with her, each of whom disputed my claims about the child's excessive violence. They said the problem was me. I felt so intimidated during the meeting that my saliva dried up and I couldn't pronounce the child's name. The mispronunciation made them even angrier.

My school once had a student whose capacity for sudden violence was terrifying. As a first grader, he kicked a visibly pregnant office worker in the belly, sending her directly to the hospital. When my colleague taught that student in third grade, the child's father used to burst into her classroom in the late afternoons, angrily ranting and refusing to leave. She had to lock the room and close the curtains so he wouldn't know she was there. If I needed to talk with her, I'd sneak around to her back door and tap our secret knock.

Over my decades of teaching, many parents were wonderful, and the vast majority were supportive and collaborative. But scary parental encounters stand out, taking a heavy toll. And nonwhite teachers sometimes face extra discrimination from parents, as do LGBTQ+ or non-Christian teachers, especially if they're outspoken.

In other words, teachers like Cassandra.

* * *

Cassandra began her teaching career in a highly polarized area of Orange County. It's where, on numerous occasions between 2017 and 2023, pro-Trump rallies devolved into violence, with pepper spray in the air and counterprotesters bashed over the head with "Make America Great Again" signs. It's where thirty-year congressional representative Dana Rohrabacher spoke in favor of housing discrimination on the basis of sexual orientation. It's where signs and bumper stickers shouting "Fuck Gavin Newsom" are plastered around town, and where giant "Fuck Biden" flags waved from the back of pickup trucks.

"It was a terrible place to be during the election and COVID," explained Cassandra. "I got laid off there because I was not silent. I fell on the sword for my marginalized kids time and time again."

A beginning teacher, Cassandra told her boss that she wouldn't teach *Huck Finn*, a required text, because the N-word appears 219 times. She argued that if the purpose of teaching *Huck Finn* was to educate students about slavery, it shouldn't be done from the perspective of a white author who used the N-word 219 times. Her boss wasn't having it; he directed her to teach the book.

"So I said, 'You want me to cover *Huck Finn*? Okay, FINE.' I pulled excerpts and used them to teach about colorism and cultural appropriation. We connected it to today and talked about discrepancies in the medical care system for Black women, and how so many problems come back to slavery. I went over all the things that the book should *not* have done. And at the end, I had my students argue whether or not *Huck Finn* should still be taught in schools."

Cassandra wasn't proposing that *Huck Finn* be banned; rather, she was advocating that it not be one of the few texts teachers were required to cover. But regardless of pro-con arguments that could be made for teaching *Huck Finn*, it was clear that this young woman had integrity and courage. I still feel shame over things I never spoke up about when I was a young teacher. In my first year, on a release day I'd been granted for observing veteran educators, I watched a longtime teacher pull a rubber windshield-wiper strip from his suit pocket and smack a fifth grader with it. I knew that the man was fluffing his tail feathers, thinking that my inexperienced self would be impressed at the power he wielded over his students. I also knew that what I'd seen was appalling. But, afraid of what could happen if I accused a school legend of hitting a child, I said nothing. I also remained silent when my principal faked his written evaluation of my performance; he'd missed the deadline for observing me, so he described watching a lesson I'd never taught.

It took a few years in the classroom for me to find my voice. Eventually, I had an established reputation as someone who would challenge authority and fiercely defend the rights of teachers and students. For nearly every year of my career, I was active in union leadership. Teachers I didn't know called me a badass, and a coworker dubbed me "Union Ninja."

But here was Cassandra, insistently speaking up in year one. I hung on every word.

* * *

When Cassandra taught John Steinbeck's *Of Mice and Men*, her class first learned that it's on many lists of banned books. So she challenged them to find other books that have been banned historically, and to research why there had been opposition to them. When Cassandra presented statistics on the recent explosion of book-banning, her students were shocked. Books have become a proxy in the current culture war, and the teens learned that topics touching on racial inequality, LGBTQ+ rights, or gender identity are among those most likely to get a book pulled.

"But if you don't like LGBTQ books or books about witchcraft or whatever, just don't read them! That doesn't mean that other people shouldn't be allowed to." It was the reasoning she heard most often from her students, young people with a hunger to learn about the great big world.

Then Cassandra had to withhold books from her own classroom library, after a student checked out a novel with a queer romance scene. A parent saw the book, read the scene, and reported it to the administration. Teachers were then directed to "clean up" their classroom libraries before the end of the school year.

"But what about books with romance scenes between heterosexual people?" I asked. "Are those books in classroom libraries?"

"Absolutely. Most of the books with romance on my bookshelf are hetero. I only have a few with queer romance scenes. But now I've closed off my bookshelf, and other teachers in my English department got rid of their books, too. 'I don't want to fight that battle,' is what most of them say."

Nearly fifty years ago, when I was in high school, I read *The Cheerleader*, by Ruth Doan MacDougall. I was astonishingly naïve—even compared with classmates at my all-Catholic school—and the book presented a side of teenage life I knew only from movies. It was also the book that taught me more about sex than anything I'd ever read, and it came from the Catholic school library. During my free period after lunch, I'd hunch down in a private study carrel at the library and lose myself in scenes of skin and sweat, love and heartbreak, finally feeling a little less ignorant of the world I knew was forbidden to me. I'd spend some time in that world each day, before whispering farewell to Sister Dominica on my way to English class. Having new information changed nothing about my doctrine-dictated behavior; it just helped me to feel a little more knowledgeable, a little more included in life, and a little less alone.

The Cheerleader, with its sexually active characters, was approved by a nun whose religion forbids sex before marriage. Today's outrage over high schoolers reading romance scenes with same-sex characters? Seems like if I were still at that Catholic high school trying to check out a queer romance book, Sister Dominica would just give me that "I know you're a reader" nod, hand me the book, and point me toward the nearest study carrel.

* * *

As the GSA adviser at her school, Cassandra had a poster on her door welcoming students to attend meetings. Then a pattern developed: Each day as her English students filed out after class, someone would rip the poster off her door. She'd tape it back up, and the next day, it would be on the floor again. She was always too occupied to notice who it was, but she asked a few kids to keep their eyes open, and the culprit was caught. She told me that it wasn't just that he was ruining her property; his actions were pointed, purposeful. She wanted to quash his efforts before they were targeted more explicitly at queer kids. It comes as naturally to Cassandra as breathing, these efforts to protect vulnerable students.

"Deadnaming" is calling a transgender student by their birth name, instead of by their chosen name. Students in the GSA often told Cassandra about the extreme anxiety they felt at the possibility of being deadnamed, so she asked her principal if she could have a slot during the start-of-year training days to teach staff members ways to avoid deadnaming students.

"I prepared a presentation with more than twenty resources. I incorporated ideas for subs, so that when teachers are absent, the subs don't deadname kids. I checked with legal. Then the district went through my presentation and cut a lot of it. 'You can say it out loud,' they said. 'It just can't be on the presentation. Because if it's in writing and someone takes a picture of it, that's when it gets dangerous. A parent could see it.'"

Cassandra was crushed that much of what she developed couldn't be shown to teachers, but she decided that the revised presentation could be a stepping stone toward the day when such conversations could be more open. So she went forward with it. The tips she gave revolved around "ask before assuming." They were simple, like taking attendance on the first day by calling each student's last name and first initial instead of using the first names on the roll sheet.

"During the presentation, lots of questions came up around fear. A lot of teachers are afraid to do things like have a conversation about pronouns. But they surveyed staff to see which training over those two days was the most important for them. By *far*, mine was the one they voted for. They kept talking about how much of an impact it made in building relationships with students."

Then she talked about the phone calls.

"In the first week of school, parents were calling and saying, 'Why are you asking my child's pronouns? Why are you asking if they use the same name at home versus in school? How DARE you! He's a BOY. He's a HE.'

"I'm just as afraid as the other teachers are," said Cassandra. "But if I get fired for something, I'd be proud if it was for a kid who felt they weren't represented."

I told Cassandra that I hoped she wouldn't get fired. But what I didn't say: If she was ever terminated for supporting vulnerable kids, I, as a fellow educator, would be proud of her, too.

* * *

Cassandra said that when she was an idealistic student in the credential program, she thought the two hardest things about teaching would be waking up early, and not cursing in the classroom. When we met just four years later, she was already incredulous that those had been her biggest worries.

"What pisses me off is that for so many parents now, we are public enemy number one. I have *four* degrees in my subject area. I know my shit! But I get questioned by people who don't know *anything* about how to teach. When would I ever walk into a finance building and say, 'Do you know what you're doing? How DARE you crunch those numbers!'"

I laughed, but her truth resonated. Distrust of teachers has risen steadily since 2020. A 2021 Gallup poll found that "Americans' belief in grade-school teachers' honesty" had dropped to an all-time low.[2] By late 2024, Gallup's new survey showed a drop of an additional 3 percentage points. Cassandra wasn't the first to tell me that the seeds of distrust burst into bloom during the pandemic.

"Parents became involved and were ready to die on the hill of their kid not wearing a mask to school. 'I don't want my kid being taught by a computer. I don't want my kid being taught by teachers at home. You can't force my kid to wear a mask.' Districts were not prepared, and so they bowed down to the parents. It was the first time parents realized they could enact change. That's powerful when it's used for positive change, but it should not mean they tell us how to do our job. Now they have a huge sense of entitlement and demand a say in everything that happens in our classrooms."

In December 2020, Cassandra's district abruptly announced plans to return to in-person instruction after winter break. Though vaccines were not yet available and COVID-19 rates were expected to spike during winter, teachers were ordered to either return to the school site or take unpaid leave. Debate was heated at the next school board meeting. Teachers implored board members to grant exceptions. One teacher wept as she spoke of battling cancer. Cassandra herself, though young, is immunocompromised. Along with panicked educators, parents voiced their opinions.

"One parent said, 'If these teachers are so scared and hiding in Biden's basement, I'd much rather have a sub teaching them, someone who's not afraid.'"

Another parent at the meeting wanted to put trackers on teachers, convinced that they were being lazy. She was certain that despite teachers' voiced concerns about being in a classroom of unmasked students, they were likely gallivanting around town, enjoying their "time off." Parents who were still speaking when their allotted time was up were allowed to continue. But when the timer beeped the end of teachers' time—including the teacher with cancer—they were cut off.

"It's a very twisted, disheartening moment when you realize how little your life is valued."

Cassandra sighed, looking bone-weary.

She was twenty-seven.

* * *

Cassandra graduated from her credential program with a group of six friends. Five years after graduation, only one of the other six was still teaching. There were plenty of jobs; the young teachers just didn't want them anymore. Though Cassandra was still in the profession, she, like so many young educators, had been laid off from her first two placements. School enrollment fluctuates every year, which means that the number of teaching positions ebbs and flows. When enrollment decreases, teachers are laid off, even if they're known to be outstanding at their job. It all comes down to seniority, and in her first few years, Cassandra had none.

"My assistant principal was the one who decided between me and one other English teacher who'd just been hired. I had more experience and was more involved on campus. I'd been recognized by both the district and the Clippers as an excellent teacher. Both of my department chairs voted to keep me instead of the other teacher.

"But he was quiet, and I wasn't."

In the fall of 2020, before the teachers in Cassandra's district were directed to return to in-person instruction, they could choose whether to teach from home or on-site. Cassandra worked from her apartment. When she'd go in to pick up her check, her assistant principal, a white man, repeatedly told her, "I didn't peg you to be scared. It's completely safe. You should be back."

"He had lots of conversations with me that felt intimidating," Cassandra told me. "He'd stand in front of me, unmasked. He knew he had more privilege and power because I was a new teacher, and I think he wanted me to act like it.

"The decision whether I'd get to keep my job came down to the end of the year, and it was up to him. And even though everyone went to bat for me, he told me, 'If I were you, I'd start looking for a new job.' That's how he did it."

Her students were as brokenhearted as she was and began organizing. They wanted to circulate a petition, but Cassandra told them it would only make things worse.

"So many teachers had already quit during the pandemic," she said. "And here they had a stellar teacher who *wanted* to stay. But he said, 'No, our school is better off without her.'"

* * *

She secured a position at yet another school. Previously, until six months into each year, Cassandra had hidden any evidence of her sexual orientation, too afraid of parents finding out. But at Back-to-School Night this time, she didn't hold back when introducing herself.

"I just told the parents, 'Oh, this is a picture of me and my wife,' and I continued. But you never know. The teacher next door had two parents fight at Back-to-School Night, because one was saying that there's not enough LGBTQ literature in the curriculum, and the other one said there shouldn't be any at all. This is the kind of stuff we have to navigate."

This spitfire of a woman reminded me of myself, with her strong opinions and enthusiasm for teaching, her idealism and vision for what the profession could be. But unlike me, she was still in the classroom, in a job that was changing with shocking speed. Cassandra said that even her friends from the credential program who had left teaching didn't understand what it was like anymore.

"It is *exhausting* to constantly wonder, 'Will I get in trouble for what I just taught? Will I get in trouble for what I just said?' I'm already burnt out.

Last October, I wanted to quit. I was depressed unlike I'd ever been. I started antidepressants because of my job."

Cassandra said that in 2021, she usually came home in tears. She'd lie in bed for days, not eating. She was incapable of doing anything in her off time. Some kids in her gang-affiliated school frightened her; one student would intimidate her daily and would either stream porn while in her class or punch the walls. She felt unsafe, overwhelmed, and helpless to do anything.

"I'd look at the kids who loved me, and I had no emotional capacity to support them. And now this year, I've had to *decide* not to emotionally support my kids. That's terrible. It sounds awful. I make them feel safe, supported, and loved for fifty-five minutes a day. But outside of school hours, I *can't*. I'm not responding to emails. I'm not doing check-ins. Because I *can't*."

The weight of her burden was palpable, and I remembered my own collapse.

* * *

Decades earlier, in my first district, I'd left the kids I loved because I couldn't bear the stress and frustration any longer. For four years, I'd fought to improve the learning conditions for the low-income students in my school that was 99 percent children of color. But it was never close to enough. We were in the flatlands of East Oakland, with 1,000 kids crammed into an elementary school designed for 750. It was so overcrowded that the district implemented a year-round schedule, sectioning the population into four groups and having only three groups attend at a time. With groups rotating in and out each month all year, our schedules were out of sync with the timelines under which the district operated.

In my second year of teaching, I served as the fourth-grade rep for our monthly planning committee. For our July meeting, "toilet paper" was on the agenda.

"We're almost out of TP, and the delivery from the district won't get here for two weeks," said Ken, a slow-talking, sleepy-looking teacher who was patient with my youthful enthusiasm. "Anybody have an idea?"

Flabbergasted, I listened as veteran teachers explained. Since very few Oakland schools were year-round like we were, the district adhered to the traditional schedules for deliveries, purchasing, and testing. Whether they had run out of toilet paper downtown or the workers who delivered it were on vacation, the dilemma was the same. The toilet tissue wasn't coming unless we made it happen.

"I have a truck," said Roger. "I can go pick some up."

Someone offered to help him, and we moved on to the next agenda item. I couldn't focus on anything for the rest of the meeting. Sure, I was naïve, but . . . shouldn't a school district ensure that each site has *toilet paper*?

By my fourth year, I was accustomed to the ineffective (though well-dressed) principal, the lack of administrative follow-through with troubled kids, and the colleague who religiously showed up half an hour after the morning bell. But my idealism had remained intact; I still believed I could solve the glaring inequities of our school's year-round schedule. That year, I had a fourth grader who struggled mightily. I could tell he was bright, but he was ten and couldn't remember how to spell his name. Why wasn't he already qualified for additional support when he obviously had extreme difficulties? His growing frustration made him increasingly angry. We were failing him.

Certain that he had a learning disability, I filled out the paperwork to refer him for screening and testing. It was only April, so there was plenty of time to assess him before he started fifth grade. After I turned in the referral, the special ed teacher found me.

"I hate to say it, but it's too late to test him this year," she said.

"But it's only April! My track is in session until the end of August!"

She sighed sadly. "Yeah, but the district won't test in the summer. The psychologists are on a traditional schedule, and they don't start anything after April."

I was outraged, but motivated. There *had* to be a way. I contacted the boy's father, and we concocted a plan. We'd attend a school board meeting together, discuss the boy's struggles, and demand that the district begin taking the year-round schedule into account, so that children could be served equitably.

When I excitedly shared our idea with the assistant principal, she sat down and looked at me soberly.

"Please don't. The district people don't want to look bad. They'll twist it and say that it's our school's fault the boy isn't succeeding."

The breath was sucked out of me. How could I function, knowing that my vision and hard work were doomed to never see results? Hopeless and powerless, I sank into a deep depression, and quit my job at the end of August. When I told my students they wouldn't see me the following year, my chin quivered, and my voice began to wobble. I put down the book I'd been planning to read. The kids stared at me, waiting.

Kao Muang patted my arm, murmuring, "It's okay. Everybody needs to rest sometimes."

* * *

Cassandra told me about her student who wrote an essay praising Kyle Rittenhouse, the seventeen-year-old who fatally shot two Black Lives Matter protesters with an AR-15-style rifle and wounded a third. The protesters were objecting to police brutality against Black people; Cassandra's student praised Rittenhouse for "getting rid of scum on earth." He'd followed precisely the essay format Cassandra had assigned, so, without the backing of her administration, all she could discuss with the student was how to improve his linguistic choices. ("Is there a way you could express 'scum on earth' more effectively?")

"A kid wrote me a note saying: 'Stop telling me to respect pronouns.' I get so angry, and then so fucking sad to my core when I think, 'I can't say THAT or THAT to my students' because I don't want them going home and telling parents. It's *constant* decision-making that is exhausting. By the time I get home, I feel like a shell of a person."

Cassandra had dreamed of being a teacher since kindergarten. When she was a child, school was her safe place, and she relied heavily on her teachers. That's why she became an educator—so she could be that kind of support for young people. When talking about kids and curriculum, she vibrated with passion and energy. Within ten minutes of meeting her and listening to her discuss educational theory and practice, I felt a pang, wishing that I somehow could have known her as a colleague during my long career, even though she hadn't yet been born when I started teaching.

Talking with her was like being able to see her beating heart. What happens when such a brilliant, vibrant young teacher feels like a shell of a person after only a few years in education?

When I sympathized, affirming how exhausting controversy can be, Cassandra's response came from way down deep.

"Saying that it's controversial that I *exist* as a queer person and asking me to hide it? That's BULLSHIT. The *controversy* is that before knowing anything else about me, people are hating my existence just because I'm queer. My identity as a queer person is not controversial. Someone existing as a Black person and being afraid for their lives is not *controversial*."

She explained how simply going on vacation is different for her and her wife; they have to research first and ask themselves if the place seems queer-friendly. They'll enter certain spaces, look at each other, and say, "Okay, don't be gay here," because being themselves could put them in danger. She decried the expectation that teachers must forever ignore their own needs. In 2021, she had an ovarian cyst rupture during class. Blood streamed down her leg, but she had to wait five minutes for someone to come supervise her class, because teachers can *never* leave a class unattended. As Cassandra was keeled over, trying to remain calm, a kid came up and said, "This is so boring." She finally staggered downstairs to the restroom, threw away her underwear, and cleaned up, hurrying all the while because it was drummed into her to not be away from her class for long. That night, it haunted her: Even while having a medical emergency, she felt pressure to go back and finish her job.

"Our job requires us to work before work, at work, and after work. The expectation is that we would do *anything* for the kids. At a meeting once, we were told, 'Just stay after school. Tutor them. Tutor them during lunch.' I spoke up and said, 'That violates all my boundaries. I will not do that. Find me a different solution.'

"We're degraded on a daily basis. All these little things add up and eat you away inside. Add all the political shit on top, and you're saying, 'What more is left of me?' It shouldn't be this hard on a personal level."

Cassandra told me she was considering leaving teaching because she couldn't envision how to continue. She said she wanted to maintain her sanity, have a semblance of a personal life, spend time with her wife and her dog, and have the emotional energy for all of that. The pressure of having to hide and then defend her mere existence was crushing. Being so committed to serving her students made it even more painful, and more impossible.

"Most of the parents with power, privilege, and a sense of entitlement are white, wealthy, and super-conservative religious people. I think of my students of color, or my other marginalized kids who are routinely silenced because of their lack of privilege, and I want to tell the powerful people that it's *only* because of the privilege they were born with that they're able to be vocal and demanding. They're only listened to because they have the means to get a lawyer. They have the means to use the right scary buzzwords to scare a principal or a district.

"But the families of color and those who need a translator . . . no one is going to bow down to them. It all boils down to appeasing parents."

Again, I thought back to my fourth year of teaching, to my collapse, to the photos of me that couldn't lie. Hollow dark eyes stare out from pictures, my thirty-four-year-old face drawn, my smile weak and pasted on. But another difference between me and Cassandra was that at my school, most parents were too overwhelmed with the work of surviving to be embroiled in debates over whatever content I did or didn't teach, especially those who didn't speak English. It was also 1993. Parents at my high-poverty school were mostly just grateful that there were teachers to help their children learn, and they left the specifics up to us. We were short on toilet paper and year-round testing, but long on curricular freedom.

Education is simply harder than it used to be. The Pew Research Center found in 2024 that 70 percent of educators reported that their school was understaffed, which results in a heavier load for the rest. More than 75 percent of teachers found their jobs to be frequently stressful, with 68 percent saying it is "overwhelming." Ninety-four percent of teachers spend their own money on basic classroom supplies, despite the fact that teachers make 5 percent less than they did ten years ago, when adjusted for inflation. Perhaps the capper: Nearly half of teachers believe that most Americans don't trust them much, or at all.[3]

With the culture wars emboldening some parents to try seizing control of curriculum, the stress is overwhelming for many. If I'd had to face constant scrutiny from parents who, instead of enrolling their children in private school, wanted to personally sculpt their child's curriculum into a sterile program with no acknowledgment that LGBTQ+ people exist, or that all students need to learn *all* of Black history, or that Christianity is not the only religion, or that we all have rights and responsibilities—well, I can't imagine I would have survived a thirty-two-year career in education. And if, in addition to all of that, parents of my students had also deemed my very existence to be controversial, leading me to constantly wonder which aspects of my identity I felt safe enough to reveal, I would have lasted only those four years in Oakland. That would've been it.

I looked at the young woman beside me. Cassandra was just finishing her fourth year as a full-time teacher.

* * *

My avocado toast long gone, Cassandra and I leaned back in our cushioned outdoor seating, enjoying the breeze, relishing the slow Saturday morning, and musing about the future of public education. Neither of us was able to envision what it will look like. Many politicians have learned that constraining, blaming, and fueling distrust of teachers can be politically advantageous. Virginia's Governor Glenn Youngkin was elected in January 2022 after he campaigned on the eradication of particular ways of talking about race and history in Virginia schools. One of his first official acts was to set up a tip line for parents to report teachers for "inappropriate behavior." In the summer of 2022, a Fox News host described public school teachers as "the KKK with summers off."[4] Another Fox host said that teachers want to "groom children to exploit them for sexual purposes," while yet another said that teachers deserve low wages.[5]

More recently, Trump vowed to cut off federal money for schools and colleges that push "critical race theory, transgender insanity, and other inappropriate racial, sexual or political content."[6] He promised to reward states and schools that end teacher tenure.

When teachers work hard, only to be accused of being groomers, pedophiles, and members of the KKK, can anyone blame them for leaving?

States with depleted pools of credentialed teachers are desperate for alternative methods of staffing each classroom. Some school districts in Texas switched to a four-day school week in 2022. Also in 2022, Florida passed a law allowing military vets—with no teaching experience and no college degree—to be offered a K–12 teaching job, as long as they'd served four years in the military and had at least sixty college credits with a C+ average.

The president of the teachers' union in Virginia's largest school district said, "When people were beating up on teachers and just being real nasty about what we're doing and what we're not doing, I don't think they were really thinking, 'Who will teach my children?'"[7]

* * *

With "solutions" like cutting one school day each week and filling classrooms with veterans, Cassandra wondered aloud if we'll ultimately have educators who are passionate about the content but not necessarily about working with children. We both knew that much of teaching is about the ability to build relationships with and among students, so her hypothesis was sobering. She couldn't imagine what she'd want to do next. Just considering a different line of work was soul-crushing to the kindergarten Cassandra still inside, the tiny child who only ever wanted to be a teacher.

"There are days when I think to myself, 'I want to run away from it,' and I'm so sad, because I didn't feel it in the beginning. I felt so in love with it. And now I think, 'I adore my kids, but they're not my identity. I'm not Ms. B. twenty-four seven. And I think I'd be happier if I wasn't at all.'"

* * *

As I walked away from Cassandra that morning, I felt proud that we shared a chosen profession.

But pride wasn't all that I felt.

I was furious.

It's enraging that racism, homophobia, and bigotry have transformed the profession so much that it could push this brilliant young teacher away from educating today's youth. Cassandra was wounded on the battleground of a war for which she never enlisted. Her desire was to teach young people about the world, and to support them in the classroom where the learning would happen. She did not sign on to be attacked for her sexuality, or for her support of the broad spectrum of students in her classes.

She was willing to work harder than she'd ever worked, but realizing her childhood dream came at too high a price. Six months after my interview with Cassandra, she went on a stress-induced leave of absence after a resentful student published her personal information online.

Two years after that, we spoke, and she filled in the details.

"He found a twelve-year-old Facebook post with my personal number and sent it out to all the students. He put me in a group chat with all the boys in my classes and was saying things like, 'Show me your tits if you're anti-racist.'"

Cassandra went on, explaining that the boy's father was upset with *her*, not with his son. He said that if she had left the group chat instead of remaining in it, the problem would have been solved. Her principal's only advice to her: "Grow thicker skin."

Publication of those ten digits wasn't just a violation. It was a threat to the only tie Cassandra had to her then-estranged family. She had only recently come out to them as queer, and relations were strained. The phone number was the only thread connecting them across the wide familial chasm. She needed to change her phone number, but to change it meant ripping open wounds that hadn't yet healed.

She walked across campus in a fog of humiliation. The thread had spread to countless students, and though many kids offered sympathy, she was continually confronting the betrayal. Teachers tried to get in on the gossip. The administration emailed the whole staff, urging employees to leave Cassandra alone. The school resource officer was brought in to talk with each of Cassandra's classes about harassment. She was mortified, unable to escape the nightmare.

Then a student unknown to Cassandra wouldn't enroll in her class. His reason? "I *refuse* to let a faggot teach me."

That was it. Cassandra went on leave and never came back. She told me, "I was juggling five jobs after I left. And I was somehow still happier than I was with my one."

* * *

For the two years after I learned about Cassandra's leave before we reconnected, I wondered and worried. Had she returned to teaching? Or was she so shattered by her experiences that she'd never again live her childhood dream?

As soon as I heard her voice when we spoke recently, I knew she had regained her spirit. Cassandra now teaches in the state college system.

"I teach and support secondary educators. I teach anyone who wants to be a middle or high school educator, and I coach student teachers who plan to teach English. And I *love* it.

"I'm able to support incoming educators in a way I never received. When I was in school, the focus was on just, equitable, and inclusive practices, but all of my professors had a lot of privilege. It was a lot easier for them to tell us how to implement inclusive practices because they weren't the targeted community.

"I'm really proud to be able to help, especially now. I'm an Arab educator. I've never had an Arab educator. I've never had someone stand against the majority and talk about how important brown bodies are, ours that get so underrepresented. And queer bodies. And the *reality* of teaching. Here, my identities are seen as an asset. My team knows the shit I've been through as a high school teacher, and they know that just adds more value. My experience doesn't mean that we all shouldn't be teachers. It just means there are things we can't control or prepare for."

She went on, explaining that she doesn't try to give her students an idealistic, sugary view of education. She tells them what she endured, but she also assures them that not every teacher will have that experience.

"It's nice to talk about education from the other side—about the good, the bad, and the ugly."

Cassandra still feels twinges of loss, even though her kindergarten dream became a nightmare. She thinks she maybe could have survived the secondary classroom if she'd just had *less* of the torment—*only* the doxing, or *only* the transfers from school to school, or *only* being targeted for her queerness.

"But I'm happy to at least still be in education. And I feel safer now."

Because Cassandra's pursuit of a lifelong goal had left her feeling unsafe. How could her experience *not* have had that effect?

* * *

For many educators today, to teach is also to be angry. I was able to carry that anger over a long career because, in manageable amounts, it fueled me to fight for change for the betterment of students and teachers. But today's personal attacks on teachers and truth are dangerous, and those who are threatened can't carry endless anger.

Because they also carry fear. And together, that's too heavy a load.

8

RAINBOWS AT THE SEA

It was 1:45 on Christmas morning of 2001, and there were only two passengers on the city bus, each of us leaving the airport after our respective travel tribulations. I was almost home, but my fellow traveler, a slump-shouldered man in his eighties, was on unfamiliar turf. He had missed the connecting flight to join his family for the holidays.

He asked the bus driver, "Does this line go near any hotels?"

Even though my exhausted body was on East Coast time, I was compelled to chime in.

"We'll go past a motel after we cross the freeway, but you probably don't want to go there, because you should stay close to BART. That's the public transit system here. If you stay on the bus until downtown, it'll cost more for a hotel, but then you can walk to BART in the morning to head back to the airport. BART starts up at eight o'clock on holidays, and if . . ."

The man turned to me with a weary sigh and said, "Are you a teacher?"

* * *

Educators often have common behavioral patterns. We talk obsessively about the classroom, as our friends and family can attest. Sprinkle random teachers into a potluck dinner and we'll find each other, posing questions about grades taught, subject-matter expertise, and the challenges of the current group of students. We bristle when nonteachers tell us it must be nice to leave work at 3:00 p.m., and we shriek with laughter when describing lessons gone awry. (To wit: A class period begins with a review of the characteristics of mammals, and my reminder to the kindergarteners that humans are included in "mammals." It ends with a book's photo of a mother cat nursing new kittens, one child's correct inference that the cat—like humans—must be a mammal, and a distressed six-year-old classmate's loud protestation: "*I* ain't no mammal! I ain't *never* drunk milk off a cat!" These experiences are meant to be shared.)

We project our voices, tend toward nurturing, and wear stain-repellent clothes that allow for sitting on the floor. Each year in August, we vibrate with nervous but excited energy as we await the morning bell that will usher in our new students, young people who for ten months will be the subjects of our discussions, dilemmas, and dreams.

And when frustration overwhelms us, we turn to other teachers. We unload our burdens, knowing that other teachers understand how hard it is. We tend to support each other, whether veteran educator or neophyte. Teaching is not a solitary sport. We need each other to make it through.

* * *

I'd been trying to reach Elisa for six months, even though I didn't yet know her name. Another teacher, Kaitlyn, had told me that a local pastor had targeted her friend on his podcast, and that a disturbing sequence of events had followed.

"Do you think she'll talk with me?" I had asked.

"I'm certain she *won't*," Kaitlyn had replied. "She's afraid for her children. She has backed off of everything."

"Could you just ask if she'll give me the date when he blasted her on the podcast?" There were far too many episodes for me to find the attack on a teacher whose name I didn't know.

Kaitlyn said she'd try, but I heard nothing more, so I didn't know any details about what the pastor had said. I figured I'd probably never learn what had happened between the mystery teacher and the pastor, but every six or eight weeks, I sent Kaitlyn a breezy text, asking if she'd heard back from her friend. I never received the answer I hoped for.

Then, in late July, Kaitlyn messaged me saying, "My friend is willing to meet with you." I was stunned, having nearly given up. I clicked on the new contact info and exchanged a few texts with Elisa. We decided to meet up the following week.

* * *

Pastor Tim Thompson's name had been shared with me by so many teachers and school board members that I kept forgetting I'd never met him in person. I'd read articles about his church and had watched videos of him preaching. In one video, Georgia Representative Marjorie Taylor Greene was giving a speech to Thompson's congregation. Until recently, his church website presented a staff composed solely of white men; it also links to his video podcast, considered part of the church's outreach. The mission statement of this podcast "ministry" decries inclusivity and boasts that the podcast is a tool to expose wickedness. Thompson says that "the government-ran [*sic*] school system is Satan's playground."[1]

Thompson is also listed as principal officer for a political action committee (PAC) in the area, a PAC with a previously stated objective of "working to stop the indoctrination of our children by placing candidates on school boards who will fight for Christian and Conservative values."[2] (The website now says it aims to elect "bold, pro-parental rights candidates.") In 2022, the PAC experienced much success toward that goal; moderate school boards in the region shifted to the right on election night, with numerous Christian nationalist candidates victorious in their races. In nearby Temecula, for example, three new board members were sworn in a month after the election, and immediately after taking their oath of office, the three-person majority voted to ban CRT from being taught in Temecula's schools.

CRT is not part of the K–12 curriculum, but their ban doesn't simply prohibit this college-level framework. It declares that teachers will "uplift" students "by not imposing the responsibility of historical transgressions in the past." It warns teachers that students must not feel discomfort or guilt due to their race, and it forbids educators from asserting that racism is embedded in everyday life or that individuals are of an oppressed class due to race.[3] District employees and students must report "racist conduct";[4] with the district's new definition of racism, it's conceivable that educators who teach about Jim Crow, redlining, voter suppression, school segregation, and the civil rights movement could be accused of engaging in reportable "racist conduct." One Temecula teacher who spoke at a board meeting wondered if she could still tell her students about being raised in the South with sharecroppers. According to the ban, racism is "long in the past."

Hundreds of community members, including students, flooded subsequent school board meetings in Temecula in protest. Students implored district trustees to allow the instruction of true history.

"It may be uncomfortable, but it *should* be," said one student. "The history of race in this country is terrible and sad, but to grow and move forward, we must all be educated."

Another said, "My peers here today are not here to promote hate toward any sort of white community. We are here because we believe that the damages of hundreds of years of discrimination will not disappear by ignoring the issue of race."

The ban remained intact, and Temecula's school board eventually moved on to its next culture-wars battle. They banned textbooks for mentioning Harvey Milk, one of the country's first openly gay elected officials. Assassinated in 1978, the iconic activist was posthumously awarded the Presidential Medal of Freedom for his civil rights work fighting antigay discrimination.

And across a wide swath of inland Southern California, some school districts joined the intensified attack on inclusivity of LGBTQ+ people, including students. As if in a live game of Whack-a-Mole, support for LGBTQ+ students was bashed wherever it popped up across the region.

A number of Southern California school districts have held demonstrations and protests over support of LGBTQ+ people. Some of the gatherings have turned violent. Board policies have been rewritten and lawsuits filed. The school board president of Chino Valley Unified School District threw California's superintendent of education out of a board meeting. He was speaking against a proposal that would force teachers to out LGBTQ+ students.

Pastor Tim Thompson is certainly not the lone voice declaring that public schools are providing "perverted sexual training" when they support LGBTQ+ students. But it's impossible to deny that he's a key player in the live Whack-a-Mole tournament. He wields a mallet. And he knows how to use it.

* * *

Mystery Teacher Elisa and I found each other in the noisy, dimly lit bar/arcade of a Southern California seaside hotel. Once again, I had caught myself unconsciously looking for a face that matched the trauma a teacher had endured. Elisa didn't match at *all*. She had playful blond braids tinged with pink, and wore adornments sprinkled with rainbows. After introductions, her wife and younger child drifted away, while Elisa told me her story, punctuated by sharp smacks of a plastic puck from the air-hockey table just behind me.

When Elisa was teaching in a neighboring school district, she came out as LGBTQ+, and seven families each demanded that their child be transferred from her class. New to being queer, Elisa didn't yet know about laws that protect her from workplace discrimination based on sexual orientation. She didn't protest.

When she moved to a different district, she came out to her principal right away.

"Just so you know, if anybody says anything, it's possible parents might want to switch kids out of my class. It happened last year."

His immediate response: "Oh, no, not in this area. That isn't *our* community. There's no way. You're going to be fine."

* * *

On Elisa's first day at her new school, it was almost time for recess. She was herding her third graders from their seats on the rug toward lining up at the door when a child's voice piped up.

"Are you married?"

As a queer person, Elisa has learned to answer questions simply, without elaboration. She said, "Yes, I'm married. Come on, kids, let's line up."

"What's your husband's name?"

Motioning stragglers toward the door, Elisa's bare-bones reply was, "I don't have one."

The inquisitive child pressed.

"You don't have a husband? But you said you're married. So do you live alone?"

By now, most of the other kids were milling about. If a teacher is not vigilant, chaos can take hold in seconds when young kids are distracted, the way an excited dog will gulp down a slippery avocado pit when a careless sandwich maker (*ahem* . . .) loses her grip.

So Elisa said, "I'm actually married to a woman. Okay, everybody, get your snacks and let's go!"

As third graders grabbed cheese sticks and apple chunks, the persistent child hollered, "YOU CAN'T KISS A *GIRL*!"

Suddenly, everyone was riveted. Elisa, all business, said, "You can kiss whoever when you're older, but we're not talking about that now. Line up." The kids headed to recess, and Elisa headed to the principal.

In the office, Elisa recounted the innocent conversation and described a book she planned to read to her class.

"It's about all the families that might raise a child. They might be grandparents, or siblings, or one mom or dad, or they might be adopted, or living in two houses. And we're a Title I school with a lot of kids who are being raised by different-looking families. It's great because the book doesn't focus on queer families. It's just saying there might be any type of family."

I had bought Suzanne Lang's *Families, Families, Families!* for my own classroom library and read it each year until I retired. Every child smiling at the adorable illustrations would feel seen and secure, knowing that their own family had its place in this world.

But Elisa's principal didn't see it that way.

"Oh, no. You can't share that. Don't bring it up again. Don't talk about your family."

Maybe that shouldn't have surprised Elisa, because one of her own children had received a similar message several years earlier, that time from a fellow teacher.

Elisa's then-kindergartener had happily announced, "I have two moms!"

The teacher hurriedly shushed the child, saying, "We don't talk about that here."

Contrary to the principal's assurance, it *was* their community after all. And already, on the first day of school, Elisa was *not* fine.

* * *

From first grade through twelfth, I attended only Catholic schools. My only public school experience before college was in kindergarten, and in the middle years when my parents sent me to summer school because they didn't know what else to do with my extroverted self.

My elementary school was St. Apollinaris, which is where I met most of my playmates. But I also made friends on my city softball team and in 4-H cooking and sewing classes, and I wished I could also see those friends at school. It was as if a part of my world was missing. I knew my parents paid tuition for us kids, and I had heard that public school kids' families didn't pay.

I knew we weren't rich. So I asked my dad.

"Why do we go to St. Apollinaris if it costs money?"

"Because your mom and I want you to learn religion at school."

I certainly understood that religion was at the heart of my education. All through elementary school, we had to inscribe the top of every math, spelling, and writing page with a tall skinny *P* and a small *x* overlay, forming the Greek symbol for Christ. We attended Mass during school hours, and once a month, all kids third grade and up traipsed over to the church next door so we could go to confession. Every teacher was a nun in a long black habit, and every classroom had a large crucifix hanging high on the front wall. I'd fix my eyes on Jesus's plaster body while the sisters led us in morning prayer, afternoon prayer, and special-intention prayers—like when Johnny Biale was hospitalized for asthma, and when Skip Long fell under a moving tractor.

Yes, religion was central. But still, I was confused.

"How come it's free for kids to go to public school?"

My Republican father explained that taxes pay for necessary services in a society. There was talk of roads, libraries, parks, and police departments.

"Everyone needs to go to school. So we all pay for that with taxes. But if people want something extra, they have to pay extra for it."

I eventually learned that tuition was twenty-five bucks a month for one child, but a flat fee of $30 for two or more. It was a good bargain for our family of four children, but the Beards had seven kids, and the Mailhots had twelve. What a deal! And if the Blackburns' FOURTEEN children—twins in my class—had all attended St. Apollinaris at once, they would have paid barely $2 a month per child. Even for the late 1960s, that seemed dirt cheap—the cost of only twenty Slurpees from 7-Eleven, 10¢ apiece.

The per-family price of Catholic education imprinted in my memory, as did the idea that taxes pay for shared needs in a society. But what I remember most from talking with my dad is that it seemed *fair* that we paid extra for private school. After all, we wanted specific, extra education. It would have seemed unfair to do it any other way.

* * *

Kids love discovering everything they can about their teacher. In my decades of teaching third and fourth grades, I've been asked why I had "a face like your thirties, but old-person hair." Students have asked how old my childhood dog was when he died, what my favorite movies are, and if I was alive when Harriet Tubman was. They wanted to know how I learned Spanish, why I thought white people voted for Donald Trump, and why I had loose skin on my elbows.

"It's like that stuff on a turkey's neck!" crowed Erik.

I laughed. He wasn't wrong.

Enoshay asked if I knew how to skateboard, saying it would be "tight" to see me "grind." Students asked if I'd ever seen the real Santa ("No, but I heard his sleighbells on the roof"), and if my parents sometimes got mad at me when I was a kid. To introduce them to the concept of including descriptive details in writing, I recounted a youthful memory while racing around the classroom, reenacting the event; they laughed, and learned that I was terrified of mice. They wanted to know if I was alive when "everything in the world was still in black and white," if I fought with my siblings when I was little, if I knew how to swim, and if a bird ever pooped on my head. They learned to wait in barely breathing silence when I'd get choked up reading beautiful books to them. Over time, they learned to read my face and would shush each other if they sensed I was about to blow. And they learned that after I did, I would often ask them to forgive me.

Before becoming a teacher, I'd never realized how far beyond academics the learning in a classroom stretches. A child who feels safe around a trusted teacher can tiptoe into asking questions that help them understand the world. In elementary school, where kids and teachers are together for six or more hours a day for ten months, the growth arrows point in all directions. I'd learn about them—as individuals and as a group—and they would come to know me, and each other. We'd expand and wrestle and argue and accept and forgive. Together and individually, we would grow.

When a sparkly ring appeared on my left hand at age forty-six, my observant students noticed and figured out I was getting married. They asked my husband-to-be's first name, and what my (presumed) new last name would be. They asked if I would have kids. Of *course* they asked these things. Hadn't I encouraged them to wonder about their world? Hadn't I modeled how to receive sincere questions and respond with respect? I answered their queries directly, without unnecessary details, giving simple, matter-of-fact answers. Then we moved on.

And I knew that some would internalize messages I never got as a child: that it was fine to marry late, or not at all; that not having children was a valid life choice; that a person can make her own decisions about her own name. That it's perfectly fine to do things differently from most, as long as we don't hurt others.

That it's okay to be who we are. That we *get* to be who we are.

That we *deserve* to be who we are.

* * *

In the landmark civil rights case of *Bostock v. Clayton County*, the U.S. Supreme Court announced in June 2020 that LGBTQ+ employees—including educators—are protected from discrimination at work based on sexual orientation or gender identity. If the Supreme Court decision had been in place when the seven families moved their children from Elisa's class, the transfers would have violated the ruling. Employers cannot consider employees' orientation or gender identity when setting class assignments.

When Elisa's principal instructed her not to talk about her family anymore, Elisa—new to the district, and without tenure—didn't push back, although the directive surely qualified as discriminatory. (Can you imagine a straight, cisgender elementary school teacher being ordered not to mention their family? Yeah, me neither.) Not knowing her own rights yet and worried about job security, Elisa wasn't sure what she could and couldn't do to support students. And she *wanted* to support them. Near the end of the 2020–21 school year, she heard that a few fifth graders had come out as being on the queer spectrum, and that some students wanted to start a rainbow club. They had even circulated a petition, gathering many signatures.

Around the same time, Elisa began attending education conferences, learning all she could about California laws that protect LGBTQ+ students and laws that enable teachers to support them. Topics included California's FAIR Education Act, which requires California's K–12 schools to provide fair, accurate, inclusive, and respectful representation of contributions of people with disabilities and people who are LGBTQ+. She also learned about rights she has as a queer educator.

California teachers earn tenure after at least two years of full-time teaching in the same public school district. Once Elisa was protected by this set of due-process rights the following year, she added "LGBTQ icons" to her classroom lineup of celebrated heritages. Most California schools recognize "heritage months," a calendared focus on various cultures and peoples, and a study of their contributions to society. Black History, Native American Heritage, and Women's History are just a few of these monthly focus areas. With June widely recognized as Pride Month, Elisa took a tenured step into visible support for LGBTQ+ kids. She and a straight, cisgender colleague bought a teacher-created unit of study, and each set up a classroom bulletin board with pictures of well-known queer people, including Harvey Milk, Neil Patrick Harris, Laverne Cox, Sally Ride, and James Baldwin. They planned to teach simple activities about the contributions of each.

Both educators first taught the lesson on artist Frida Kahlo. But when the other teacher received two complaints—from a parent and from a fellow staff member—administration told her to take the bulletin board down. Elisa took hers down, too. But she also contacted the district's new equity and diversity director.

"I'm passionate about this. I'd love to work with you. What are your goals? Let me help!" the director told her. Throughout that summer of 2021, Elisa kept checking in. The new director sent cheery "I'll be in touch!" replies but never was.

While at a fall conference, Elisa learned that when a school allows other noncurricular clubs on campus, LGBTQ+ students have the right to form a club, too. So she emailed her new principal.

"I want to start an LGBTQ support club. We already have other clubs," she explained. "Kids have gathered eighty signatures. They want a rainbow club."

When the principal rejected the idea, Elisa informed her that she legally *couldn't* say no. She presented her with laws, videos, and statistics, adding, "I didn't just wake up deciding to start a club. Look at the signatures. Those kids know what they want!"

The principal said she'd need to get the district involved.

The district *did* get involved.

And so did Pastor Tim Thompson, mallet at the ready.

* * *

Over the next weeks, there were nine meetings, multiple district administrators, and hot tears of frustration.

"You need to know this neighborhood," said the administrator in charge of LGBTQ+ inclusion. "We're on a seven-year plan, so it's too soon for a rainbow club."

"Seven *years*? We don't have seven years! Kids need support *now*, and they won't get it anywhere else. I grew up here. My wife and I live here, so I *do* know the area. There are places we can't go, and things we can't do."

Ultimately, a unity club at Elisa's school was allowed, under strict conditions. Meetings would be student led, with Elisa facilitating only if inappropriate conversations started. Kids would need signed permission slips, and Elisa would have to turn in a list of activities planned for the entire year.

In January 2022, the first meeting of the new Unity Club was held. At the gathering, kids wrote why they wanted to join, listed their pronouns, and thought of one thing they wanted to change about their school. Then Elisa got COVID-19 and went out on sick leave. In her absence, all hell broke loose, though Tim Thompson would probably say it was heaven-sent.

* * *

Elisa believes it was a particular churchgoing staff member at her school who brought her name to the attention of Pastor Tim Thompson. That shocked me—not because a fellow teacher disagreed with Elisa's support of LGBTQ+ students, but because the staff member had brought the concern to *church*. If truly worried about the welfare of children, it seems the person would have followed district protocol and gone straight to the principal, who could dictate what Elisa could and couldn't do. But by bringing the concern to a pastor with a massive social media following and a practice of posting inflammatory videos for many thousands of viewers, it seems that the intent was more far-reaching than just shutting down the Unity Club.

Mere days after Elisa fell ill with COVID, Thompson and a videographer showed up at her school, apparently without an appointment. In the school office, Thompson calmly addressed the principal, asking if she was aware that a teacher had been passing out LGBTQ+ flags and literature, pushing children to use different pronouns, and speaking to them very graphically about sex.

In the video of the encounter, Thompson identifies himself as a pastor and spiritual leader of the community; the implication is that this justifies him taking the time of public employees. Thompson maintains a composed demeanor, his velvety voice repeatedly informing the principal that he is merely asking questions. The two go around and around. Thompson asks, "Are you aware that the teacher is doing this?" and the principal replies that she was aware of the Unity Club but not of the charges he is leveling. She assures him that things are under control but asserts that she's not going to specify what is and isn't happening there. Finally, she tells him that she won't answer his pointed questions about what she is aware of, and urges him to contact the school district office if he has a complaint.

Thompson and the videographer immediately pounce, demanding, "Why? Why won't you answer those questions? So are you okay with a teacher doing that? There's no reason why you can't answer!"

After the principal says goodbye, Thompson addresses the office receptionist with his parting words.

"I'm not happy that [the principal] is *clearly* allowing children to be exposed to this.... She's going to regret not standing on our side with this. It's going to end up being a larger issue than it had to be because of her unwillingness to work with the spiritual leaders of this community."

Thompson's words communicate that he had hoped to work with the principal. But the feeling I get from watching the video is that things played out exactly the way he wanted.

* * *

Watching the recorded interaction, I couldn't help but think of the last principal I had before retiring. When I taught a third grader who had a genetic mutation making him prone to outbursts of wild rage, Principal John directed me to send a one-word text if I needed immediate help. When summoned, he'd sprint down the hallway, yank open my classroom door, and contort himself to sit underneath a table—while wearing a suit—to soothe the distraught child. From early morning until late afternoon, John was on the go: meeting with parents, observing and critiquing classroom lessons, revising budgets, and dealing with young instigators of recess aggression. Each day's varied crises were myriad and widespread; in his first eight weeks at my school, John covered so much ground rushing across the large campus that he lost fifteen pounds. I often found him by the staff microwave at 3:15, heating up the shriveled baked potato he hadn't had time to eat for lunch.

Teachers, principals, office workers, counselors, librarians, instructional aides, cafeteria workers, paraeducators, speech therapists, and custodians at a public school are often overworked, and usually underpaid. So to see Tim Thompson demonstrating his expectation that public employees owed him their time—it rankled. He communicated a clear message by bringing a videographer instead of sending an email or making a phone call. He wanted to stir things up and make a show for his audience, which was primed for his performance. I thought of the long-ago conversation with my father, and his clear explanation that public schools could not give children an education centered on religious principles.

Tim Thompson must not have received a similar message from his dad.

* * *

The two men went to the district office, where they recorded an administrator identifying Elisa as the teacher behind the Unity Club. At a school board meeting that same night, Thompson named Elisa before the large crowd, then railed against her for starting the Unity Club, for "pushing transgender ideology" on her social media posts, and for organizing a meeting for local LGBTQ+ educators. Then he blasted the school board, calling one trustee evil and telling them all to "put your big-boy pants on and get ready for November, because we're coming."

Within days, Thompson featured the school visits on his video podcast. One clip got well over a hundred thousand views. He posted additional videos about Elisa, including one where he states, "This is clearly a groomer in our school system. She is a danger to society."

He wasn't done. Thompson published a picture of Elisa's Facebook profile, saying, "So right there, you know that this is a woman who clearly is open about her homosexuality and *went out of her way* to marry another woman." He posted a screenshot of an article Elisa had written about her prior experience of being traumatized by the church, and declared, "She has it out for anybody that would adhere to sound Biblical doctrine about sexuality." Finally, he reposted Elisa's notice from her union's private Facebook page. It was a friendly invitation for LGBTQ+ educators to gather for a meeting, and it included Elisa's personal phone number. Suddenly, her private information was out there for over a hundred thousand riled-up viewers to see. Adding betrayal to fear, she realized it must have been a fellow union member—a teacher—who shared the private post with Thompson. No one else would have had access to it.

The commenters got to work.

Oblivious to the fact that Elisa was sick with COVID, one respondent said, "She's not there, so she's already been put on leave." Someone else wrote, "I found her address. Let's all go camp outside her house or her school and confront her." One commenter recommended that she be stoned, as in biblical times. Strangers flooded the school with daily phone calls, asking, "Does that teacher work here? Do you know she's doing this?" The office manager told Elisa that eight of every ten phone calls came from out of state.

Elisa is public in her support of LGBTQ+ students, and in one impassioned TikTok video, she declared that she would stand up for LGBTQ+ kids until she was dead. One commenter said, "Where's the gun? I'll gladly put you in your grave." She was called a pedophile. Her social media videos were reposted by Ben Shapiro, Charlie Kirk, and Libs of TikTok, the group focused on exposing queer teachers.

Still on sick leave, Elisa contacted district administrators in a panic.

"He made a video about me. He shared my private information, and now people are threatening to come to my house. I'm concerned for my safety."

The district ordered Elisa not to respond to Thompson or his followers and assured her that the situation was being monitored. She followed the directive, but it pained her. She couldn't help feeling like the district's silence was an admission of her guilt.

When Elisa returned to work, colleagues wouldn't talk to her. She'd pass people in hallways, and they'd turn away. She'd greet teachers, but they'd walk past without speaking. Ostracized and feeling unsafe, she reached out to the district.

"I'm being isolated. Almost nobody will talk to me, but I haven't done anything wrong."

The district's response was to inform her that she was under investigation, pending further review.

* * *

Elisa understands that parents worry about their children. She is a parent herself; both the teacher and the parent within her pound the constant drumbeat to keep children safe. Yet here *she* was, being investigated while still reverberating from being targeted, threatened, and doxed. She felt cornered; the big loud voice she'd found in support of LGBTQ+ children and families was being taken away and used against her.

The stress was overwhelming. Two close friends at school walked her to and from her car that spring. Whenever she entered a room, she could feel that everyone knew. For months, she didn't go out in public. Would someone who'd seen the videos attack her? A public reading that she'd organized was canceled; it was part of the national Human Rights Campaign, an organization that fights for the rights of LGBTQ+ people. A small coffeehouse had agreed to host the event, but when Thompson's followers inundated the business with threatening phone calls, the manager phoned Elisa.

"We're so sorry, but we can't afford to shut down."

There was no doubt who was behind it. The callers had all identified their church by name.

* * *

The investigation dragged on into the 2022–23 school year, and Elisa was still largely being shunned. When she spoke to her principal, the response was, "Well, other staff members are healing, too."

"Healing from *what*?! They weren't investigated or doxed!"

When Elisa suggested that she was being discriminated against, two straight teachers were looped into the investigation, though the reason for it was still murky. If she'd ask her grade-level team to meet about a curricular issue, she would be told, "I don't know if we can. Let me ask admin." She was depressed, lonely, and confused. There had been no parent or student complaints against her, and the principal had said, "This has nothing to do with your teaching. You're a great teacher!" She knew she was being watched; the principal was aware when kids stayed indoors with Elisa during lunch, and quickly shut down this common practice that had not been an issue the year prior.

Finally, Elisa learned that Tim Thompson was not behind the investigation at all.

"It looks like the complaints came from staff members here who attend his church," she said. "The main complaints against me were that I was 'refusing to collaborate with my team,' that I was 'promoting the LGBTQ agenda,' and that I was being 'inappropriate on social media.' I can't prove it, but it's pretty obvious which teachers complained about me."

When Elisa had come back from sick leave, the behavior of a few teachers had stood out. It wasn't just that they weren't talking to her. Some had instructed their students not to visit Elisa during their recess or lunch. Those same teachers would leave the room when she would talk about her wife.

"There were teachers who *clearly* discriminated against me, but I had always put it off as something else. I already knew those people didn't 'agree with my lifestyle'—I *hate* that saying—but I had assumed it was me being paranoid. Then it became clear to me that it was in fact discrimination. It *wasn't* something else."

The eventual verdict was that Elisa's posting on social media had not violated any policies, but that she had indeed failed to collaborate with her team members, whose teaching beliefs and methodologies were very different from hers. The investigation also determined that Elisa had been promoting "the LGBTQ agenda."

But what does *that* mean when coming from a place where she was unjustly ordered not to discuss her family? A place that initially refused to allow a state-sanctioned LGBTQ+ support club? A place where a teacher complained when Elisa wore rainbows or shirts that read "Protect queer students" and "Stand up for LGBTQ rights"? A place where a teacher once filed a complaint because a (closeted) gay man was teaching kindergarten? He was moved to a higher grade level, and when he ended up on the same team as the complaining teacher, his work environment became so toxic that he left the profession.

The investigation called for a forty-five-day period during which Elisa would take extreme care to follow the rules, with a reconvening to verify her compliance. Elisa's union lawyer urged her to move to another school, but she was unwilling to leave her own child behind at the school or force them to move. So she stayed, even though it was painful. Her two close friends left, having chosen different sites with more welcoming colleagues.

One day, Elisa was speaking with her child's teacher.

"It's weird!" said the teacher. "Nothing I've heard about you is true!" She told Elisa of the rumors that were still being spread.

Elisa continued to fight false claims, and to push for district support.

To one district administrator, she said, "Our district policy, board policy, and California Ed Code all say that we protect LGBTQ kids and families. You won't make a statement against Tim Thompson, but will you at *least* reiterate publicly that our district will keep supporting *all* families and students?"

The hemming-and-hawing reply was mostly "I don't know" and "I'm not sure."

Making another effort, she said, "I do trainings for CTA [the California Teachers Association], and have presented several times for the National Education Association about support for LGBTQ students. I'd love to help our district with training. I can explain to teachers what the laws are."

Nope.

She forged ahead.

"I'm not the only one," she told the district administrator in charge of inclusivity. "And not only am I a queer teacher, but my kids go here. I'm a *parent* here. We have an African-American Parent Advisory, and a Latinx Committee. We need to have an LGBTQ Parent Advisory."

Meetings were held, with haggling over the composition of the proposed advisory. The district wanted it to be for "nontraditional families," including foster parents, grandparents, and parents of unhoused children. Elisa protested that the issues faced by these groups were entirely different.

Should that have to be pointed out? Is it not obvious?

She is weary of battling.

"They keep asking me which other districts in the area are inclusive to LGBTQ youth and families. But when I tell them, nothing happens. And they think I'm the only queer teacher in the area."

Clearly, she's not, but she's one of the few who are out. Her union president has affirmed that other queer teachers say they'll *never* come out in her district. It's not hard to understand why.

"An administrator asked me, 'Who else is Tim Thompson targeting?' And I said, 'Well, I have a public social media where I am willingly out as a queer teacher in elementary.'"

"*Well . . .*"

The one-word implication: that Elisa had brought the abuse on herself.

No wonder she's weary.

* * *

In addition to the remarkable Principal John, it was my grade-level colleagues who got me through the excruciating year of distance teaching. Certainly, there were times when I was overwhelmed by stress and hopelessness, like that dreary February day in 2021 when, overwhelmed by it all, I signed off from my young students after class, closed my laptop, and drove to Muir Woods, a forest of ancient redwoods. Standing alone in the dark woods, I wept in the rain.

But rarely did I feel truly alone; despite the fear and desperation and appalling workload, the collaboration and camaraderie among the three of us third-grade teachers are what saved me. We each taught ourselves technology tricks, then made video tutorials so the other two could learn them, too. Our creativity exploded as we developed virtual lessons seven days a week, sharing everything with each other. Every few days, one of us would crack, and the other two would shoulder a bit more of the load. Our text threads were endless strings of quips, encouragement, and hilarity, tales of lessons gone wrong and soaring successes that felt like miracles. Shared laughter sustained us, as did the constant support, as unshakable as the towering trees under which I'd wandered in the rain. Teachers need the support of administration, and they need each other to make it through. When you're the only adult in the room all day, in a high-scrutiny job requiring unending patience under often stressful circumstances, you lean on the ones who understand, the ones who can listen, encourage, laugh, and commiserate. Without the support of faithful coworkers, I couldn't have made it through the most difficult period in my thirty-two years of teaching.

But Elisa usually stood alone during her most tortured time. And the thought that a churchgoing colleague had likely been the one to steer Tim Thompson in her direction—that cut deep. Walking in the redwoods wasn't going to heal that wound.

* * *

The CTA lawyer urged Elisa to move sites, warning that detractors would hound her until they found a way to take her job.

At first, she considered it. Then she thought, "Wait. Why do *I* have to move? That would make administrators' lives easier, but not mine."

Elisa explained that "just go to a new school" means something very different for her than for straight, cisgender people like me. It means coming out to at least fifty new people, probably many more. That's draining and, after what she has been through, daunting. But going back in the closet is not an option.

"I *can't* not be me again. I *can't* not support my students and parents. Teachers email me after I do trainings and tell me they now have rainbow clubs at their schools. I *love* doing the trainings, and helping people who are starting clubs. But I *hate* that while I'm doing this, my district is still saying, 'This is not for YOU.' That eats away at me.

"At night, sometimes I scroll online, wondering what I can do instead of teach. Everything I thought I'd be as a teacher has been obliterated because of this. I feel like a basic C student. I'm not really great at anything. I'm very shy, and social situations stress me out. But *this*—it's something I have a voice for. It feels like a calling."

She fed me statistics about the effect of caring teachers on queer kids. The Trevor Project's 2023 data show that when LGBTQ+ young people reported that teachers were accepting of them, they had 43 percent lower odds of an in-the-past-year suicide attempt.

"I'd love a position where my voice and story are used in a positive way. But they'll never hire me at this district to give trainings or be their inclusion person.

"They think I'm that one lesbian who has a loud voice, and maybe they think I'm grooming kids. I don't know what else they think I'm doing. But what I'm *actually* doing is reading them books, showing them rainbows to say I love them, and giving them a space where they can be and say whatever they want, to identify as whoever they want."

* * *

Elisa and I reconnected in June 2025, when I learned of her latest struggle.

After one year of relative peace, she started the 2024–25 school year with a student on her fourth-grade class list who was known for his challenging behavior.

It's very common for teachers to display a few family photos on the wall behind their desk and on their individual "About Me" page on the school website. A supportive colleague who knew the challenging student spoke to Elisa.

"You might want to consider taking down your family pictures," he said. "Just be really careful."

The student left no doubt about his conservative family's viewpoints. When Elisa took attendance on day one, instead of responding "Here" to his name, the student announced, "I am Donald Trump." He would raise his hand in class, but when Elisa called on him to answer questions, he'd say, "Do you know there are only two genders?" or "Do you know what your constitutional rights are?"

By focusing on his positive behaviors instead of on his attention-seeking bait, Elisa developed a decent rapport with the child. Things were going well.

Then one day, while the children silently read books they'd chosen from the classroom library, the student approached her, holding a book.

"I found something inappropriate."

Elisa said, "Why don't you show me what's upsetting you?"

He put his finger on the word "transgender."

It was in *A Kids Book About Being Inclusive*. Containing only speech bubbles with no pictures, the book displays a dialogue between two children who teach each other what the words "inclusion" and "inclusive" mean. While there is brief mention of being transgender, the book's central message encourages acceptance of others, because everyone feels happy when they're accepted for being themselves. A representative excerpt reads,

> People can feel excluded because of their skin color, or their religion, their gender, the way they dress, if they have a disability, what language they speak—and for so many other reasons.
>
> Even though we're all different from one another, we all want to be part of the group. We all want to feel included.

The page that the boy complained about reads, "I always felt like I didn't fit in or didn't belong. At the time, I wasn't quite sure why until I found the word to describe who I am . . . That word for me is transgender."

Elisa's explanation to the complaining child was, "It's actually not inappropriate." When the boy protested, she continued. "If you don't want to read it, you don't have to. I'm not requiring you to read it. You could just put it down."

The student responded, "I don't agree with that."

Elisa said, "It's fine if you don't agree with that at your house. But in this classroom, we accept everyone, and we have books like that so that everybody can feel welcome in our classroom."

* * *

Elisa called her administrator immediately.

"I know where this is going. We need to message the parent so they don't feel like we're hiding."

The administrator asked Elisa to put the book in an envelope and deliver it to the office, telling Elisa she preferred the "wait and see" approach.

The parent lodged a complaint within half an hour of dismissal.

* * *

Two days later, the student informed classmates, "We're going to have a sub tomorrow." Elisa corrected him but later received a call telling her to report to the district office the next day instead of to her classroom. There, she was told that there had been complaints about books in her library and that she was being put on paid administrative leave.

Within a few weeks, the child moved to a different district school, and his new teacher emailed Elisa, asking if they could talk. Later, Elisa learned why.

"She said that when he introduced himself to the class, he announced, 'I just got my last teacher fired.' His new teacher was freaking out."

With the child no longer at her school, Elisa thought she'd be allowed to return. But her union president learned that the child's mother had been standing outside her classroom, telling other parents Elisa was grooming kids. Four other families joined the complaint.

Months passed, and the district periodically grilled Elisa, who was still on paid leave. How did she select books for her library? At least twelve titles had been pulled from her room, deemed "inappropriate" by the district. What websites did she use to guide her selections? Why did she consider the twelve titles acceptable for fourth grade?

"Parents find them inappropriate," said one administrator. "You and I will have to agree to disagree."

Elisa spoke with various attorneys. The response was consistent: Nothing could be done since the district wasn't firing her.

One lawyer added that if other teachers on her staff had the same books, they could prove Elisa was being singled out.

"But you're the only one. That makes you an easy target."

* * *

At the end of the 2024–25 school year, Elisa was told she'd be moved to a different elementary school, with conditions.

"You will no longer be allowed to have a personal classroom library unless it's approved by the district," said her administrator. "And—this is *not* a directive—if students ask about your family, I would say, 'My family is personal, and I like to keep it private.'"

Now in tears, Elisa responded, "So let's say I do that. What happens when my son talks about his family? We're on the same campus. People will figure it out. It just doesn't seem fair. What about family pictures?"

"You can have one picture on your desk."

"But other teachers' families aren't '*private.*' My son's teacher has her husband in her classroom *every single day* volunteering! This is not equitable!"

For months, Elisa had believed she'd be reassigned to the continuation school. She was relieved; similar complaints at the secondary level seemed unlikely. But being sent to another elementary school felt like a setup, a placement where she was doomed to fail. And a new condition of her employment was that if there were another investigation of her which involved the "LGBTQ+ agenda," it could be grounds for termination.

The advice from her union's legal consultant?

Don't have *any* personal books in a classroom library. Don't wear *anything* with rainbows—not a pin, a shirt, a hair accessory. Don't have a sign about the classroom being a "safe space" unless the district approves it.

Fly under the radar.

Be invisible.

Be silent.

* * *

After we said goodbye, I thought about Elisa's rainbow adornments on the day we'd met, nearly two years prior. Her future students might not get to see her rainbow pins, earrings, and hair accessories, but her support and acceptance for them will still shine through.

Because when seaside fog blocks the sun, the light is still there. It hasn't gone away. It's still shining brightly, just above the low-lying clouds.

9

THE THING ABOUT DISCOMFORT

Quick—what image pops up when you imagine a high school librarian busy at work? Your only hint is that she's a woman. What do you notice about her posture, her demeanor, her clothing? Is she whispering to a student, pointing toward a shelf? Perhaps quietly reshelving books?

Sorry, but whatever you're picturing, it's wrong. The photo in my hand showed this teacher-librarian in one of her favorite places to perform her work duties: perched on the padded seat of a heavy cargo bike. Clad in a helmet, leggings, a T-shirt reading "Alternative fact checker," and a huge smile, Jennifer projected an enthusiasm and energy that pulsated from the image on her phone. Though the vehicle is technically a tricycle, it's known around town as the Book Bike, and Jennifer's hope is that it will one day be a mainstay at school events, football games, and local parades. The two oversize front wheels support foldout cabinetry packed with books, most available to students for free.

Jennifer and I were sharing a sidewalk table on this steamy summer morning, and she bubbled over with book talk.

"We bring the library to kids who say, 'I don't go to the library.' The library comes to you!" She laughed, her eyes bright behind polka-dot-rimmed glasses.

I was captivated by the idea of a Book Bike, and by Jennifer's infectious spirit. Over the next two hours outside a downtown café, she told me her story as the two of us shifted our chairs to follow the migrating shade. I hung on every word, except for the ones I missed when rumbling trains screeched their arrival at the station across the street.

* * *

Jennifer's offhand mention of earlier life experiences conveyed the endless possibility of young adulthood. In college, while studying Paolo Freire's *Pedagogy of the Oppressed*, she taught in prisons, conducting art workshops. She then joined the Peace Corps; several years after returning, she traveled to Cuba, where she partnered with a grassroots nonprofit. Though skateboards are contraband and not sold in the island nation, Jennifer taught local skateboarding kids to use GoPros and digital cameras to document their lives while kick-flipping and nose-grinding across tropical asphalt.

Between the Peace Corps and Cuba, Jennifer had become an English teacher in California, and she was troubled by the massive disparities she saw. The wealthy, high-achieving students at her school cruised through AP classes, while struggling students were grouped into classes openly named "far below basic." The pressure from parents paralleled kids' academic levels. Parents of struggling students focused on just getting their kids to show up, while parents of high-level kids hammered her with a single, unwavering message: *My child needs an A.*

Weary of the stress, Jennifer earned an additional credential to teach art, and began teaching photography classes in addition to her English courseload. The disparity was still there—some students had beautiful cameras, while others had none—but teaching art helped keep Jennifer grounded in why she had entered education.

"It's not about *photography*. It's about building communities with kids."

It's how she's wired: to connect with others, and to help young people connect with the world.

* * *

Most teachers experience moments that spark them, jolt them, stop them mid-step to remind them why they chose a profession that can be isolating and demoralizing, exhausting and demanding. It's because teaching can be miraculous, too. Those magic moments can blind us to all the difficulty and awake in us a sense of wonder at the beauty of educating young people. For many, those moments revolve around the power of "community." For me, one of those moments came with Alejandro and the young kids who sat at his feet.

Alejandro rolled up onto the balls of his feet when he walked, giving him a jaunty air. He appeared slightly off-balance and looked awkward performing tasks like using scissors, throwing a ball, or zipping his coat. He qualified for speech therapy in multiple categories. His brain had trouble expressing thoughts with language, while a physical speech impediment hindered him in replicating sounds in both English and his native Spanish.

Alejandro didn't know the sounds of the alphabet but was clearly very bright. He remembered details in math word problems after I read them aloud only once, and he quickly grasped the gist of his modified assignments. The day I taught the class alphabetical order while using a dictionary, Alejandro was the first to successfully hunt down each word I projected on the big screen, though he couldn't read a single one.

Despite his intelligence, Alejandro couldn't retain his classmates' names, which seemed to get tangled on the journey from brain to mouth. Only rarely did he use my name. With lips pressed together, brow furrowed, and forehead flushed pink down the center, he still said my name as "Zan-grella" instead of "Gran-zella." Alejandro was also severely colorblind, and his eyes didn't track in tandem. When one faced forward, the other angled a shade off from straight.

Yet Alejandro remained undaunted, always cheerful, friendly, and kind.

Writing was the hardest; the string of consonants Alejandro scrawled bore no resemblance to the words he intended. When the class wrote true stories from their own lives, his were unintelligible jumbles of letters, the same few over and over. Neither he nor I could read his drafts, and with so many students, I couldn't take dictation.

So I'd hand him my old iPod Touch and he'd tell his story aloud, recording himself while I hustled from kid to kid. At night, I'd listen, typing what I could understand. Even after I would replay it several times, some words remained a stubborn mystery.

When a kid finished writing and illustrating a story, the student would set up my $50 karaoke machine, read the piece through the mic, and receive classmates' feedback. They all knew the drill: listen carefully, applaud at the end, give compliments. On the day Alejandro was ready to share his first piece, I was uneasy. He'd need help with all of it. These kids were kind. But still—they were only eight. How would they react?

Alejandro tiptoed his way to the shabby rocking chair. With his back straight and feet swinging a few inches off the floor, he switched the microphone on and pressed his lips into the thin line of concentration I recognized. He was ready. The only problem: I knew he couldn't read a single word. He knew it, too.

As a final desperate appeal, my eyes begged the class to be silent, and I started whispering beside Alejandro, feeding him his own words, three at a time. *"The dog came . . . to my house. . . . My mom said . . ."* As he echoed me, I shot glances all around, ready to extinguish sparks of laughter. But there were none. The kids were rapt, silent, listening.

As he plodded onward, my worry turned to wonder. Nobody whispered, *"She's reading it for him!"* No smirking, no fiddling with shoes, no giggling. The only laughs were at appropriate moments, when Alejandro described the comical aspects of dog ownership. The kids acted as if nothing were unusual. They were focused on the speaker, as I'd taught them. When Alejandro ended with *"And I never . . . saw my dog . . . again,"* the class broke into applause, and their hands shot up.

Like a benevolent king surveying his subjects, Alejandro gazed upon his classmates. Then he pointed his chubby finger at one after another, inviting feedback. Their compliments were simple: his description of the dog's spots, the humor, and the morsels of dialogue.

"Thank you, thank you," Alejandro repeated. Then he grinned, seeing my raised hand. Pointing at me, he asked me my name.

A kid who couldn't name his *teacher*? Surely now the others would laugh.

But my worry was unnecessary. No one reacted as I fed him my name, adding, "I liked your last line. It really made it sound like the end."

* * *

By the next morning, I'd decided to tell the class how much they'd impressed me with their gentleness. It wouldn't be easy; it's risky for a teacher to discuss an individual child with the group, and I didn't want to draw the wrong kind of attention to Alejandro's difficulties.

Once he left for speech therapy, I brought them all to the rug.

"Have I ever talked about someone in our class when the person isn't in the room?" I asked.

"No," they chorused.

"Well, I'm going to talk about Alejandro now, because I need to say how proud I am of you." A few kids' eyebrows crinkled in confusion.

"Does anyone know why I'm so proud of you all?"

Joshua always knew where I was headed.

"You're proud because we didn't laugh when Alejandro read his story."

"Yup." Suddenly, my throat quavered; I blinked hard and took a few deep breaths.

I gestured toward a few talkative kids. Mia complied.

"We listened to him read his story. And it was a good story."

That's it. Powerless to speak, I just shook my head and patted the flat of my hand on my chest. The kids rustled and squirmed.

Finally, I found some voice.

"Remember when I explained that everyone has different doors into their brains? Well, Alejandro has different doors than the ones I'm used to, and I still need to find the right doors to help him. Reading and writing are very hard for Alejandro. But that doesn't mean he's not smart! He's *very* smart! He just needs a little more help."

Voices popped up from all sides.

"Alejandro is *really* nice."

"He's good at math."

"He helped me pick up my crayons yesterday."

"Alejandro is funny."

"He never makes fun of other kids."

I smeared my hand across wet cheeks and tried to smile at these young people.

"Alejandro will have a happy life, because he knows how to treat people well. And so will you all, because *you* know how to treat people. You are very good *human beings*. I am proud to be your teacher," I said.

Grabbing a tissue, I motioned them back to their desks.

Later that morning, when one child whispered to another, "Do you need help?" I smiled a silent thank-you. But they didn't really need the extra encouragement. They were used to thinking of others, and not just of themselves.

Even at age eight, they knew the sweetness of community.

The memory still takes my breath.

* * *

When Jennifer returned from her sabbatical in Cuba, she went to a teacher conference and fell in love. Not with her husband—that had happened in the Peace Corps—but with the spirit of collaboration at the school hosting the conference. It was a chronically underresourced high school very near her home, but what stood out to Jennifer was the collection of educators. She knew their job was hard, and they showed up every day, working together to give students their all.

She had long valued working and living in the same community, and yearned to join this group of "amazing humans" on staff. She approached the principal.

"There's such a good vibe! I want to help. What do you need me to do here? A magazine or something?"

When he told her he needed someone to staff the library, Jennifer deflated. She didn't hold the right degree.

But he continued.

"You can help students find resources and books, help them do projects. With your English degree and all your digital knowledge, we can cobble something together."

Cobble, they did. It wasn't a new position—just the regular librarian position reimagined, spiced up to incorporate the diverse skills of a media specialist. Jennifer glows when discussing her job, the one for which she returned to school to earn her master's.

"It's the perfect marriage of everything I love! It's storytelling, my English experience, my digital knowledge, and relationships with kids."

This school, in a fairly liberal pocket of California, officially promotes the power of community. About fifty seniors per year participate in a special intensive program, one that welcomes all twelfth graders, not just those who would normally enroll in AP courses. One goal of the program is that it will reflect the diversity of the entire student population. The belief is that greater diversity injects a wealth of perspectives into class interactions, which enriches the experience for everyone.

I remembered Alejandro and long-ago third graders who listened to him "read" when reading was still impossible. The heart of this school's goal resonated. More enriching for all? Undoubtedly.

It's how we humans learn empathy.

* * *

Jennifer threw herself into the teacher-librarian position, driven by her desire to immerse kids in all forms of reading. She's an enthusiastic ambassador for literacy, energized by the wealth of twenty-first-century ways to stimulate kids' interest in learning information.

"It's a full media center," she said. "Yes, it's a library. But there are computers, podcasts, and videos. All reading counts. All thinking counts!"

She still wants kids to read more; she dreams up incentives to get students reading books, but also welcomes moving beyond text held in the hand.

"Kids who don't want to read a book can work with media, like pairing a podcast with a piece of art and an infographic," she says.

Students' needs guide her actions. In November 2022, when kids' stress levels were peaking, Jennifer read children's picture books to the high schoolers in the library.

"I told them we were going to start having story time. We brought in a little fake fireplace that just blows air, and we bought some real logs. It was cute! I told them we wanted them to remember what they loved about the library when they were little. A lot of these kids came from Latin America and never even had that early library experience. So we were giving them that, too."

Jennifer often said "we" instead of "I." Yes, she had an assistant, but I suspect that doesn't fully explain the "we." I think she inherently sees herself as part of a supportive team that nurtures students, and it would grate on her to speak as if she acts independently. I kept wishing I could turn back time and use a Book Bike with my own students. Listening to her enchanted me, as if I were one of her students, curled up by the fake fireplace.

Jennifer continued.

"I read them *Julián Is a Mermaid*. It's a beautiful story of a little boy who wants to wear his grandmother's robes. I just thought, 'For a minute, let's forget about math, forget about science, and just remember being little kids, wanting to dress up.'"

* * *

When selecting books for the library, Jennifer always tries to look at it through the parent lens.

"Look, I *get* it that some books are hard. But if a book is on a recommended list of an organization I rely on, my answer is YES, because I don't know who that book might speak to. I always think of kids who are holding a lot of questions inside, so I'm able to live with something that might be a little too graphic for others.

"I always bring it back to my own kid. There are some books I know she *definitely* won't pick up, but if she wants to—great! And we'll talk about it. But I will *absolutely* have those books on my shelf."

She told me about Maia Kobabe's *Gender Queer*, a book at the center of many banning controversies. When she set up a display for Banned Books Week one year, an adult helping in the library spotted it.

"That was the first book that made me feel like a human," he said.

Isn't that enough right there? Isn't it our hope that books can teach young people about the world and help them believe that they belong in it?

It's especially hard, says Jennifer, when the controversy is over not just a book's topic but the maturity level as well.

"Sure, there's a certain book here that might make more sense for an adult. But I'm keeping it, because we don't know what kids are going through.

What's gross to one person might be life-saving to another. They can see a way of life they never thought was open to them."

Jennifer knows that some parents worry their openly LGBTQ+ child is not actually queer but instead is just responding to today's prevalence of acceptance among progressive teens regarding sexuality and gender. They wonder if their child has decided to "try on" being queer because they've absorbed so much talk of spectrums, pronouns, and fluidity.

Though it's easy to imagine parents wondering about that, to Jennifer, it's clear.

"My answer is, 'So what?' Would you rather have a young person sit in silence and wrestle with this? And then internalize the judgment he thinks his parent will have? Or would you rather have this open dialogue and let them know that you love them no matter what?"

* * *

Scrolling through Facebook one evening several years ago, I came upon a photo and stopped. The girl's face glowed, and she was draped in a rainbow flag. Around the picture was a rainbow frame emblazoned with the words "Proud Mama." Once, this girl was in my third-grade class, and now, on her mother's Facebook page, the eleven-year-old had come out for the first time as gay. The post had more than a hundred likes, and the ribbon of comments overflowed with rainbows and hearts.

I added my own message and returned to her picture. There was the wide smile I knew so well, but there was also an excitement layered atop the quiet serenity she had always exuded, unusual in a child so young.

Not long afterward, on the weekend of San Francisco's Pride parade, she popped up on Facebook again, this time next to her father. Side by side, they stared into the sun, the dad's arm slung across his daughter's shoulders, a hint of defiance in his stance. The stocky man wore a floppy hat, a solemn expression, and sunglasses obscuring his eyes. He stood with his shoulders back and chest out, his chin tilted up as if daring someone to challenge the message on his black T-shirt. In huge white letters, the shirt proclaimed, "Proud dad of my girl."

His daughter was pressed against his side, painted flowers splashed on her bare legs below the hem of her shorts.

Her shirt said simply, "I'm his girl."

* * *

Crazy Hair Day at my old elementary school showcased the exuberance of youth. No parade, no contest—just a little fun for the smattering of kids who enjoyed playing with their look. They wore faux-hawks, glittery hair gel, rainbow powder, and unicorn hairbands. My usual nod to the day was an orange pageboy wig, six bucks at Party City.

Many of my kids ignored Crazy Hair Day, so nine-year-old DeShawn didn't stick out when he showed up that day with his daily 'do, closely shorn tiny black curls. But outside at recess, when he streaked past me, I gasped. The wig must have been stuffed in his coat.

Long, loose black curls cascaded down his back. This was no Party City wig; it had to belong to his mom. Thick and luxurious, the lustrous locks framed DeShawn's face, highlighting his shining eyes and spectacular smile. How had he secured the wig so perfectly? He looked amazing.

As he raced across the playground, I could see what I somehow hadn't noticed before: His movements, mannerisms, and demeanor hinted at "feminine" more than they suggested "masculine." My eyes followed him as he ran past me then stopped short, dipping his head low only to whip it back up, curls flipping back over his head and bouncing on his shoulders. He spread his fingers, running them through shiny black coils before tossing the hair again. Flip, finger-comb, toss, caress, laugh, bounce, arrange . . . it was a breathtaking display. He looked so natural. My yard duty partner was staring at him, too.

Thoughts whirled through me. What a brave child, this third-grade boy flaunting hair so unabashedly feminine. But then again—*was* it bravery? Or was it more a relief, a day of absolute freedom to appear as he never had at school, maybe in a way he'd always wished he could? He looked as genuinely joyous as I'd ever seen him.

I thought of his mom, the wondrous wig's presumed owner. Had she worried for her son when he asked for it? I suspected it wasn't the first time he'd worn it, but had he been out in public with it before? I imagined his mom encouraging DeShawn to wear whatever made him happy, and I swelled inside with appreciation for a woman I'd met only twice. For DeShawn to appear so carefree, so confident, wouldn't his mom *have* to shower him with acceptance, exactly as he is?

But maybe the real story was much simpler. Maybe DeShawn was straight and cisgender, now an adult with a closely shaved head, a man who smiles when he remembers wearing his mom's wig to school at age nine. I'll never know.

But that day on the playground? I just kept calling out, "Wow! You look great!"

He tossed his hair in response, and ran his fingers through the curls.

* * *

When the pandemic started and teaching went virtual, Jennifer's job became a lonely one. The building was closed, and no students were assigned to her. She offered to oversee fifty kids with their long-term research projects and meet with each of them once a week.

She also saddled up her own bike, outfitted it with a basket, and rode around town delivering books to students. It helped her connect with kids, but she also loved the simplicity. She remembered seeing a book bike in a different city and realized that this was the moment to get one for her school.

So she applied for a grant, and the Book Bike was born. Her assistant principal was impressed.

"Usually, people get a toy and then don't play with it. But you're on it all the time."

Once the school reopened to in-person instruction, the Book Bike began attending Friday-night football games. Jennifer arranged for donations from bookstores' back stock and stuffed the foldout shelves with free books.

"I'm going to get this one for my mom!" she'd hear.

Soon, students racking up service hours were staffing the bike near the stands, offering story time for little ones too young to care about football. Jennifer delighted in the students' enthusiasm for the mobile "library," and noticed that the Book Bike also provided a way for anxious high schoolers to attend a football game without having to confront their social discomfort. They had a purpose. They were cultivating a love of reading, helping to build literacy.

Jennifer also developed an "ambassador program." Students needing service hours volunteered in the media center during their free period, helping to shelve books, schlep boxes, and make TikToks and Instagram videos. The video PSAs toured fellow students around the media center, keeping energy up about literacy.

"We grew from four kids the first year to eleven this year. I applied for a grant to buy swag, so they feel like a team. They wear ambassador T-shirts and teach other kids to print, check books out, and do research."

Jennifer tries everything she can think of to engage students in school.

Until last autumn, that was the biggest challenge she had.

* * *

Jennifer's own eighth grader was at her school that Wednesday, previewing high school. When her seventh-period ambassadors entered, the principal was with them. She thought he was there to see her daughter.

"I need you to check your email," he said. "NOW."

The email from a writer at Fox News Digital read, "My understanding is that your library maintains an extensive collection of sexually explicit, pornographic, and radical-left books which are broadcast: one, on your website; two, on your Instagram; three, on your TikTok account." Jennifer's mind swirled in confusion. *This isn't real . . . Wait, TikTok? I have four followers . . . It must be a bot . . . I only use TikTok to create things . . . This isn't real . . .*

The email listed the books in question, sometimes giving reasons for the writer's objections and sometimes not.

By now, Jennifer was shaking.

"Holy shit. What is this?"

The principal said, "What do you want us to say as a response?"

Acutely aware of her daughter and the ambassadors standing right there, Jennifer's reply was strong.

"We don't ban books." Then she added, "Besides, I don't know if this is even real."

"Oh, it's real all right," the principal said grimly.

Banned Books Week and its flurry of activities had just ended, so Jennifer was primed, knowing she had the backing of the American Library Association and other organizations against book banning. Her mind raced, but she spoke with confidence.

"If we even *think* about banning books, we're in a whole lot of trouble as a society. We need to make it clear. Say that, and something like, 'We preserve everybody's right to choose what they want to read.'"

The principal nodded. "I'll forward it to the district and see what they think." Then he was gone, leaving Jennifer reeling.

Puzzling over the mention of TikTok, she suddenly remembered her seven-second video that got millions of views, thanks to book lovers and Swifties who'd loved the poster of Taylor in the background. The TikTok simply showed mountains of donated titles and urged kids to come grab some free books.

It was homecoming week, so Jennifer and her ambassadors rode the Book Bike in the evening parade. During quiet moments of the weekend, she pondered the Fox email. As a digital expert, she knew about algorithms and clicks, and refused to Google the writer. She took another look at the "problematic" titles in the email. Among them:

Antiracist Baby, a number one *New York Times* bestseller written by Ibram X. Kendi, professor and founding director of the Boston University Center for Antiracist Research.

White Fragility, the bestseller with the subtitle *Why It's So Hard for White People to Talk About Racism.*

The 57 Bus, the bestselling nonfiction book by award-winning journalist Dashka Slater. It explores multiple perspectives of a crime that took place on public transportation, when an agender teen wore a skirt and another teenager lit the skirt on fire.

That same weekend, Jennifer posted on Instagram the content from the American Library Association on banned books. Previously, she had printed out and displayed the same content at school during the designated week but, sensing the changing climate, had opted not to also post it on Instagram.

I don't need to necessarily be advertising this, she had thought. *Kids see our display.*

But after the unsettling email, she expressed her position online.

"I reran the whole 'These are the ten most commonly challenged books. This is why people challenge books. Lest anyone forget, we don't ban books.'"

Feeling good, she left it at that.

Monday morning, Jennifer was at the library desk, titling a document: "What Jennifer Wants to Say, but Won't." Making the list were things like:

"Do you really consider twelve books out of twenty thousand 'extensive'?"

"Do you know how libraries work?"

She'd never say those things to the writer; listing her thoughts helped her process the Fox email. Even as she typed the retorts she would never express, she thought, *This models good behavior for kids.*

Then a new email came.

> You're a disgusting human.
>
> Why are you talking to kids about sex?
>
> You deserve to be in jail.

It said a lot more, all of it cutting, horrifying to Jennifer. Five of her ambassadors were at her side, watching, listening to her whisper, "Oh, my *god*," as she clicked and scrolled, eyes glued to the screen.

When she noticed one girl staring at her, Jennifer realized she only had a few seconds. Unwilling to break down in front of students, she instructed the five to sit at the desk while she ran across the hall.

Coming upon a coworker on break, she blurted, "Can you please go in there? I'm going to cry."

Then she ran to the principal.

"Something is happening," she told him. "I got a terrible email."

He assured her he'd figure it out, and turned to his phone to contact the district office.

Meanwhile, Jennifer started talking to herself. *Pull it together. Assume it's a one-off. My principal said he's on it.*

At this point in telling me her story, Jennifer started to cry.

"I'm sorry, I'm sorry," she said. "I knew I'd cry at some point, but I didn't think it would come this early. Usually I just cry at the beautiful parts."

Beautiful parts? This hardworking, big-hearted teacher only wanted the best for students.

"It was such a terrifying email," she continued. "There was no threat of 'We're coming to find you' or anything. But at that moment, you suspect everybody. I was thinking, 'Oh my god. Is there a kid in here who's mad at me?' Because there are conservative kids that maybe feel like we're not seeing them. So that was my first thought."

But within thirty minutes, the principal had determined that the email was not tied to any account in the district. It was a relief, in a way. But something was happening. She just didn't know what it was.

Though she had never closed the library, that day she shut the doors at lunch.

While debriefing with a colleague, it hit her.

I bet that Fox lady who emailed me published something.

Her mind flashed back to the email from the week prior. The writer hadn't asked questions; she'd merely made a statement about Jennifer's book collection. She'd also said, "My deadline is five p.m." Deadline? For what?

"So there I am in front of my colleague who's not really getting it, not really understanding what I'm all upset about. I honestly think I blacked out.

"I went to Fox News, and typed in the author's name. There's the article, and the picture with it is of Tucker Carlson on his show. You'd have to see the headline to understand how scary it is."

She showed me a screenshot. Above the article about this devoted teacher-librarian was a headline splattered with words like "sexual," "pedophile," "explicit," and "porn."

"Then I saw the second paragraph, listing my name and my place of work. That's when it hit me."

She was furious, with the words "How DARE you!" roaring inside, accompanied by "all the expletives." As Jennifer ran back toward the office, the words "Okay. It's happening!" pounded with the beat of her steps.

Absurdly, at that moment she remembered a clip from the TV show *The Office*, when the incompetent manager directs his employees away from an office fire.

"Okay, it's happening!" shouts the manager. "Everybody stay calm. Everybody stay calm. STAY FUCKING CALM!"

She entered the office, shaking. Seeing the school secretary, Jennifer blurted out, "It's unacceptable that Fox News can ruin people's lives like this!"

She told the assistant principal that she needed to close the library to handle things, though she didn't even know yet what that would mean. She just knew she couldn't be at the desk, in front of children.

Breathless after running back to a computer, Jennifer started screen-grabbing images of the article, determined not to click any links.

No way in HELL am I supporting this link! she was thinking. *That's exactly what she wants!*

Next, she locked down her social media, to separate her home life from this mess. She contacted Dashka Slater, author of *The 57 Bus*; Slater had visited Jennifer's school four years earlier, and just that morning, Jennifer had seen Slater's Instagram post showing a cart of banned books being wheeled out of a Texas library.

Jennifer's message to Slater read, "It's happening here. Look at this email. Nothing has been taken out yet, but they mentioned your book in this article."

Slater sent Jennifer a phone number and said, "Call them immediately. There's someone there keeping a database of attacks all around the U.S."

PEN America is a group that "stands at the intersection of literature and human rights to protect free expression in the United States and worldwide," and it was tracking efforts to ban books.[1]

It dawned on Jennifer that a whole community stood with her.

She wasn't alone.

There are already people on it, she thought. *I'm going to be okay. I need to tap into people who can support me.*

After the first email the previous week, Jennifer had contacted a district administrator who had said, "I'm new at this job. Can I ask you—is it true?"

"Is it true? Yes, they're on the shelf. But that's not how we classify our books. We have criteria for choosing them."

Maybe she shouldn't have had to explain that to administrators, but they needed to understand that harassment over books was unacceptable. Now she needed their support even more. Her media center was near the school's front door; she felt unsafe and exposed. She didn't want to be a victim, placed on involuntary leave while the district investigated. District personnel hadn't seemed alarmed the week prior, but this time, Jennifer wanted to ensure they grasped the seriousness of what was happening. They reassured her and offered her a day off to deal with the unwanted interruption to her job.

* * *

What does a devoted teacher-librarian do when she learns she's been targeted by name on Fox News? That's not covered in teaching credential programs. Jennifer figured it out as she went.

> *I need to call the public library. They're my biggest collaborators. I need to let them know it's happening.*
>
> *My principal said the assistant superintendent is trying to reach me. Have to call her.*
>
> *Call the union.*
>
> *Guess I need to call my family to warn them in case the article pops up on their feed. Ugh . . .*

Jennifer's community responded. The city librarians were solidly supportive and comforting. Her union reps were glad that she'd taken the day off, and began drafting a statement that would later be signed by many members and sent to the school board. The statement affirmed union support for Jennifer and her book collection, and declared that she was neither a pedophile nor a groomer interested in porn.

When she finally reached the assistant superintendent, the woman simply said, "Can I have your autograph?"

Relief poured over Jennifer.

"So is this the highest point in my career, or the lowest?"

"Oh, it's *definitely* the highest," said the assistant superintendent. "If you got their attention, you're doing something right."

The administrator then shared her own experience. Once, she'd suspended a kid, and Rush Limbaugh picked up the story. She knew what Jennifer was going through.

Jennifer hung up thinking, *This probably feels a lot bigger than it really is.*

* * *

Despite the momentary relief, it didn't take long for the self-blame to start.

> *Maybe I brought this on myself.*
>
> *I mean, I* did *ride the Book Bike in the parade last summer as an "alternative-fact checker."*
>
> *Maybe people didn't like my "Everybody's welcome" sign.*
>
> *Oh, shit. I did this to myself. Forget social media. It was me.*

But before long, her sight turned outward.

"The minute your trust is broken or violated, you start finding everybody suspicious," she explained to me.

She remembered early in the pandemic, when she would collect donated books in parking lots, not knowing if the covers were even safe to touch. A man had gifted a collection of historical papers from the Civil War era, and Jennifer had passed them to an interested community member months later. She later learned that the woman who'd received them had been at the January 6 insurrection. Had she been set off by something she'd seen in the library when she'd picked up the papers?

Next, Jennifer thought about another visitor to the library, who'd spoken of her plans to start a nearby teen center.

Teen center? They're all in school, Jennifer had thought. But she welcomed the woman, who took many pictures while there. Had she noticed the trans person volunteering in the library? Had that somehow sparked the terrible emails?

During that same dizzying week when she saw her name in the Fox News article, Jennifer attended a Zoom town hall meeting. The big topic was a hotly contested ordinance to allow a gun shop across the street from her daughter's school, and very near to the city library. The woman who owned the land where the proposed gun shop would be had been at the insurrection. Jennifer and many others in attendance were demanding a stay of the ordinance.

When it was her turn to speak, Jennifer focused on remaining calm. But, propelled by stress, the words exploded out.

"People keep talking about the Second Amendment rights. But this old-timey interpretation of the Constitution is driving me wild when our FIRST Amendment rights are being challenged every day in our LIBRARIES!"

It had burst out of her. She muted herself, but still heard her rage-filled voice inside. She couldn't silence it. It was too much.

Oh, god. I need some help.

* * *

Jennifer stopped going to the gym, thinking, *I don't want to be in water aerobics and have people say, "Oh, you're* that *person . . ."*

She shared her theories with friends.

"Remember that woman? She went to the insurrection? Maybe it's all connected!"

Concerned friends said, "You know, you're starting to sound a little crazy . . ."

The thought ran on a loop through her head: *I don't want to be everyone else's problem. This can't be my personality now.*

So she withdrew from activity for a while, and started therapy.

* * *

Hate email periodically appeared in her inbox—not in a steady stream, but just often enough to keep her unsettled. Still, over the next weeks, her vision shifted from cloudy to clear.

"I kept thinking, 'Wow, what have I done?'" she told me. "But it wasn't like, 'Poor me.' It was more like, 'I'm here because I can handle this. I *will* handle it. It's just going to suck for a while.'"

The next revelation came six weeks after the hate emails started.

"I saw the post of a Minnesota teacher I follow on TikTok, and she said, 'Okay, I'm back now after the whole Fox News thing.'"

Jennifer was stunned. It turned out that the same writer at Fox News had attacked the Minnesota teacher because she'd given a survey to her students that asked their preferred pronouns. The writer had conducted a whole smear campaign against the Midwestern middle school teacher.

Puzzle pieces began snapping into place.

A few weeks back, Jennifer had attended a school fundraiser for the Dream Club, whose members were kids from immigrant families. There, a neighboring district's board member told her that one of their teachers was also getting harassing emails every day. The next morning, at a "United Against Hate" civic event, Jennifer ran into that teacher, who told her that she'd been hounded by the "insurrection woman."

"She won't stop emailing me," said that teacher. "Ever since Coming Out Day when my seventh graders read a book to third graders, one of the third-grade parents won't stop bothering me. She's a friend of the insurrection lady."

Coming Out Day.

Right around Coming Out Day is when the harassment started for both of them, and for the Minnesota teacher. The same Fox News writer even profiled a high-ranking member of Joe Biden's administration, blasting her for raising topics including white privilege and racism.

Together, the educators decided that conservative writers must have been on a mission to find public schools promoting Coming Out Day and other topics opposed by the far right. It was election season, so exposing those teachers as if they were criminals could be a tactical move to continue the attack on public education.

It all made sense.

It turns out that from May 2022 through May 2023, one writer at Fox News wrote nearly one hundred articles targeting specific teachers, librarians, schools, administrators, board members, and other school staff. Her articles railed against discussion of gender, sexuality, and systemic racism in schools, and multiple educators whom she named were ultimately doxed, harassed, fired, sued, or forced to resign. After she attacked a California trans teacher in five separate articles, bomb threats were received for both the teacher's classroom and the school district offices. The assault on education accounted for nearly half of all articles written by that reporter that year.

Jennifer wasn't glad that others were being tormented, but it made her realize the whole mess was bigger than one librarian and her media center. No one was directly challenging her books and ordering her to take them off the shelf. The hate emails that had continued in the weeks after the first two—sure, they called her a pervert and fumed that she should be in jail, but there was no one calling for official action.

It wasn't about *her*. She was part of a larger group, a community of sorts.

It can be an odd comfort, knowing you're not special.

* * *

Her students, though, would beg to differ. On the day she took off to straighten out her life, word spread to parents and students about the article with the horrible headline.

"The first day back, it was a love fest in the library the whole day," said Jennifer. "It was so emotional. Kids were coming in, 'Are you okay? Oh, my god.' One kid said, 'I'm going to write this woman a letter!'

"I didn't want to tell him what to do, but I had something to say."

Then this Book Bike–riding, TikTok-making, fake-fireplace-stoking librarian told me what she said to her students.

"You need to worry about your safety," she'd said, "because this is not a joke. No way do I expect anyone to stand up for me. I'm good, folks. I'm going to stand in this discomfort *for you*, so you don't have to."

Emails from parents began streaming her way, and soon, she had a collection of touching, appreciative, grateful notes.

"So really, it turned into being a very beautiful day."

* * *

We don't ask for much.

The simplest things can turn a teacher's day from mundane to magic. A child with autism is screaming, overwhelmed, and a classmate rushes over with the plushy pink stuffed octopus to offer comfort. You read *Holes* aloud, and when you close the book, your fourth graders cry out, "Just one more chapter! PLEASE!" You let your fifth graders wear costumes each day for reading because it makes them so happy, and during a surprise fire drill, they lead the parade, wearing top hats and chef toques you scored at garage sales.

A brilliant kid with dyslexia writes the third-person bio, *Axel struggled with reading until third grade, when he learned he's a great writer.* First graders are too young to catch a pointy ball, so when you cover "football" in your PE teacher curriculum, you play "Puppy Bowl," and all they do is throw and "fetch." A fourth-grade student visits his homeland and wants to Zoom with you, the class, and the principal to share his pride in his native country.

You're sick inside because one student has threatened another, but then you find a letter that a different student has written to her friend, speaking of caring and kindness. You teach English to new immigrants, and when "song" is the theme of your "Walk-and-Talk," the high schoolers share favorite tunes in a musical mosaic of Spanish, Chinese, Arabic, and Korean.

You find a crayoned note on your desk reading, *You are sunshine to me.*

You've been retired for two years, and when you're looking for an art video you posted in Google Classroom back during distance teaching, you are stunned to discover that many kids still visit the obsolete page, leaving messages to their old classmates, and to you. You read, *We're in sixth grade now. We went through hard things in third and we made it together.*

We don't ask for much.

* * *

Teachers are famously underpaid, and that reality often gets translated as societal permission to disregard teachers' needs. It's as if teachers' demonstrated willingness to educate children is seen as our public acknowledgment that we deserve any abuse we get. We knew we'd be underpaid, working in dilapidated buildings with insufficient heat and no air-conditioning, buying our own classroom supplies at Target. And we chose to enter education anyway.

We deserve what we get. We knew what we were walking into.

I heard it at the bargaining table when we argued for a long-overdue raise.

> *Our district can't afford it. Teachers don't go into education for the money.*
>
> *Every percent of teacher wage increase costs the district half a million because there are so many of you.*
>
> *If we give you more money, we'd have to raise class size. And that's not good for kids.*

California teacher salaries are so disproportionate to the sky-high rents that early in the 2022–23 school year, a Bay Area district asked parents to rent out rooms to teachers. (In *The Legend of Sleepy Hollow*, teacher Ichabod Crane lived with students' families. When I read it to my third graders one Halloween, we all howled with laughter just imagining it. The story was published in 1820.) California educators have the nation's highest pay, averaging $58,409 in 2024 for starting teachers and $101,084 for teachers who've lasted for years. But when adjusted for inflation, teachers make on average 5 percent less than they did in 2015 and 9 percent less than the peak in 2009–10.[2] And by most ranking systems, California trails only Hawaii for the highest rent and home prices, with densely populated regions being the worst. For example, the minimum living wage for a single adult in my county is over $62,000, and for an adult with one child, it's nearly $121,000. In the neighboring county, those numbers are about $12,000 higher.[3] It's commonplace for friends and families of educators to fill GoFundMe grants to stock classrooms. Teachers spend hundreds, often thousands, of dollars to outfit their own rooms.

That's not new.

But attacking those same educators for teaching true history, for protecting students' right to privacy about identity and orientation, and for stocking shelves with books that reflect the children reading them—that *is* new. And many educators are deciding they've had enough.

Jennifer isn't quitting the media center position that is "the perfect marriage of everything [she] loves." But other educators who've been targeted *have* quit, in increasing numbers that should frighten all of us.

Teachers *want* to educate kids. They know it's grueling work, but the privilege of helping young minds expand is worth it. All they ask is that people respect their expertise, recognize that public educators serve *all* children, and support their efforts to do this essential labor.

We really don't ask for much.

* * *

On "Love Fest in the Library" day, Jennifer addressed her student ambassadors.

"It's my job to make sure that *everyone* sees themselves on these shelves. And that's worth being a little uncomfortable. It's not discomfort over the material, but in knowing that *some people will be uncomfortable.*

"So I'm going to stand in this discomfort for you. It's exhausting, but it's necessary. Give me the books. They can talk about me all they want. These books are staying on the shelf."

Their librarian. Their supporter. Defiantly, stubbornly, unfailingly—their teacher.

* * *

Nine months later, Jennifer still gets flickers of anxiety when checking her email.

"That's the most difficult part about being an educator right now," she said. "You just don't know when it's going to rear its ugly head."

She has survived this first round. Not everyone does.

* * *

Jennifer has drawn inspiration from Martha Hickson, a New Jersey high school media specialist who won the American Library Association's 2022 Lemony Snicket Prize for Noble Librarians Faced with Adversity. Hickson was slandered as a pornographer and pedophile because of books in her library. She endured hate mail, personal attacks, threats, and vandalism. Her blood pressure and anxiety shot so high that her physician removed her from her job.

Yet she was unshakable. On *The Daily* podcast, Hickson said,

> You know . . . you're 14 or 15 years old. You walk through a crowded library. You find a book on the shelf that is labeled in big block type as clear as day, "This Book is Gay." It's got huge rainbow stripes on the cover.
>
> You carry it back through the crowded library, to this 62-year-old bag sitting in front of the computer who you hardly know, and hand it to her, and say, "I'd like to check this out."
>
> I think in this day and age, especially when we hear what's going on at our board meetings, that takes a lot of courage for a kid to do. . . . No way are you taking that book away from those kids.[4]

Struck by Jennifer's frequent use of the words "comfort" and "discomfort," I wondered aloud yet again, "Why do we put such importance on other people's comfort? We don't learn when we're *comfortable*. Learning happens when there's grinding, disequilibrium, something we can't mesh with our understanding. Why is 'comfort' the goal?"

Jennifer nodded.

"I wanted to have a statement for teachers who wonder what to say if they're asked about it all. So my statement to the principal is this: *The feelings of acceptance for marginalized folks outweigh the discomfort of those who've always been part of the narrative.*"

The words hung there, heavy in the summer heat.

"Someone has to say it," she said. "So I will be that person.

"I'm ready to be uncomfortable."

10

JOURNEY TO MISFIT ISLAND

A long-ago fourth-grade student of mine never turned in homework. Her mother said that since her nine-year-old daughter was forgetful, she wanted me, the teacher, to unzip her backpack each morning, find the homework, and turn it in for her. There were thirty-one students in my class, and multiple mini-crises in the hubbub of early-morning entrance. Was she *really* expecting me to stand in line between Julio and Markenya and wait my turn to drop pages into the green basket?

Other parental requests are reasonable, not requiring me to step away from managing the whole group. A mom asked that I always place her son in my car on field trips, since she trusted me to drive safely. No problem! A grandmother suggested that her boy's desk be up front, since he tended to mess around with friends if I wasn't right there to stare him down. Good idea! A mom said that if her daughter were ever quiet instead of talking nonstop, I should call her immediately, because "quiet" meant "sick." For another, could I encourage a kindhearted kid to invite her son to play during recess? Her boy loved to engage with others, but he had autism, and approaching kids was difficult.

Of course.

But another parent directed me to supervise her son in the classroom during each recess, even though that was my only time for the restroom. She was tired of the principal's calls about playtime violence her child provoked, so she wanted it to be my job to keep him from getting in trouble. Another parent instructed me to ignore her daughter's frequent complaints of stomach pain, even if the girl cried. Some parents asked me to stop teaching and call whenever their child was off-task. A few others snapped at me when I did call, whether about off-task behavior or something more serious.

"You shouldn't be bothering *me* with things like that! You're the teacher!"

Parents aren't infallible, and their desires are not uniform. Most people understand that teachers can't bend to every request; parents can't demand a change each time there's an element of their child's experience they don't like.

But some refuse to accept that aspect of public education. Somewhere along the way, some have become misled about what "parental rights" means when it comes to matters more significant than homework and goofing around in class. California's Education Code grants certain rights to parents and guardians, but public schools are not lumps of clay, ready to be sculpted according to each parent's liking.

Parents have the right to opt for a private education for their children. But if they choose public schools, they have "very limited rights to prevent their children from receiving the entire range of instruction available in public schools."[1] They have the right to *examine* curriculum materials of their child's class, but parents don't have the right to demand that certain materials be excluded from the classroom just because they disagree with the content.

They can't have it both ways. If they choose public education for their kids, they are choosing an education that cares for the many, not one that is molded for the few. Public schools can't cater to individual parents, whose wishes can change with tomorrow's afternoon breeze.

* * *

PragerU is a company that creates free, online videos promoting "pro-American values," videos that purport to cover history, civics, and science topics for kids. PragerU says it "offers a free alternative to the dominant left-wing ideology in culture, media, and education."[2] One of its "educational" videos depicts a cartoon Christopher Columbus implying slavery wasn't a big deal because it was so widespread; another describes George Floyd as a "Black man who resisted arrest" and decries "the false claims of racial targeting" of Black men by police.[3] YouTube has removed two anti-trans videos from PragerU's primary channel for violating hate speech policies.

When PragerU's Jill Simonian criticized a Southern California educator for teaching about LGBTQ+ people, her video cohost Aldo Buttazzoni warned teachers, "Whether or not you disagree with the parents' viewpoints, you are still paid to do what the parents want. You are a tax-funded school. . . . So you can disagree with the parents, but at the end of the day, your job is to do what the parents want you to do."[4]

* * *

On a Saturday morning, I left the noisy motel that charged way too much for beach proximity and pointed the rental car east. I'd be driving for a while, so there was time to think. I was nervous; it was hard to believe that, after everything she'd been through, this elementary school teacher was willing to meet. Would my questions retraumatize her? Leaving the coastal chill behind, I headed toward the low, rolling hills.

Rachel Cohen's school community sounded a lot like my old district. Like me, she had taught third grade at a Title I school, where a large majority of students qualify for free or reduced-price lunch. Similar to my old school community, Rachel's was composed largely of first- and second-generation immigrants, with most students still learning English. The student population was diverse—as are many suburbs in the counties around Los Angeles—with a mix of white, Asian, and Latino kids. One very big difference in Rachel's school community, though, is that most of the immigrants are religious conservatives.

I arrived at our meet-up spot, and within minutes, we were seated with a pile of pastries between us. After laughing about our shared love of dogs, she began telling me her story.

When Rachel received the late 2020 district email asking educators to pilot teaching materials from Learning for Justice, she jumped at the chance. Learning for Justice (formerly Teaching Tolerance) is a project of the Southern Poverty Law Center, which is "dedicated to fighting hate and bigotry and to seeking justice for the most vulnerable members of our society."[5] Even though she'd been teaching for thirty-two years and was deep into the pandemic's distance teaching, Rachel was still eager to learn.

"I come from a family of Holocaust survivors," said Rachel. "For me, teaching tolerance and acceptance of others is extremely important. I've always taught about tolerance and different people's religions and cultures. Everyone's different, and we need to learn and appreciate people's differences."

She was accepted into the pilot program. As one of only two lower-grade teachers in the test group, she didn't find much in the teaching materials that would work with her young third graders. She turned to her supervisors, the district's teacher specialists who conducted the training.

"Can we supplement and find other materials?" she asked.

"Of course!"

So she incorporated Learning for Justice lessons into the structure she'd established earlier during that year of distance teaching. Each Friday, with her eight- and nine-year-old students attending "class" at home on laptops, Rachel led them through activities paralleling that month's "heritage" focus, such as Black History and Hispanic Heritage.

When June came, Rachel decided to teach about Pride Month; in her thirty-two years, she'd never before taught lessons about LGBTQ+ people, but she knew about the FAIR Act and believed in the importance of inclusive education. When she couldn't find anything on topic in the Learning for Justice materials, she searched YouTube Kids and found four videos. With those videos as the backbone, she planned three lessons, one each day for the last, short week of school.

She knew that one student's parent always sat off-camera, watching her teach. On the day of the first Pride Month lesson, with so many little boxes of kids' faces on her screen, Rachel didn't notice that the watchful parent's child disappeared during the session. She didn't see the mom's message until after instruction was done for the day.

The text from the mom read, "When you finish teaching sexual orientation, please let me know, and I will let my daughter back in Zoom."

"I got really nervous and scared," Rachel told me. "I thought, 'Oh my gosh, maybe I shouldn't have done that. I'm going to email my supervisors and give them the links to the videos and see what they say.'"

So on June 7, 2021, Rachel wrote this: "Today I talked to my class about LGBTQ pride month and played 2 short videos from YouTube that were geared toward kids. A parent who heard the lesson and discussion made her daughter leave zoom and texted me asking me when I was done discussing sexual orientation so that she could let her [kid] back into zoom. I was planning on doing more lessons tomorrow and Wednesday, but now I'm afraid to. Here are the videos and lessons I was going to do with my class."

Within thirty minutes, Rachel's district supervisor, a specialist in restorative practices and positive behavior intervention and support, wrote back. In addition to saying, "Do not be concerned or afraid," he added specifics about the four videos. He gave three his full support. The fourth video, one that Rachel had shown, featured Canadian comedian and TV personality Jessi Cruickshank having a two-and-a-half-minute "round-table discussion" about Pride Month with four earnest and giggly little kids.

The tone of the video is sweet and a little goofy. Balloons are bobbing everywhere, and the kids are adorable. They say things like, "I think gay marriage is just regular marriage," and "My auntie . . . she's gay and she hasn't married yet, and I'm just wondering if I'm going to be her flower girl!"[6] When one child explains that "coming out of the closet" refers to playing hide-and-seek and being discovered in a closet, comedian Cruickshank just says, "Makes sense," and smiles into the camera.

When Cruickshank asks the kids if they know any gay celebrities, she can't suppress her comedic impulses. She wisecracks about Jodie Foster causing her to question her sexuality when she was young. She says that Foster was nude in *Nell* and then drops her voice and speaks quickly out of the side of her mouth, saying, "Not that I remember watching it several times as a child . . ." It is very obviously a "wink-wink" to the audience.

Addressing that video, Rachel's supervisor said that though the tone was positive, it used the word "sexual," which could be a red flag for some. He said that Rachel should "reconsider" using it but added that there was really nothing wrong with it. He never instructed her *not* to show it.

Rachel was too frightened to tell him the Cruickshank video was one she'd already shown. Telling herself, *I will be brave,* she continued with her Pride Month plans the following two days, since she'd been assured she had nothing to worry about. The watchful mom again removed her daughter from Zoom during the lessons, and Rachel notified her once the lessons were over.

"I figured she was fine with me teaching it. She didn't tell my principal, and she didn't tell me it was wrong that I was doing it. So that was the end of that."

Except it wasn't.

If not for that one sentence by a comedian in a children's video, would *any* of what transpired next have happened? Probably so, though it might have happened to someone else instead of to Rachel. Her Southern California school community had been enraged by the restrictions of the pandemic. A significant portion of the local population was composed of an ethnic community of extremely conservative Christians actively engaged in culture-war battles. Her school district community was a California forest of bone-dry tinder, ready to explode into a firestorm at the flicker of a flame. Rachel was just the unfortunate one holding a candle.

* * *

When a long-ago student came out as lesbian years after she sat in my third-grade classroom, I realized that I needed to be more explicit about being inclusive in my teaching. We were all little once, and though everyone figures their identity and orientation out on a different timeline, silent messages are absorbed from a very young age.

So I asked LGBTQ+ friends of mine what they wished they'd heard when they were young. I was also invited to the nearby middle school for a meeting of its GLOW (Gay, Lesbian, or Whatever) Club, and I asked the students there what they wished their third-grade teacher had said when they were little. Finally, I invited the GLOW students to respond to an anonymous online survey about behaviors at school around LGBTQ+ issues. The answers from both my friends and the students pierced me because their wishes were so simple.

My friend Andy said he wished there had been TV commercials that featured two dads.

"You know, like a commercial about laundry detergent," he said. "If I had seen two dads folding clothes, that would have meant the world."

A seventh grader in the GLOW Club said, "Just read books to kids so they know that some people are gay, or whatever." A large majority of the GLOW kids said that a simple sign would help, just a visible signal that they were accepted for who they are.

"It doesn't even have to be a flag," said one kid. "Just a piece of paper taped outside, maybe with a rainbow, or something about being safe."

When the students were asked what would have helped them feel more supported, their survey responses included:

Knowing it was okay to be this way.
Having a family that would accept me.
If some of my friends would understand.
Maybe a box in the office for LGBTQ members to report things that made them feel uncomfortable or unsafe.
If people didn't use "gay" as an insult.
That no matter if you're a part of LGBTQ or just an ally, you matter. No one should judge you for being yourself.

When asked what advice they'd give to teachers of young children, the middle schoolers said,

Maybe have a lesson about equality.
Accept everyone for who they are.
Make eye contact with your students.
Explain that being LGBTQ is normal.

It's a good thing that Aldo Buttazzoni of PragerU didn't become a teacher. He would have given students a very different message. Here he is on the topic of Pride Month: "I am 5'10". Should I be proud of that? I have brown hair. Should I be proud of that? Our immutable characteristics and the things that they claim are not a choice—it's just who you are—again, if it's just who you are, then why are we celebrating it? Why are we going over and over and over and talking about it?"[7]

What Buttazzoni doesn't understand is that a straight, white, cisgender man doesn't need to celebrate his pride in himself, because people like him are celebrated all over the country every day of their lives. Straight, white, cisgender men don't have to justify why they use a certain bathroom, and they're able to walk alone at night without fear of being shot or raped. There's no need for them to consider whether it's safe to reveal their orientation. Their opinion gains respect before it is earned, their salary is higher, and they're far less likely than others to be harassed at work. People with power and privilege don't have to waste energy worrying about all the things that could block opportunities. They don't need special recognition just for being themselves.

But people without societal power *do* need to be celebrated. The ones who long for a detergent commercial with two dads, or for a picture book featuring gay characters, or for a colorful piece of paper taped outside a classroom, or for a mailbox in the school office—*these* people need the reminders that they matter, that they have value, that they are worthy of being celebrated. When queer people don't see themselves reflected in our world, or when they experience derision or worse, Pride celebrations can be a balm.

"There are others like you, and we're all beautiful," proclaim the banners, the flags, the rainbows. "You're not alone. We're happy you're here. You belong with us."

No matter if you're a part of LGBTQ or just an ally, you matter.

* * *

In July 2021, one month after Rachel showed the Pride videos during distance teaching, several individuals quietly began filing Public Records Act requests, the California parallel to federal Freedom of Information Act requests. It's uncertain whether either of the two most frequent requesters was even a parent in Rachel's school district.

They wanted school district correspondence and documents containing keywords including "Critical Race Theory (CRT)," "teaching tolerance," "gender identity," "restorative justice," "gender support plans," "social-emotional learning," and "anti-bias." They demanded to see a list of "race-conscious, anti-racist, and inclusive resources for adults and kids," the whereabouts of book titles that show up on many "banned books" lists, and a PowerPoint presentation on gender identity. From July 2021 through April 2022, thousands of pages of copied documents were turned over to those who requested them.

Rachel didn't know any of this.

It was April 2022, nearly a year after she'd shown the Pride videos. It had been an exhausting school year with students back on-site. After having spent more than a year at home, kids were unaccustomed to being back in a large group, in a physical classroom with structure and different expectations. Many students struggled mightily. Wild behaviors, trouble getting along with others, outbursts of rage, and inability to focus on academic work made it an extremely difficult year for teachers and students alike. Rachel was spent, and on one April evening, she and her husband were quietly celebrating his birthday. As they were eating cake, she saw a notification from Messenger light up her phone.

"Hey, you don't know me," the message read. "But your email is posted on Facebook on a group called Valley Parents Voices."

Rachel had never heard of the group, so the stranger sent her a screenshot. She immediately panicked. There was the email she'd sent to her supervisor ten months prior, informing him of the Pride videos she'd shown. The parents in this group were outraged that LGBTQ+ people had been discussed in a third-grade classroom.

Abandoning thoughts of her husband's birthday, Rachel clicked "follow" on Facebook. Maybe the Facebook administrator wasn't paying attention; Rachel was admitted to the group. She began reading comments. They were all about her.

"There were maybe a hundred and thirty comments, saying things like 'She shouldn't be teaching sex,' and 'She's a pedophile who's grooming your kids.' They were horrible, terrible things."

When she showed up at school the next day, the principal assured Rachel she'd take care of it. Her version of "taking care of it" was to call a special Zoom staff meeting a week later, during which she repeated the vague, cryptic warning, "Remember, emails that you write are in public records. So it's public information." The second half of the meeting was an unannounced training on "LGBTQ in the classroom." Rachel was the only one who knew why the disparate topics were the subject of the abruptly called meeting. She didn't know yet that the principal had been deluged with emails and phone calls from riled-up parents.

Over the next few days, Rachel watched the Facebook page, where things were getting heated. She warned her principal that the next school board meeting would be explosive.

"I'm sure it'll be fine," said the principal. "Yes, the parents are concerned. They're sending me emails because they're worried that you're teaching LGBTQ in the classroom. The district is getting emails, too. But we're going to have a Zoom call with the director of elementary."

Rachel's understanding was that this director—the head of the entire Learning for Justice pilot program for her district—would be explaining the program to about forty concerned parents on the call. She didn't know that she would be sacrificed in the process.

"He threw me under the bus," Rachel told me. "He said that the video I'd shown was not a district-approved video, and it wasn't age appropriate."

Many people in the community felt that the Cruickshank video was innocuous enough, and that Rachel had done nothing wrong. But even if one believes she shouldn't have chosen the Cruickshank video, it seems clear: Rachel, a stellar teaching veteran of over thirty years, did the best she could to follow state law and teach about inclusivity and diversity when she had been given neither guidance nor materials.

Most parents were placated by the Zoom call with the director of elementary and understood that the isolated incident was unlikely to be repeated. But a small group was not. There was talk about having a big protest against Rachel in front of her school, but the small group decided they'd speak at the next board meeting instead.

Speak, they did. As Rachel and her husband sat on their couch and watched the live stream in horror, the first speaker—who was not a parent at Rachel's school—called out Rachel and her school by name, then read the year-old email Rachel had sent to her supervisor. Next, the speaker quoted parts of the supervisor's response, finding hidden messages in his reassurance.

"He gives more media recommendations to the teacher," says that parent, "but says to steer clear of content that says 'sexual' or 'coming out,' since it may raise red flags. In other words, he's *coaching this teacher on proven methods to push your agenda, but to stay under the radar*."

After declaring that "the systemic indoctrination is abhorrent," she ceded the mic to the next speakers, who continued the bombardment. Only one person spoke in generalized support of Rachel. A teacher on the union's Equity Team, he affirmed students' need to see themselves reflected in their classroom and urged the board to follow through on their "responsibility to protect the educators who create inclusive learning environments for [district] students."

Watching video of the board meeting, it's clear the parent speakers are opposed to teachers ever mentioning LGBTQ+ people during class. There's no acknowledgment of the FAIR Act's mandates, and no recognition of the need for every student to feel included in their school community. However, there were multiple mentions of religion. One speaker said, "The level of disrespect that has been shown to Christian conservative parents is becoming very obvious." Another said, "You guys don't see us coming here and asking you to teach our children about Christianity or Catholicism."

It's as if some see it as a trade: *We aren't allowed to have our religion represented in schools, so you're not allowed to talk about LGBTQ+ people.* As if speaking of LGBTQ+ matters were giving airtime to a religion.

A religion that these people really, really oppose.

* * *

One year when I read the penguin book to my class, we covered the basics when the book was done: that males more commonly partner up with females, but sometimes couples can be two males or two females. I told them that people can be in same-sex partnerships, and that however people are is fine, as long as they're kind to each other.

When I asked if anyone had any thoughts or questions they wanted to share, it was pretty quiet. Then a girl said, "I have an idea—can we do a fishbowl and talk about it?"

"Fishbowl" is when a few kids (maybe four) sit in the middle of the whole group and have a discussion, while everyone else sits in a circle around them, listening and observing conversation skills. I was surprised she even remembered "fishbowl"; we'd only done it twice, months earlier.

Kids cried out, "Yes! Let's do fishbowl!" Hands shot up, and I pointed at students until there were five in the middle.

"That's enough," I said. Then I realized—why would I limit the number of kids who wanted to speak?

So I said that anyone who wanted to could take a place in the center, and about ten kids formed an inner circle with their chairs. I handed the microphone to one of them, and they began their non-teacher-led discussion.

I was a little on edge; without me structuring the conversation, would somebody say something that could get me in trouble? But my worry was unnecessary. After a couple of comments, I grabbed paper so I could take notes on their observations that were sweet, innocent, and deep all at once.

The back-and-forth was like a game of ping-pong.

> "I don't understand how a boy loves a boy."
>
> "The book reminds me of when Ms. K read us a book about penguins in first grade."
>
> "Why did they think a rock was an egg? Were they just not very smart?"
>
> "I think they just wanted a baby so bad they weren't thinking clear."
>
> "Why did those two fall in love with each other?"

My favorite proffered answer to that last question was, "I think they probably just spent a lot of time together and figured out they were both nice."

When people hear that a third-grade teacher has discussed LGBTQ+ topics in class, some jump to a conclusion that we must be talking explicitly with children about sex.

Even though it took me way too many years to bring up topics of queer people in the classroom, the students who participated in those discussions with me knew that sex wasn't the topic.

We talked about love.

And kindness.

And how to be an ally.

Those conversations were some of the moments when I understood most profoundly what a privilege it is to be a teacher.

* * *

Rachel drove to school the morning after she and her husband watched angry speakers rail against her as if she were a criminal. Rachel's workplace had no parking lot, so she did what all her coworkers do: find a spot in the neighborhood and walk to school.

Except she couldn't. Once she parked her car that morning, her heart began pounding, and she started sweating. Paralyzed with fear, she was physically unable to get out of her car. How could she walk the streets—alone—near school after what had just happened?

She called her husband, saying, "I don't know if I can get out of the car. I don't know if I can walk into school. I'm terrified. I don't know what to do."

He offered words of encouragement, Rachel assured him that she'd be fine, and they hung up.

But she wasn't fine. Still in her car, still unable to move, she heard the words whispering in her: *I need to talk to a counselor.*

So this third-grade teacher who had shone brightly for thirty-four years called a crisis counselor. The person calmed Rachel until, after half an hour, she was finally able to leave her car. She walked the still-dark, tree-lined streets, past apartment buildings, not knowing who was watching her from behind kitchen curtains.

Still terrified, she went in and taught her young charges as if nothing had happened.

On the advice of her union president, Rachel filed a formal complaint with the district, saying she feared for her safety at work. Painfully aware of how she had been betrayed by the director of elementary, she listed three needs in the complaint.

"I wanted a letter from the school district's attorney, ordering the parents who verbally attacked me at the board meeting to stop publicly harassing me or the district would pursue legal action. I wanted a public statement from the district, affirming that other teachers and I are teaching standards in accordance with the FAIR Act. And I wanted the board and the superintendent to refuse to allow speakers to call out specific teachers and slander them."

The response was swift. "We will look into your complaint. We will take care of it."

Rachel assumed she'd have legal recourse due to privacy laws, so she asked her union for a lawyer. When she eventually began working with the lawyer, the attorney's goal was to protect her teaching position and to prevent anyone else from requesting public records with her name. But at the initial meeting, it was just the head of HR, Rachel, and her union president.

First, HR urged her to take a job she had once interviewed for: teaching independent study, away from her school site.

"I don't know you," he said. "Are you the type who'd rather hide? I could make sure you get this transfer."

"No, you *don't* know me," she retorted. "I won't run away and let those parents win."

Then he told her she needed to sign a form for worker's comp stress leave.

"We want to show we are offering this, that you can get help, and you can take a stress leave of absence. We need it within three days."

Rachel was uncomfortable. Why was he pushing her? She didn't *want* to go on worker's comp. She wanted to finish out the remaining six weeks with her students.

Another rushed meeting was held, with more higher-ups on both the union and district sides. Rachel had been told that her complaint about an unsafe environment would be addressed at this meeting, so when she was asked about the complaint, she mentioned one additional thing.

"I told them there is also a history of anti-Semitism I have felt in this school community. But my focus for this complaint is my fear for my safety."

Then the meeting took a weird turn. The district personnel began pushing Rachel about the video. Had she shown the Cruickshank video that parents were so riled up about? Had she shown the other three? They kept pressing for details until Rachel became rattled. She'd taught the lessons in June 2021, and now it was April 2022. Her mind was a swirl of confusion. She knew the videos had been in her lesson plans that year, but had she shown the kids all four? Why didn't they show up in her YouTube history? Which videos *had* she shown before everything went so wrong? Why couldn't she remember?

HR wanted to see her lesson plans, but Rachel stepped outside with her union rep.

"Do I have to answer?" she asked. "Am I going to incriminate myself? Am I going to get fired?"

She told HR the truth: She didn't remember. So the district personnel reverted to their prior fixation and told her to file for worker's comp.

"You've been given two chances, and it's past the deadline."

Rachel reiterated that she didn't want to file for a worker's comp stress leave. So HR said he was *directing* her to file.

The union leaders were incredulous at the directive and refused to accept its legality. An argument ensued, and HR finally agreed that if she waived her right to worker's comp, she could reverse it later if needed. Rachel knew that agreeing to stress leave meant being grilled with personal questions she was in no state to answer. She didn't want the leave.

So she finally signed the waiver.

As soon as she laid the pen down, the HR director said, "Thank you. Since we want to address your safety, we've decided to move you temporarily to independent study. Starting Monday, we've arranged for a sub to take over your class. We recommend you go to your room and gather some of your personal belongings."

Stunned, Rachel cried, "I don't understand!"

The head of HR reiterated that the move was for her own safety.

"How *dare* you do this to me after thirty-four years!" she said, shaking with rage. "This was the hardest school year I've ever had! I worked so hard to develop a rapport with my students. I was making progress. They were learning, and it was *hard* for them. It was hard for me. And now you're telling me that I don't get to finish the school year with them? *Unbelievable.* It's *unbelievable* that you're doing this to me!"

Outraged, her union president protested, citing Rachel's adherence to district curriculum, the district's lack of support, and the appearance of retaliation. What message was being sent to the community?

It didn't do any good. The matter had been settled.

Rachel stormed out, and her note-taking coworker left with her. It felt like a punishment. Still trembling with anger and shock, the two of them grabbed some of her things from her classroom, and they left.

* * *

Every teacher I know says that the 2021–22 school year was even more difficult than the 2020–21 year of distance teaching. Kids floundered, having spent more than a year burdened by isolation, fear, depression, and loneliness. More than anything, students that year needed stability, patience, normalcy, and predictability.

Yet that's when the district abruptly pulled Rachel out of her classroom and away from her students, two weeks before the state test she'd prepared them for all year. They didn't even let her say goodbye. Distraught nine-year-olds and their parents sent messages to her.

> "Mrs. Cohen, where are you? Nothing is working! Please come back. Everyone misses you."
>
> "Mrs. Cohen, we are worried about you and sad. We want you to come back! Epsipa loves you!"
>
> "Oh, Mrs. Cohen, I'm so sorry to hear something from other parents. Justin really was worried. He loves you by the way. Thanks for this year. We miss you."

Meanwhile, a video clip of parents reaming Rachel at the April 2022 school meeting went viral. It was picked up by myriad right-wing news outlets, which raged about Rachel's alleged "conspiring" with district officials to teach forbidden topics. The district changed Rachel's email address so she wouldn't get more hate mail, but she was deluged with frightening messages on Facebook and Instagram from people around the country.

There were some letters of support. A friend wrote, "As teachers, if we want to make the world a safe place for ALL students regardless of their race, color, religion, gender identity, disability, or frankly anything that makes them different, we must educate and provide an environment of tolerance and acceptance."

But a pastor sent Rachel this: "Ms. Cohen . . . the best I can hope for is that you are fired from your job and lose your teaching credential . . . if you continue this same course you are following, one day He will judge you and cast you into an eternal lake of fire!"

There were more threats. Besides the pastor who wrote about sinners being weighted down with heavy objects and cast into the sea, a woman who lived a hundred miles away left a chilling message on Rachel's phone. Filled with profanity, it stated, "You guys are like the devil. You're going to get what's coming to you. . . . Somebody will be outside your house, I'm sure, a mob." The caller referenced Rachel's husband, saying she could tell that he "likes it up the ass," and that the couple should end up in jail.

The message was so disturbing that Rachel reported it to the police, who sent a detective to her house. Once the detective's report was written, Rachel and her husband fled. They spent the night at a friend's, and then traveled to Northern California, where they stayed with a relative for several days. They drove back for the Dodger game on Sunday. It was baseball's Teacher Appreciation Day, and Rachel longed to hear words of gratitude toward teachers.

She felt relief but couldn't fully relax. Certain she was being recognized and watched, she hid behind sunglasses and a hat, dissolving into the crowd.

* * *

Those months were the worst of Rachel's life. She felt paralyzed, unable to function. She had trouble sleeping and eating, and was paranoid. Nightmares haunted her, dreams of being at her old school and hiding so she wouldn't get caught. Overwhelmed by shame and guilt, she was powerless as thoughts cycled through, over and over. *Maybe I did something wrong.*

Maybe I shouldn't have shown that video. I'm a terrible person. I'm a horrible teacher.

She was deeply depressed, and for a time, she was suicidal. She told her husband, "The only reason I'm still on this earth is because of you and our three kids." It was thanks to the support of friends and her family that she made it through.

At the next board meeting in May 2022, those supporters were ready. And they weren't just defending her; they were defending the state imperative to teach about LGBTQ+ people's contributions to society, to pull them out of their silent, invisible void in education.

One nonbinary student stood at the mic, repeating, "Please, stop playing politics with my life," over and over until their allotted time ran out. A group of teachers assured LGBTQ+ students and their parents, "Your teacher allies are not going anywhere." A seventeen-year-old gay student said that when queer topics are voiced and LGBTQ+ history is taught in schools, queer kids grow up to understand themselves better and know they have community.

Rachel's adult daughter spoke, expressing outrage at the district's failure to defend her mother against "the defamatory and horrendous statements made by a vocal minority." Rachel's husband spoke of his wife's never-ending devotion to her students. "Parents have the right to disagree with state-mandated and school-mandated curriculum," he said. "But they have *no* right to personally attack the teachers who deliver it."

Rachel herself gave a scathing review of the district's failure to stand up to the group that was "furthering a hateful agenda" and maligning her character.

"By joining the program, I had hoped to make my classroom a safe space," she said, "and that I could teach my students to love and accept others no matter their differences, even if some of them had been taught to disapprove or hate others who were different from them." Fuming that she'd never felt so *un*appreciated on Teacher Appreciation Day, she turned from the mic to head back to her seat. There, facing her, she saw a mass of teachers wearing red union T-shirts. Throughout her speech, they'd been standing in silent solidarity behind her.

"When I turned and saw everyone, I couldn't believe it," she told me. "I barely made it to my seat, and I thought I was going to faint. But even though I'm an introvert and I hate being the center of attention, it was more important for me to stand up for what was right and tell my story."

As she dropped into her seat, she felt a tap on the shoulder. It was a reporter, asking to speak with her.

With two police officers standing guard outside a small side room, the reporter said, "First, can I give you a hug?" They embraced, and he continued.

"I want to thank you so much for being a warrior and for standing up. I was bullied in school for being gay. It's because of teachers like you that I'm still alive. I just want to thank you."

NBC News was there to report on the meeting, along with other media outlets. As Rachel was escorted to her car, onlookers screamed at her.

I wonder if the words of the gay reporter reverberated in her loudly enough to drown out the shouts of her detractors.

* * *

Rachel's involuntary transfer to the "temporary" placement turned out to be permanent. She says the district never investigated her complaint, except for the claim of anti-Semitism, which they decided wasn't substantiated. When she'd been transferred to teaching independent study back in April 2022, she'd taught from home. But now that it was August, she needed to clear more than three decades' worth of her own materials from her classroom and set up in her new—permanent—location for teaching independent study.

To her surprise, it was a good fit.

"I learned it, and made new friends. Then I found out it's like teacher jail over there. It's where they put the misfits. We call ourselves misfit teachers on Misfit Island. We all have a story to tell, and we have the best time together. I've bonded with them."

But the respite didn't last long. In December 2022, California's Commission on Teacher Credentialing wrote, telling her she'd been accused of misconduct. Unbeknownst to Rachel, the parent who had removed her daughter from Zoom while Rachel was showing the Cruickshank video had recorded the lesson without Rachel's permission. She had shown the recording to a friend, who then complained about Rachel to the state.

They were trying to take away her teaching credential.

* * *

She was assigned a new union lawyer who specialized in defending credentials, and collected sixteen letters attesting to her character and her excellence as a teacher. When Rachel and I spoke and she reached this part of her story, she handed me a file of papers: screenshots of social media posts, letters defending her character, and notes from strangers and friends.

A parent wrote, "I am so sorry for all of the hate you endured. . . . I was so upset to read it and can't even imagine what it must have felt like. The world is crazy and I am grateful teachers like you exist. . . . I wish [my older son] could have had you when he was smaller. There are lots of people [who] admire and support you—know that there is one in me."

Several notes were from her former students:

> "Omg, that's my fourth-grade teacher Mrs. Cohen!! 😱 🥺"
>
> "Mrs. Cohen if you ever see this, please know that I greatly appreciate you for supporting the LGBTQ+ community!"
>
> "Thank you for your courage and dignity. . . . It is truly sad to see the result of what was supposed to be an act of love. . . . I just received my diploma yesterday and graduated six months early. As someone who wants to pursue a path in law and public service, your situation is certainly another reason for me to stay committed."

The president of a distant school board wrote to Rachel's district officials, "Our school system is dealing with a change of radical proportions. . . . We are recognizing that our educational system was not set up in a way that truly helps our most-marginalized children—such as students of color, from low-income families, and those that do not conform to traditional cis-heteronormative sexual identities. . . . I believe Ms. Cohen and the curriculum she taught . . . is on the right side of history, and I know [your district] will be if it supports her."

A friend added, "[Rachel and I] have both lost family members to the Holocaust. During those dark days, it wasn't just Jews who were killed, it was LGBTQ, disabled people, anyone who didn't fit in. A part of Rachel's passion and strength comes from that connection and duty to teach tolerance."

From a coworker: "She is an invaluable member of the teaching community . . . and in no world should she be punished for trying to promote acceptance in a world where it seems to be increasingly harder to find."

A gay seventeen-year-old student said, "An LGBTQ history in schools is extremely important. Students educated on these topics, especially gay students . . . don't feel isolated, and they are able to connect with the people around them. . . . These conversations are important for cisgender heterosexual students, too, because students are able to get a great understanding and respect for their peers, and [it] leads them to grow into empathic, understanding people."

While reviewing documents collected by the state, she read the complainant's words: "[Mrs. Cohen] is Jewish and has taught her third-grade class a lot of Jewish religious rituals and the Jewish people. . . . It was not appropriate for third-graders."

It then dawned on Rachel that other teachers who'd been harassed by the conservative Christian community were also Jewish.

"When I was absent for Rosh Hashanah and Yom Kippur, I told the kids about it," she said. "And in December, we talked about Las Posadas and Kwanzaa and Hanukkah and Christmas."

Something clicked, and she realized that if she'd belonged to the conservative Christian community and had shown that video, there was *no way* the parents would have turned it into a witch hunt. She's probably right. I'd streamed hours of her district's board meetings, and was struck by how vehemently members of this conservative community argued their "right" to have their religious beliefs upheld in public schools.

The findings of the state were that Rachel showed a video not appropriate for the grade level and not approved by her district. She was given a private admonition and a warning that would stay on an internal record for three years. While the attorney and Rachel were both upset that the state had found any wrongdoing at all, they reluctantly agreed it wasn't worth fighting.

* * *

From all of the pain and fear came a few sparkles of light.

Her vice principal at her new site wrote a stellar letter when she needed to save her teaching credential, saying that if his kids were younger, he would have wanted them in Rachel's class. She heard from former students, now adults, who thanked her for being brave and supportive.

And in June 2022, the LGBTQ+ organization in her city honored her with their Crown Jewel award for being a supporter and ally to the queer community. Photos of her with the award were posted all over social media by the organization, and news outlets—not just right wing—ran with the story.

The California State Senate passed the School Employees Protection Bill because of what happened to Rachel. It would have made it a misdemeanor to "subject a school employee to threats or harassment for reasons related to their official duties while they are away from a school site or after school hours." The governor vetoed the bill, though, saying that credible threats of violence and acts of harassment against anyone can already be prosecuted as a crime.

Rachel eventually filed a grievance against the district for the involuntary transfer. When she was first removed and sent to Misfit Island, she longed to return to her third-grade classroom. After months of back-and-forth, though, she decided she didn't want to go back after all. Her old principal had initially assured her she'd write a glowing letter to help Rachel keep her credential, but then caved to district pressure and reneged. Why would Rachel return to the school with a principal who'd demonstrated she wasn't wanted and supported? And with time, she realized the superintendent never would have put her back with the same group of parents still ready to revolt. The grievance was settled with an agreement that Rachel would never be involuntarily transferred again.

It must sting that the small group of parents basically got what they wanted—Rachel was removed from their school. But in an ironic twist, Rachel is maybe more directly an ally to LGBTQ+ kids now than she was before. When she started teaching middle school students in independent study, two of her students were nonbinary.

One had chosen a different name from what was on the school record, so each time they'd meet on Zoom, Rachel would immediately change the name on the screen to their chosen name. Independent students come on-site each week, so Rachel and the student developed a real relationship, and Rachel learned that the child was only placed in independent study after being bullied for being nonbinary and overweight. The student's family had moved from Texas, thinking their child would be safer in California.

Another of Rachel's nonbinary middle schoolers had extreme anxiety, perhaps connected to their gender identity. Rachel and her colleagues had adorned their rooms and offices with LGBTQ+ flags and signs all around reading, "This classroom is safe." Though the student kept most of their story to themself, the reassuring message must surely have helped.

Some parents coming to the independent learning site belonged to the conservative Christian community and objected to the signs.

"That's the devil! This shouldn't be here!" they cried.

One of Rachel's coworkers had a student whose parent refused to let his children into meetings because he didn't want them to see rainbow signs reading, "This classroom is safe." When the coworker told the vice principal that the parent wanted the signs removed, his response was, "Don't take them down. We're not doing it."

That vice principal was not one to be bullied into backing down. He'd already proved it. When kids returned to school after the pandemic's early days, he enforced mask mandates, which enraged parents, who then complained to the district. District leadership caved in to the parents and transferred the vice principal to Misfit Island.

Just like the other island dwellers, he had his own story to tell.

* * *

Reflecting on the Cruickshank video, Rachel said, "The funny thing about it is that the humor was so quick it went over most of the kids' heads. But the extremists, they focus. They blow it up and make something bigger than it actually is. Would I show that video again? Hell no."

I remembered a video I wished I'd never shown. My good intention was to explore an educational topic that fascinated my young students. I was too exhausted on a Friday afternoon to lead kids through the science experiment I'd written in my plans, and because my decision to show the video was spontaneous, I didn't preview it. It came from the school library; of course it would be fine. But the purchasing website had miscataloged it, and it was actually intended for high schoolers. No teacher at my school had ever checked out the video before me. Without going into detail, I'll say there was a surprise body part, accompanied by the screams of shocked third graders.

Remembering, I still shudder.

Nothing happened to me. But Rachel was targeted with death threats, slandered from across the nation, and nearly left without a teaching credential.

Teachers are human beings, and most try desperately to do what's right. Just as in any profession, there are a few who don't.

But Rachel is not one of those. She added, "Knowing what I know now, no, I wouldn't show it. But I *would* teach the idea again."

It's not over. In June 2023, more than a year after Rachel was targeted at a board meeting and two years since she showed the video, there was another board meeting explosion in her district. Five hundred people gathered outside before a school board meeting, when a proposal to declare June 2023 Pride Month was on the agenda.

Proud Boys and January 6 insurrectionists were solidly in attendance, along with other anti-LGBTQ+ community members. They carried American flags, while pro-LGBTQ+ people waved rainbow flags. The two sides clashed and a brawl erupted, with demonstrators knocked to the pavement. Police helicopters swarmed overhead, while ground officers made arrests. When the arrests didn't stop the fighting, police declared an unlawful assembly and ordered the crowd to disperse. The boardroom went on lockdown. Then-Representative Adam Schiff later released a statement reading, in part, "We will not go back. We will not apologize for celebrating the strength and diversity of our LGBTQ community."

An insurrectionist Proud Boy took a photo of Rachel at the demonstration and posted it on Instagram, inflaming commenters once again. He messaged her to tell her he'd posted; horrified, she read his frightening language, intended to intimidate and enrage.

By now, she knew that Attorney General Merrick Garland had instructed school employees receiving credible threats of violence to contact the FBI, so she did. The FBI came to her home two weeks later and listened to her and two others tell the whole story.

When the FBI agents were leaving, one said, "You probably won't hear from us again. But that doesn't mean we're not doing anything."

The harassment continues off and on. In August 2023, two months after the demonstration-turned-brawl, Rachel learned that posters of her and a few others were displayed around town; her name and a large, smiling photo of her were shown under the heading "GROOMER WATCH." Then Wanted posters of her were put up, though immediately taken down. It felt like she was on a hit list.

What's next?

* * *

Oh, and at that board meeting where the brawl happened?

The board voted unanimously to recognize June as Pride Month.

* * *

After the terrifying events that changed Rachel's life, two of her most persistent tormentors ran for the school board. One of them based her entire campaign on continued harassment of Rachel.

Parents, teachers, unions, an LGBTQ+ group, and community members who support inclusive curriculum poured everything they had into supporting student-centered candidates, and in March 2024, both extremist candidates failed in their bids to be seated on the school board.

Because of the dissent and upheaval of the previous few years, one of the newly elected teacher-supported board members wanted to demonstrate his support of teachers. So he contacted one of them to ask that she do the honor of swearing him in at the meeting when he took office.

You already know who received his call.

Even though the district ultimately didn't allow teachers to swear board members in, Rachel Cohen attended the meeting, standing tall as she applauded the new trustees, cheering and hoping for a better future for students, and for those who educate them.

11

PAST, PRESENT, FUTURE

Nearly fifty wineries are tucked into the outskirts of Southern California's Temecula, on gentle slopes blanketed with acres of vineyard, bordered by long white fences that crisscross distant hillsides. I grew up in northern wine country, but it didn't resemble this foreign land, these unpaved roads of sand that whirled in small tornadoes past my car. In Temecula, I felt off-balance, repeatedly thinking I faced the familiar only to learn I was all turned around. And it wasn't just the unfamiliar landscape.

A coffeehouse I found felt like an old Berkeley hippie spot, with its gluten-free and vegan treats, its beat-up easy chairs, the fake-distressed wooden cabinets, and floating strains of guitar music. But then I caught some lyrics:

Can I get a hallelujah? Can I get an amen?

I wandered toward a display shelf, thinking it housed secondhand novels until I saw the books were all Christian. There were stacks of "Our Daily Bread" pamphlets and a framed Bible verse about fear, fools, and wisdom.

Then I noticed the enormous banner hanging from the ceiling, a black-and-white American flag with one blue stripe. Some say this flag represents professional pride among law enforcement and is a tribute to fallen officers. But it waved alongside Confederate flags during 2017's violent Unite the Right rally in Charlottesville, where white supremacists and neo-Nazis marched, chanting, "Jews will not replace us."

Toto, I don't think we're in Berkeley anymore.

In Temecula, signs of Christianity are all over. When old friends picked me up after a teacher interview, one said, "Have you noticed? Strip-mall churches are *everywhere*."

There are evangelical billboards, and the first vanity license plate I saw in town proclaimed an abbreviation of "Jesus loves you." In a parking lot, I overheard the words "Bible-centered values" from a mom buckling her child into a car seat. On a corner by the high school, a woman carrying a rainbow sign waved a rainbow flag.

Nice! I thought. *A supporter of queer kids.*

But up close, I could read her sign:

Transgenderism mutilates children. It's evil.

* * *

The Temecula region is home to pastor Tim Thompson, the same man who went to Elisa's school and grilled her principal about Elisa's support of queer kids, and the same Tim Thompson who founded a PAC and a widely followed video podcast. Thompson spreads his powerful influence into multiple school districts across the expansive county, generously sharing his microphone with far-right extremists. When a church member convicted of January 6 crimes was pardoned by Donald Trump, he received a standing ovation at Thompson's church before speaking to the congregation about praying in prison. In 2022, Sheriff Chad Bianco spoke at a fundraiser for Thompson's PAC, the group that funded Christian nationalists recruited to run for school boards. Sheriff Bianco, who donated $5,000 to the PAC, previously belonged to the Oath Keepers. The emcee of the fundraiser was British commentator Katie Hopkins, famous for her racist, anti-Muslim, anti-immigrant writing.

Five of the seven Christian nationalists backed by Thompson's PAC were victorious in school board elections in November 2022, and the three wins in Temecula flipped the school board to a far-right majority. On a Saturday morning mere weeks after Temecula's three were sworn in, teachers Janice, Renee, and Gina met with me upstairs in a cavernous coffeehouse. To keep them straight, I attached mental descriptors to each.

Beside Renee's name in my phone, I'd typed a cheerful curse. She'd texted it to me to underscore her eagerness to talk, and now I kept wanting to giggle. She was spirited, a powerhouse.

Dejected by bigotry in her home state, "Midwest Gina" moved to diverse Temecula, hoping to find it a welcoming place. She has a master's in Holocaust and genocide studies. She knows what a lack of acceptance can lead to.

As for Janice, she was a school board trustee in neighboring Murrieta.

"Wait," I said. "Don't you teach in Temecula? You do *both*?"

Janice nodded.

Over the summer of 2022, people kept begging her to run for a seat on the Murrieta board. Despite teaching full time in a nearby district, she filed election paperwork just before the deadline.

"I never would have thought of running for school board. I like helping people *behind* the scenes. I just felt like it was the right thing to do now because I realized what chaos these people cause in public schools."

Far-right extremists won two of Murrieta's three open seats. Janice took the third by less than a percentage point.

Full-time teaching *plus* school board trustee. Two different districts.

Even imagining it made my heart race.

* * *

On the night Temecula's new board members took office in December 2022, their first action was to adopt an "antiracism" resolution, and then to ban Critical Race Theory. The CRT ban whitewashed the definition of racism, and the new antiracism resolution directed employees and students to report "racist conduct." Under the new definition, though, "racist conduct" could include teaching kids about the slave trade, redlining, Jim Crow, or the civil rights movement. Teachers could no longer discuss racism as being embedded in everyday life or affirm that some individuals are of an oppressed class due to race. Teachers who did could be accused of "racist conduct."

The three board members claimed that CRT assigns generational and racial guilt for conduct and policies that are "long in the past." One trustee claimed that "America has spent a lot of time, money, and blood breaking free of its racist path." It's an impressively sunny outlook on race relations in the United States.

But if we've broken free of our racist path, why does Tim Thompson promote his podcast by showing video of white churchgoers in the 1950s while he speaks longingly of the good ol' days when church was where everyone discussed what was good and bad in the community? And when his promotional video talks about where we've gone wrong, why does it show Black people wearing Black Lives Matter T-shirts? And when he condemns the left for naming as "good" that which is "evil," why does he show images of a Pride parade?

* * *

As the three teachers educated me about Temecula, the word "cartoonish" sprang to mind. Not because their stories were funny—far from it—but because some characters seemed too absurd to be real.

Aside from the sheriff / former Oath Keeper, there is Temecula's white mayor who resigned in 2020 after he sent a racist email that went viral. As of 2024, he's back in the mayor's chair.

There's the outlier Black man commonly railing against CRT at board meetings and holding anti-LGBTQ+ signs outside schools, harassing children. He recites Bible quotes at board meetings, called the state board of education "perverts," and threatened to "destroy" Governor Gavin Newsom. His jarring actions have some teachers wondering if he's being paid.

Then there's the white city council member who likened 2021's mask requirements at council meetings to what Rosa Parks endured.

"[Rosa Parks] took a stand. At what point in time do we?" she said. "I'm getting pushed to the back of the bus. This is what I'm telling you I feel like."[1]

She was roasted by Stephen Colbert for her remarks. Neither the back-of-the-bus comments nor her 2022 homophobic tirade about Pride month caused her to lose her position. Neither did her declaration at a council meeting that the Bible, not the Constitution, is her authority.

* * *

After November 2022, Temecula's school board had three new Christian nationalist characters. Trustee Danny Gonzalez said the board's ban on CRT wouldn't "undermine the teaching of *true* American history."

Trustee Jen Wiersma posted that she was "honored" when the local chapter of Moms for Liberty endorsed her candidacy. At the swearing-in meeting, she stated that "every skin color has both *been* a slave and *owned* a slave," and lamented that ethnic studies has an "overemphasis on white supremacy."[2]

"She refers pretty much to all teachers as groomers," said "cheerful curser" Renee. "During her campaign, she went door to door . . . saying that elementary schools have gay panels indoctrinating kids into becoming homosexuals."

Joseph Komrosky, the new board president, blew off a conference he'd already committed to, wasting $1,200 of district money. Instead, he and the other two extremists attended a right-wing workshop where some believe the three prepared their CRT ban, copied from another district's.

James, a public official, talked with me about the Brown Act, legislation designed to avoid secrecy in government. Outside of a public meeting, board members can't communicate with each other in any way that would lead to a majority developing agreement on an action. Yet the first time all five trustees gathered, the three newbies presented their CRT ban, printed out and ready to go. And they had already decided on Komrosky as their president.

The three teachers and James all believe the Brown Act was violated.

"So will it be prosecuted?" I asked James.

He said the district attorney is supposed to follow up on Brown Act violations.

"But unfortunately, we have a really bad sheriff who was an Oath Keeper. . . . And the district attorney is one of his cohorts."

* * *

Most K–12 educators don't even know what CRT is, so school boards that prohibit CRT tend to say, "If you don't teach it, why are you opposed to banning it?"

The question plays dumb, though, because it disregards the reason why the bans are written. K–12 educators may not teach the scholarly framework, but it's impossible to teach U.S. history accurately while avoiding the central tenet of systemic racism. As Columbia University professor and economist Jeffrey Sachs says, "It's a way essentially of preventing teachers . . . from being honest about a lot of the uglier sides of American history and contemporary society."[3]

A key component of CRT bans is the stipulation that instruction can't cause kids to feel "discomfort, guilt, anguish, or any other form of psychological distress" based on race.[4]

But what if kids just feel it on their own?

Renee teaches high school English, and a large proportion of her AP students are white.

"I've never had a kid say, 'I feel bad reading this book.' They're mostly like, 'Oh my GOD, this happened?'"

Renee told her students of a Black Temecula man who was released from prison in 2018 after serving twenty years for a murder he didn't commit.

"I'll bring that stuff in to show this happens here, too, not just in the South. But now, I worry about the way [the antiracism resolution] encourages parents, teachers, students to tell on someone."

Renee teaches Bryan Stevenson's book *Just Mercy*, about a lawyer and his legal practice that serves the poor, the wrongly condemned, and the people trapped in our criminal justice system. It's not an easy read; themes of racism, poverty, and injustice run throughout. After the first time she taught it, Renee surveyed her students, asking what she should continue doing and what she should stop.

"Every single kid said, '*Just Mercy*. Keep teaching *Just Mercy*.' And when I talk about *The Immortal Life of Henrietta Lacks*, they say, 'Keep teaching Henrietta Lacks. We didn't know this happened.'"

When I wondered aloud about kids feeling discomfort, Renee was clear.

"They *should* feel bad about it. . . . That's called empathy."

* * *

After George Floyd's murder in 2020, Renee heard from a former student. Now in college, the student asked Renee to Zoom with a group of other Temecula graduates, some of whom Renee had taught. It was a mixed group, including both white students and students of color. At least one young person was gay. Seven or eight of them logged on from UCLA, Berkeley, Stanford, and other universities.

"These were kids who love the school system and thrived here," said Renee. "And they were *angry* that it took them leaving Temecula to learn about the real world."

"We're in college, and we didn't read stories about people like us," one student told her.

Their unified message: "We need you to tell people to do better. You HAVE to do better at this."

* * *

Julie's name was everywhere in articles about Temecula schools. Though she teaches science elsewhere, she lives in Temecula. When we met, I couldn't hide my surprise.

"You're so *young*!"

I apologized for condescending, but I still marveled, already knowing a little about her activism. How the heck was someone in her early thirties already such a community leader?

"Growing up here, it was very religious, and very conservative. I kind of felt like an outsider," she said. In high school, her economics teacher once spoke about a ballot measure on abortion and parental consent. As he launched into a speech against abortion, Julie stood up.

"I stepped in front of the class and said, 'One, this is inappropriate. And two—how DARE you!'"

Julie, who is white, didn't read a story with a nonwhite character until tenth grade.

"It was so eye-opening when I read *Native Son*, having the perspective of a Black man in the Jim Crow era. Or Amy Tan's *The Joy Luck Club*, with the experience of Asian Americans. I had never had that window."

Julie attended college in a distant town that was Temecula's "complete opposite," where she studied molecular biology and dove into politics and public health. She also worked in rural counties with people unable to access medical care. When she started teaching, it was in a very diverse district with high poverty.

"It opened my eyes to the cycle of trauma and poverty and how those are intertwined," she said. "It *really* made me want to advocate for my students."

She leapt at an opportunity to teach AP chemistry for two years in China, at a school where California-credentialed teachers prepared Chinese nationals to attend college in the United States. There, Julie learned about a different kind of trauma. When Chinese President Xi Jinping held a meeting in her city for Communist leaders, Russian President Vladimir Putin came to town. There were barricades everywhere, and Black and Latino teachers were searched every day.

"There was this weird privilege I had being white in China," she said. "It made me want to advocate more at home. And it made me so appreciative of the Constitution and our First Amendment rights."

Since the school used California textbooks, they were censored for U.S. history. White tape covered objectionable text, and pages mentioning Tiananmen Square had been ripped out. When the Communist Party heard about the school's student body election, they showed up unannounced. Teachers raced around, pulling down campaign posters.

"Because you can't have an election," Julie explained. "You don't want kids getting used to voting and having freedoms they don't really have."

Reflecting on her early adulthood, Julie said, "I've lived in very liberal areas. I've lived in a Communist country. I've seen books banned. I've seen curriculum challenged.

"I do what I do because I've seen things."

* * *

Julie returned from China in 2019. Days after George Floyd was murdered in 2020, Temecula's mayor sent an email that went viral, fueling Julie's sense of purpose. It read, "I don't believe any good person of color has been killed by police." The mayor blamed his dyslexia and a dictation app for inserting the word "good," and claimed he was only referring to killings in the *local* region.

His excuse was feeble. It also denied history.

In 2016, Temecula resident Matthew Tucker, eighteen and Black, was distraught after a breakup. He asked his mother to call the police because he was suicidal. He was in the garage with a hunting knife when police shot him. The fatal shot was to his back, from at least fifteen feet away. He died within earshot of his baby niece, sister, and mother, who couldn't hold her dying son because police restrained her.

In June 2020, immediately after George Floyd's murder and four years after Matthew was killed, Matthew's brother published an opinion piece in *The Washington Post.* "I'll never forget the haunting screams from my sister over the phone as she held my niece," he wrote. "I hope he's not another Black man that America will forget."[5] He'd penned the opinion piece because the words of Temecula's mayor had ripped open his wound. Those same words catapulted Julie into action.

"I *know* this family," she said. "We've done candlelight vigils and protests for them."

Julie's first move was to challenge the owner of a local pizza parlor who announced after Floyd's murder that he was giving local law enforcement discounts on pizza.

"I wrote in the community forum that it was disgusting," said Julie. "I said, 'If you do not feel that this is racist or culturally insensitive, then you need to give the same offer to people of color who are grieving and hurting right now.'"

At first, Pizza Man agreed. But when Julie responded with, "Cool. Let's have a roundtable with people in the community," his reply was, "Well, these Black people you're bringing . . . who are they?"

"Nope," said Julie. "We're done. *You* don't get to dictate that."

She organized an event called Unity in the Community, held in June 2020.

"We decided to have a place of listening and understanding, where people of color would have the platform to talk to law enforcement and city leaders, who would need to just listen."

Julie invited local sheriffs, police departments, city council members, and the mayors of Temecula and neighboring Murrieta. Though it was early in the pandemic, a small group of local Black business owners and residents still showed up, posing questions to law enforcement. People of color who'd grown up in the area told of oppression they'd experienced, including from racist teachers.

"In my friend's tenth-grade English class, she said she wanted to be president. And her teacher said, 'No, Black people can't be president.' That was around 2004."

Real police reform would require rebuilding from the bottom up, but tough questions were asked of law enforcement that night, and dialogues took place. The group continued working together and eventually helped push the city council to approve a commission to focus on matters of race, equity, diversity, and inclusion. The commission drew eighty applicants, the most in the city's history.

"The 'work' was really just a Facebook group, Temecula Unity," explained Julie. "We don't have money. We're just a group of people who write letters and have meetings with people in city hall to lobby for good governance."

In late 2022, just months before the election, Julie's friend from Temecula Unity suggested forming a PAC.

"We had over a thousand engaged members, and we were doing good work but without any money. We couldn't run any candidates. And if we had a PAC, we could fundraise and put teeth behind the political advocacy."

So the One Temecula Valley PAC was born, with Julie heading community outreach.

The Temecula Unity Facebook group was unapologetically progressive, but Julie and other leaders insisted that the PAC remain moderate.

"No matter where you are on the spectrum, our North Star is that you're advocating for *all* people, not just one side. It's that you're listening to all, with dignity and purpose, using data and reasoning and evidence, not feelings.

"In our very different ends of the political spectrum, sometimes it's nasty," she said. "But that's where *work* happens. It's where people get engaged."

Julie says residents can't ignore a five-alarm fire.

"When you live in a place where people all think the same, you can ignore what you want, because you don't have to see it.

"But when you live in a place where people go to school board meetings and say that teachers are pedophiles and groomers, and that books need to be banned, and people are being rude and nasty, that's when change can really happen."

I understood. After I switched school districts, things ran smoothly under experienced administration. But when an ineffectual school board began hiring problematic superintendents, there was a new urgency to fight for change. That's when we educators organized protest marches, flocked to board meetings by the hundreds, and nearly went on strike.

Julie said more than 90 percent of PAC donations come from residents of the immediate area, making $10 or $20 monthly donations.

"It's not coming from people with deep pockets. It's moms, teachers, concerned citizens, and grandmas. We have this internal motto: 'Make Temecula boring again.'"

Boring. It's an admirable goal.

They're not there yet.

* * *

During the pandemic, board meetings became dangerous because of the schools' masking policy. After antimaskers pounded on windows, demanding entrance into a building already at capacity, meetings were moved to the high school. Teachers told me that violent rhetoric shut down one meeting. At another, an audience member was screaming at the board about Jesus.

"It was like what you see in the South on TV," said Midwest Gina. "Now they had something to do with their lives besides go to church."

But once the new board took office in 2022, a whole new faction rose up at board meetings: the students.

* * *

Teachers estimated that about thirty students spoke at the big December 2022 meeting. On a school night, Black kids, white kids, Native kids, and other students of color begged the board not to ban CRT; they knew the real ban was against teaching the truth about race in America.

Here are some representative words from a few student speakers:

"Feelings shouldn't be part of the politics. . . . This is education. This isn't about your feelings and how your white fragility can't take what your ancestors did." (From a senior)

"You want to pretend that my history didn't happen, for the sake of your children's feelings. But what about how *I* feel?" (From a junior)

"It may be uncomfortable, but honestly, it should be. . . . The history of race in this country is terrible and sad, but to grow and move forward, we must all be educated." (From a sophomore)

"Students cannot be expected to navigate their past while being provided a blurry version of it. If we do not intend on tampering with the students' freedom of opinion, then we must not tamper with their right to knowledge." (From a freshman)

"The board did not listen to anything they said," fumed Renee. "We were there until twelve thirty in the morning. We were all exhausted. Jen Wiersma said, 'I'm doing this to protect you. I want you to know that you are more than your race.'"

Despite the condescension and dismissiveness from board members, the students weren't done. Three days after the CRT ban was approved, hundreds of Temecula's high schoolers held a student-led walkout. Michelle, a local special ed teacher, described the students' efforts.

"They were ignored by the board, and harassed, ridiculed, and name-called by adults in the audience," said Michelle. "We used to be a little divided by high schools, but now we're seeing these three schools work together to create amazing, peaceful protests."

James, the public official who'd spoken with me about the Brown Act, walked alongside marching students. The right-wing board majority and Tim Thompson's church blasted James, accusing him of leading the protest.

"It was totally organized by the students," James told me. "Their message was, 'You're trying to erase history. You're trying to ban our education. You're trying to prevent us from learning the truth about what happened in this country, how minority people have been treated in this country. . . .

"'And by banning CRT, all you've done is make us more eager to learn about it.'"

James said he wrote to the sixteen-year-old student who'd organized the walkout. He told her, "Stand up for what you believe, and don't ever back down. Don't ever let people tell you you're wrong. Because you're 100% right."

* * *

In between my multiple trips to Temecula, I traveled hundreds of miles north that winter and met with a teacher who spoke to me about race. Damon, who teaches high school English, longs to help students develop a greater sensitivity to matters of race. It made me think about what students miss when teachers are prevented from discussing the history and lived reality of racism. And it made me think about how much I'd never been aware of in the mostly white environments of my youth.

When deciding which college to attend, I didn't have to think about what many young people must consider. I never thought about my skin color, wondering if I'd feel at home with fellow students. I didn't consider my orientation or gender identity and search for a safe, inclusive school. My calculations were basic. I wanted to be reasonably near my parents, and to avoid big cities. I chose UC Davis, in a quiet Central Valley town with orchards of fruit trees and golden, allergy-inducing grasses. The university attracted pre-vet students, and the dorms nearest the horse barns smelled like manure. There were more bikes than cars in Davis. It suited me perfectly.

But Damon had different calculations. This young Black man was raised in a rural county where Black people make up barely 2 percent of the population. As a kid, he yearned for a cultural connection. So for college, he moved across the country and attended an HBCU (historically Black college or university). That deep need to connect is what steered him into education.

"I never had any Black teachers until I went to the historically Black college," said Damon. "I wanted Black students to see a role model in front of the classroom, to let them know this kind of profession is accessible to them. I wanted them to see themselves in this role of being a positive influence, as opposed to how society tends to portray Black culture. I'm hoping that my career as an educator contributes to that cause.

"I love being in the classroom with teenagers!" he said while I settled into a student desk in his room. Damon's passion and positivity were palpable, his face alight. And even though he teaches in an area with a fairly low Black population, he described how matters of race permeate everything that happens within those classroom walls.

Every English teacher Damon ever met has spoken in reverential tones about *To Kill a Mockingbird* and how it's THE book to cover with ninth graders. As a student teacher, Damon learned the book was richer than he'd expected. He even fostered a tentative love for it and taught it in his first year.

But during the national awakening spurred by George Floyd's murder, he identified the source of his nagging discomfort.

"I was a Black educator using a 'white savior' story to teach about Jim Crow," he said. "Of all the books we've published in this country, there *had* to be other books to teach about that era."

So in his second year, Damon dropped *Mockingbird* and taught Melba Pattillo Beals's memoir, *Warriors Don't Cry*. Beals was one of the Little Rock Nine, a group of Black students who faced down angry mobs in 1957 when they enrolled at formerly all-white Central High School in Little Rock, Arkansas. The enraged crowds and the infusion of the National Guard and the U.S. Army lasted nearly a month before the nine teens could finally attend school. But that didn't end it. The students were tormented by white classmates and their parents for years. The home of the youngest of the nine was bombed just weeks before she graduated.

Not only is the harrowing story told by a person who lived it, but the heroes are Black teenagers. And Beals ended up living in Northern California like Damon's students, which must make the book even more alive for them. It would be very powerful for young people of any race to learn from this kind of narrative.

Which made me wonder if *Warriors Don't Cry* is on national lists of frequently banned books. So I checked.

It is. Of *course* it is.

* * *

Damon is troubled that some districts still require traditional texts like *Huck Finn* and *To Kill a Mockingbird.*

"We can recognize these books might have *been* great," he said. "But if they were great seventy years ago when status quo was that you don't teach anything to Black students, or that Black kids had to go to separate schools to get an education—what does that say about us if we're not even *questioning* those texts? There's no reason we should be married to these texts with all the things America has been through."

When Damon was in eighth grade, his class read *Uncle Tom's Cabin.* Years later, as a student teacher, he was stunned to hear his white mentor reading the N-word aloud while teaching *To Kill a Mockingbird.*

"I couldn't even take notes. I couldn't pay attention. It brought back all these emotions as a young eighth grader before I even knew what I felt about this word being read out loud in a classroom.

"So to read *Huck Finn* or *To Kill a Mockingbird* and use the excuse that, 'Well, the author is just trying to portray what it was really like in that time,' is . . . I think it's fucked up. Because if you're being honest, the only students who need to know what it was like in that time are white students. Black students know what it was like. It really hasn't changed that much. It's still the same world they live in."

* * *

Damon advises the Black Student Union (BSU), fulfilling a long-held dream. He understands being a Black adolescent and not seeing much representation around him.

"You kind of form to the majority. We see lots of Black students saying wildly inappropriate things about Black culture. I think they either face macro- or microaggression so frequently they think it's the norm, or they think, 'I must adhere to this in order to be accepted.'"

Damon searches for multicultural material to enrich the curriculum for his students, many of whom are Latino. He structures class discussions to encourage critical thinking, without leading any ethnic group to feel blame or shame.

"I remind them things like, 'When I say white, I'm not speaking to ALL white people. I'm speaking to this specific subgroup,' or 'Is everybody doing okay? I don't want anybody to feel targeted.'

"I ask for anonymous feedback on paper, like, 'How do you feel about talking so heavily about race and these things?' Overwhelmingly, it's positive."

His students trust him. And, because it's the real world, things come up.

A graduate once reached out to Damon. The former-BSU student informed him that the newly elected student-body president, a white girl, was in multiple online videos using the N-word.

Many parties were looped into subsequent meetings, including a specialist in restorative justice. Damon and the BSU were pushing to remove the girl from office. The girl's parent pushed back, claiming that the upset over her use of the N-word was an example of CRT.

"We wanted it to be an educational opportunity," said Damon. "We didn't want to yell and shake a finger in her face. We wanted her to understand exactly what she said, how it affected her Black peers, and why it's problematic to use such language."

So Damon helped the girl and affected students through the time-intensive restorative justice process. She really listened to fellow students as they described the pain her actions had caused.

Having heard the voices and feelings of her peers, the girl decided to resign. Damon believes she walked away a better person for it.

"It worked really well. I saw her frequently throughout the remainder of the year, and she always stopped to talk to me. There's no ill will."

Resolution wasn't just important for the Black kids. It was important for *all* the kids.

* * *

Issues that BSU students bring to Damon are often uncomplicated, and most get resolved. An older white teacher innocently suggested a phrase students could use instead of cursing, but a student pointed out its racist roots. As with each issue Damon's students brought to him, the BSU backed the student, and the matter was brought to the administration.

"Almost every time, the teacher ended up apologizing to the student, recognizing their role and why it was wrong."

"Almost," because resolution is sometimes elusive. Damon often tells his freshmen, "Next year, you can take ethnic studies if this is interesting to you." Recently, a white student sought out Damon.

The kid was stellar: taking a full course load, playing varsity soccer, and engaging in school activities. In a meeting to discuss his classes for the following year, he asked his adviser about ethnic studies.

"Oh, you don't want to take ethnic studies," said the adviser. "That's just a bullshit class."

This time, when Damon conferred with the administration, it was different.

"My voice was shaky, my palms were sweaty, and I was very emotionally invested," he said. Later, Damon learned this adviser was a well-known Trump supporter who was vocal about political ideologies.

"But if I can talk about systemic racism in the classroom without condemning white people," he told me, "there's *no* reason why you can't advise a student about academics and not allow your political ideologies into that conversation. And not blatantly steer a student away from the class simply because you don't believe in it."

The counselor stubbornly denied saying anything, so nothing happened besides the inclusion of a piece of paper in a file at the district office.

Damon ended with this: "I didn't expect right-conservative pressure to come from inside the school itself. I was picturing a parent, school board, or community member. I wasn't picturing, 'Yeah, I got to fight a counselor at my own school.'"

You fall down, and get back up—usually bruised, a little more wary, maybe bitter, maybe a little jaded. Perhaps more motivated.

That's what it's like to live in the present, where racism is not "long in the past."

* * *

Back in Temecula, I met with a Black pastor and teacher named Deon Hairston, who shared a chilling story from his family tree. It gave context for his outrage over the school board's efforts to silence education about race.

In 1949, seven Black men were arrested for the alleged rape of a white woman in Martinsville, Virginia. Interrogated without legal counsel and threatened with a lynch mob, each man "confessed" to involvement in the rape. Six of the seven were twenty-one or younger, and some were unable to read the confession they signed. In jury selection, prosecutors rejected all potential jurors who were Black. Six trials were held in rushed succession, not one lasting more than a day.

Seventy-two white men convicted the seven Black men of rape, and all seven were sentenced to death. The Martinsville Seven were executed in 1951, in the largest mass execution for rape in U.S. history. Between 1908 and 1951, Virginia executed forty-five men for rape. All of them were Black.

In 2021, Virginia's governor issued posthumous pardons for each of the Martinsville Seven, recognizing that they hadn't received due process and that the executions resulted from systemic racism. For decades, family members of the seven had advocated for pardons. They sobbed when the governor told them his decision.

Three of the Martinsville Seven bore the surname Hairston, the name of the largest extended family in America. The family has thousands of members, Black and white. Today's Black Hairston families are the descendants of enslaved people.

Which brings us back to Pastor Deon Hairston, longtime resident of Temecula.

Three months after banning CRT, the extremists on Temecula's school board voted to hire a CRT "expert," a white man named Chris Arend. Arend was from Paso Robles, nearly three hundred miles away.

Temecula's CRT ban copies Paso Robles's ban verbatim, and Arend was on the Paso Robles school board when it banned CRT in 2021. In March 2023, after Arend lost his board seat, this new "consultant" led a Temecula panel discussing CRT.

During public comment, Pastor Deon Hairston gave an impassioned speech against racism and the CRT ban. As he returned to his seat, a white woman called out, telling Hairston he should get out of the country.

Hairston repeated her comment for the crowd, and Komrosky, the board president, said, "Sir, that's your first warning. The second warning, you'll be asked to leave."

Livid, Hairston shouted, "She told me to get out of the COUNTRY! *My family has been here since August 1619!*"

Komrosky calmly directed sheriff's deputies to escort Hairston out.

Chaos ensued.

Many in the crowd began booing and shouting, while others applauded. Komrosky threatened to empty the building. A nonmajority board member argued with Komrosky, telling him to eject the woman instead.

A portion of the crowd chanted, "Take the woman! Kick her out!" The two nonmajority board members left the head table, separating themselves from the three extremists. One of the two left the dais and stood among the people. When the white woman was finally escorted out, cheers and jeers erupted, and the board president called a ten-minute recess.

Major media around the country ran the story.

And in the myriad articles about a Black man descended from enslaved people getting kicked out of a public meeting after being told to leave the country, there was no mention of racism being long in the past.

* * *

Once Temecula's CRT ban was in place, the board's far-right majority really got busy. They prohibited Black Lives Matter and Pride flags, as well as any banners other than county, state, U.S. military, or American flags. They wrote policy ordering teachers to out transgender and gender-nonconforming students to their parents. They fired the district's popular superintendent without cause, despite accolades she'd received for improving school safety and instructional quality. They listed "objectionable" books and called for their removal from school libraries.

Five months after being sworn in, the board majority vetoed the purchase of K–5 social studies textbooks because the books mentioned Harvey Milk, whom Komrosky denounced as a pedophile.

After California's governor threatened to deliver the textbooks himself and fine the district $1.5 million, the board reversed its decision.

But by then, those opposing the board had had enough.

It was time to hit the streets.

* * *

EnACT Temecula is a group of Black moms and educators advocating for inclusive learning environments. They had the idea to recall the three Christian nationalist board members. The president of EnACT said, "I'm not a Democrat, I'm not a Republican . . . I'm a Black mom. [I'm going to make] sure that Black voices and marginalized voices are heard and our issues are addressed."[6] After she openly criticized the school board, EnACT's president faced intimidation, including social media harassment and unfamiliar cars beaming their headlights into her home.

The One Temecula Valley PAC began collecting recall signatures in June 2023.

It was a daunting prospect. Residents could only sign the petition for the board member representing their own area, and since about five thousand signatures were required for each of the three board members they wanted to recall, organizers would need to gather about fifteen thousand signatures. Julie (who'd taught in China) and her husband led the volunteer effort. From August until the December deadline, she and her husband pounded the pavement each Saturday and Sunday, eight hours at a stretch. Droves of community members joined them.

Already outspoken at board meetings, Julie now became even more visible in her community.

"It's not easy, and it can be scary," she told me. "I've been accosted by men in the dark. My friend had her car vandalized with red paint. I have people harassing me every day on Instagram about what a horrible, evil person I am."

The publication *Capital and Main* wrote of pro-recall teachers and students being targeted online by board supporters. Photos and addresses of some were posted. Others were followed to their homes or jobs.

One Black teacher said an op-ed appeared in her school mailbox about the history of Black people who owned enslaved people. Renee was doxed twice on Instagram and was harassed at board meetings. She and another teacher requested extra security for Back-to-School Night.

More security. For teachers. At work.

* * *

My district was a proponent of "restorative practices," activities designed to build a strong sense of community in schools. Restorative practices can "teach interpersonal skills, repair harm when conflict occurs, and proactively meet students' needs . . . so misbehavior is less common."[7] One example of a restorative practice is to hold regularly scheduled community-building class meetings.

For these meetings, my third graders and I would sit in a circle on the shabby rug I'd bought for a hundred bucks at Home Depot. Twice weekly, we'd start with a quick warm-up and then would talk about current issues in our classroom. Usually, there were group concerns, though problems between two individuals were also common. Sometimes I'd bring up my own frustrations, and occasionally, a brave child would raise a concern about something I'd done.

(Once, I told them I was tired of struggling to get their attention; they countered, pointing out I'd abandoned the use of our agreed-upon signal for quiet. They were right. When I needed quiet, I was supposed to say "waterfall," and they were supposed to respond with "shhh" while sweeping waggling fingers downward to simulate running water. But I'd usually forget to say "waterfall" and would instead don a long-suffering expression, sighing heavily. One gentle student was an expert at reading my face, and when he saw The Look, he'd catch my eye and urgently whisper, "Waterfall, waterfall, waterfall!")

Typical matters discussed during class meetings included:

"Kids in our class are too loud in the cafeteria, so the lady calls us last for recess!"

"Kids get too mad at tetherball, and now the yard duty said we can't play it for a week!"

"Some kids always run to be first in line, and it's not fair!"

After working through the conflicts, we'd end on a happy note by giving compliments to each other and then get back to work.

But sometimes, our format for class meetings didn't fit.

CJ was beloved by his classmates. A natural comedian, he didn't do much classwork but was the first to make sad kids feel better. Children recognized his big heart and wanted to sit next to him or be his partner for math games. For nearly an entire school year, CJ was the only child who knew that the mother of a new classmate had died at the end of second grade. The grieving child had told me not to tell anyone, but he confided in CJ, the first kid who had befriended him months earlier. (When CJ told me he knew about his friend's mom, he said, "I told him my hamster died, so I knew how he felt.")

One afternoon, before we could start our meeting, CJ hung his head and began sobbing. Eyes popped wide in shock. CJ was the one who made us laugh, arms waving as he spun a story, pretending he didn't know how funny he was. On Grandparents' Day, CJ posed a deadpan question to the panel of guests: "Are all of you hamster people?" I don't think the grandparents noticed the twinkle in his eyes.

But CJ was inconsolable, despite the kids on either side who looped arms around him.

"What happened?" I cried.

"I was supposed to go over to Eric's house after school today . . . but he just told me I can't come, because his parents don't want Black kids to come over."

The collective gasp of horror almost drowned out CJ's wailing. I embraced him, patting his narrow shoulders and murmuring inadequate words of comfort. All the while, I was hyperaware of Eric, sitting behind where I crouched. Were the other kids glaring at him? He was such a nice kid, and he and CJ were great friends. Why had he repeated those awful words?

In a public school classroom, topics like racism sometimes arise. How could they not? Nearly all of life happens within those four walls. My students quieted, awaiting my response.

I didn't know what to say.

Being overly talkative comes in handy sometimes. Words flowed as I told CJ we all loved him, and my students chorused agreement. I said it was always wrong to judge someone by their skin color, and though I couldn't know exactly how he felt, I knew it was terribly painful. I said he was beautiful exactly as he was born, as all people are. As I spoke, my eyes darted around the circle, scouting for anyone who might be scowling at Eric. Nobody was. They still looked stunned.

Then I instructed kids not to blame Eric for something his parents had said, and that was the hardest part. I did *not* want to excuse the racist sentiment, but neither did I want to insult Eric's parents in front of him. Additionally, I'd taught the older son of these immigrants from Southeast Asia, and they'd been nothing but lovely—to *me*, anyway—over the years. But "lovely" and "ugly" can coexist, and I didn't want to be that white person who dismisses racist displays.

Later, I dashed to the principal, who spoke at length with both boys. He updated me after school, saying he'd spoken with Eric's parents, and genuinely believed they had not said what Eric claimed.

With the principal, Eric had confessed to being irritated when extroverted CJ kept pestering him for a play date. Eric also admitted his parents had never said CJ wasn't welcome. According to the principal, Eric was annoyed with his friend; lacking the skills to say, "Maybe another time, because I need some space," Eric had likely dropped a bomb to end the conversation.

I'll never know the truth. Did Eric decide the lesser of two evils would be to take the hit for something his parents said? Or was he simply exasperated with his persistent friend, and said the most hurtful thing he could think of?

The answer doesn't really matter, because whether originating from adults or a child, those words of "good" versus "bad" slash to the bone. Maybe it would've been worse if Eric came up with them himself, reminding us that eight-year-olds understand the deep injustice of excluding people based on skin color. Reminding us that kids absorb so much.

It's never easy to discuss the pain of racism with a classroom of children. But teaching allows you to see how much kids can learn, and change. They absorb the bad, but they also absorb the good, the beautiful. Their capacity for growth inspires. Their innate drive to be bigger, better, brighter—it brings us hope.

But if schools ignore the truth and refuse to discuss race, teach empathy, be uncomfortable, and teach true Black history—where will that get us?

It sure won't lift a sobbing child off a drab carpet from Home Depot.

* * *

During summer's heat in 2023, as Temecula teachers and parents walked countless miles gathering signatures, seven students and three teachers—including "cheerful curser" Renee—filed a lawsuit against Temecula's school board, claiming that banning CRT had taken away students' fundamental rights to an education. The suit alleged that the board's actions censored teachers and violated the California Constitution, infringing on students' rights to receive information and violating their rights to equal protection. The board's actions created a "hostile environment to teach and learn," according to the president of the teachers' union.[8]

In an article on EdSource, teachers, students, and parents described the bleak reality of Temecula schools, "where teachers are afraid to teach about Black history and race, and, as a result, discourage student discussions on the topic out of fear of retribution from administrators." Teachers spoke of colleagues called into administrators' offices "to discuss the appropriateness of a mural or the display of the image of a civil rights leader on their classroom walls."[9]

The article goes on to quote a Temecula government teacher, who said, "We are being intimidated, and the students feel it. It affects them every day, and makes them feel unsafe."[10] One parent said her son's class had read Martin

Luther King Jr.'s "I Have a Dream" speech the previous year, but after the CRT ban, he received no similar lessons during Black History Month. At the news conference announcing the lawsuit, one teacher broke into tears while reading a student's statement, which read in part, "Young people [immediately] became targets for social media harassment, not by children, but *adults*."

Speakers at the news conference described increased intolerance toward students of color and LGBTQ+ youth. One plaintiff's parent said, "[The ban] has created an unsafe, discriminatory, and dangerous environment for our Black students, students of color, and LGBT-plus students. In particular, the Black students who have voiced opposition have suffered an ongoing campaign of harassment by primarily adult supporters."[11]

The goal of the lawsuit is to have the CRT ban be declared unconstitutional and revoked. While waiting for a ruling, teachers and parents continued gathering signatures in dogged pursuit of a recall.

"Vacation" for many Temecula teachers wasn't very restful in the summer of 2023.

* * *

Board meetings continued to be contentious. Komrosky, desperate to exert control, anointed himself a referee and implemented a system of yellow and red cards. When he deemed an audience member had crossed a line, he'd wave the yellow card. If the same attendee offended him again, he'd flash the red card, and the person would be ejected. In a public meeting, Komrosky declared, "This is our meeting, not yours," and multiple times threatened to clear entire audiences.

In late 2023, one of the board's extremists resigned his position and moved to Texas. That left four members on the board, two on the far right. By now, the volunteers working toward a recall had concentrated their efforts to ensure a vote on recalling at least one, so they halted efforts to recall "honored to be endorsed by Moms for Liberty" Wiersma and put all their eggs into the "Recall Komrosky" basket.

In December 2023, a year after the three Christian nationalists were sworn in and days after the recall petitions were turned in, the ACLU filed a lawsuit against the Temecula Valley Unified School District, the school board, and Komrosky himself. On behalf of two women—including "she taught in China" Julie—the suit alleged violations of both free speech rights and California's open-meeting law, the Brown Act. (Word of advice: Maybe don't trample the free speech rights of a brave, brilliant teacher who taught where white tape covers up history.)

Both women had been red-carded by Komrosky for objecting to his free speech violations. Neither woman had disrupted the meeting, which the First Amendment requires before a person can be kicked out.

That lawsuit was successful. In April 2024, Komrosky was ordered to follow California law and give verbal warnings instead of merely flashing color cards.

Julie responded to the ruling.

"It's important that our rights to petition the government and air grievances shall not be infringed by a school board president on a power trip." An attorney for the plaintiffs said, "Debate is *democracy*, not disruption. The settlement protects the people's right to engage with their elected officials, free from unlawful censorship."[12]

Komrosky could no longer "determine that members of the public are being disruptive and order them removed merely because he disagrees with the viewpoint of their speech." This, despite Komrosky's belief—as he expressed on Tim Thompson's video podcast—that the "conventional First Amendment" does not apply to board meetings.

The district was ordered to pay $75,000 in legal fees. Julie and the other woman did not seek damages.

"I'm a *teacher*. I don't want to take money from programs, from public education. But I *had* to sue. He doesn't think you should be able to criticize him, but the Constitution doesn't say that you have to be nice. [I lived] in China—not having freedom of speech, not having freedom of peaceful assembly, not having the freedom to petition the government, not having the freedom to read books in a library.

"To see someone trying to do even a little bit of that in the United States in 2024? No fucking *way*."

Mere weeks after the ruling, Komrosky was already violating the Brown Act again by allowing attendees at board meetings to make speeches against his recall. He was belatedly rewarded.

By a razor-thin margin, Komrosky lost the recall election in June 2024, but he ran for school board again five months later and won. It was a devastating blow to the exhausted teachers and community members who'd poured so much into the recall.

But they'd proved that they won't surrender to bigotry.

No fucking *way*.

* * *

The refrain I heard most in Temecula is that the Christian nationalist extremists aim to dismantle public education.

"They have no genuine desire in anything to do with education," said James, the public official. "They ran as part of the Christian nationalist agenda because *they're* the ones being 'discriminated' against." His eye roll spoke volumes.

I remembered Tim Thompson's PAC, with its expressed goal of electing candidates who will "fight for Christian and Conservative values" in public schools. (His PAC's website was later scrubbed of any mention of Christianity.)

"I think this was an outside group," James continued. "The three [board members] live here, but they were funded by an outside group that came into our community to foment this kind of discord."

It was what I'd heard earlier from the three teachers, Renee, Gina, and Janice. Gina had made sure I understood that point.

"They planned on taking over the school board and making 'public' schools for Christian nationalists," she'd said. "They're getting on boards, and they have their own agenda. It's not about the kids, or teachers, or education. It's about getting their own agenda accomplished."

As I streamed past Temecula school board meetings, what I watched in the present kept morphing into visions of a possible future, one that so many teachers, parents, and students are working desperately to avoid.

It's not hard to see what many teachers, officials, and parents of Temecula have in common. It's not their ego, or a desire for power, or money.

Their common concern is the students. That's it. They vibrate with care for their kids, the ones who will carry this present moment into their future.

"In fight-or-flight, I'm a fighter," said Gina. "This doesn't scare me—it pisses me off. I'm here because I want to make sure my students are always protected, every single one of them. I want to teach more of the truth."

* * *

At the board meeting back on the night CRT was banned, a psychiatrist with thirty years of experience treating mental illness spoke. She said,

> In order for any of us to make changes in ourselves, we have to first confront the things within us that we want to change.
>
> The same goes for our society. Some members of this board would deny our country's history of slavery and its residue that has extended into the Jim Crow era and beyond. They believe that teaching this history will harm white children, when, in actuality, I believe it's more harmful not to.
>
> Teaching our children the truth about our history helps them understand how, when we fail to be aware of and confront our racism, we miss a vital opportunity to create a better world. . . . Human growth can only be accomplished by acknowledging where we have failed, or need to do better. Don't we teach them that in their academics? If they make a mistake on a math problem, don't we show them how they made the mistake and help them to correct it? Don't we do that in sports? . . . Why would we deny them the same opportunity to learn from our country's past, and the mistakes and past behaviors of our ancestors?
>
> I'm telling you this, reluctantly, as the great-granddaughter of a KKK member. He was married to my great-grandmother, who was a part of the Underground Railroad. And I want you to know that I have to embrace both of those if I'm going to learn from the mistakes and the success of my ancestors.

> I would ask you to give our children the opportunity to know the whole truth, no matter how ugly, about our nation's past, so that they can learn from those mistakes, and we as a society can move forward with a commitment to make our future brighter.

* * *

In a stunning victory for students, a California court declared in May 2025 that Temecula's CRT ban violates students' educational rights. Pointing to the district's vague definition of CRT, the presiding judge said, "Teachers are left to self-censor and potentially over-correct, depriving the students of a fully informed education."[13]

According to the attorney for the jubilant students and teachers, it is the first ruling of its kind in the nation.

* * *

But whether Temecula schools will face a brighter future remains unknown. With Komrosky back, will educators worn out by the hostile environment leave the district, as some have claimed they might? Will Tim Thompson's PAC carry new Christian nationalists to victory in upcoming school board elections? They'll have the money. Eric Trump was a VIP at Thompson's May 2024 PAC fundraiser. Tickets for a meet-and-greet went for a cool thousand.

The story of Temecula must include Komrosky and Thompson. But it also can't be told without spotlighting the community, the parents, teachers, and students who have refused to quit.

Who refuse to erase the past. Who pull the past into the present.

Who are determined that Temecula's students learn painful truths that will change them as they march into their future.

12

JUST PEOPLE

Jerrell, my former third-grade student, rarely put pencil to paper. Seldom would he open a book or attempt even basic math. He'd try an assignment only if it appealed to him; encouraging, pushing, coaxing, or insisting had no effect whatsoever. When he occasionally would try classwork, it was according to his own plan, on his own timeline. His academic skills were desperately low. I suspected a learning disability, but his parent would not allow us to conduct tests to find out.

Despite his extreme difficulties, my greater concern was his submerged anger, which usually led to self-sabotage. I couldn't always predict when his quiet seething would bubble over, but when it did, he'd go from sunny to destructive in a flash. He sometimes destroyed other people's things, but usually turned his hurtful actions onto himself. I had a sense that if this bright child could get the help he needed, his desire to engage with classwork could follow. His utter refusal to attempt most academic work struck me as his way of taking control of one tiny part of his world. His listening comprehension was exceptional, so I just hoped he was absorbing *something* as he occupied himself with his own game plan.

Jerrell loved art. While others worked on math and reading, Jerrell snipped mounds of paper bits, pilfered my Scotch tape, and left uncapped markers scattered around the room. His creations were mystifying, nothing like what third graders usually produced. Once, he crafted a gas mask from a paper plate and two small paper cups, and wore it out to recess for a week. He made long, wispy figures out of toilet paper, eerie faces with no mouth, and body parts attached with staples.

One day, I couldn't handle the mess anymore and told him that artists have a *studio* where they create, instead of making piles in their kitchens and bedrooms. I kept him in at recess for a few minutes, and as we Googled images of "artist studio," his eyes popped wide.

"YES!" he cried, when I asked if he'd like a classroom version of his own.

With paint, an empty desk, tape, and large sections of cardboard from disassembled boxes, he busied himself, and a few classmates helped him when they finished their assignments. No one complained that I was letting Jerrell paint while the rest of them were working on academics. Maybe they were relieved he'd taken a break from ruining the communal markers.

Once the "studio" was finished, Jerrell's artwork changed. Instead of fashioning his floaty, twelve-inch translucent figures with stapled-on appendages, he made a flat, life-size replica of himself. He called it "Little J." Little J even had "bones" (giant-size popsicle sticks) so its arms and legs could bend.

Little J was very popular with the other kids, who encouraged Jerrell by embracing the paper version of his troubled self.

One day when Jerrell was angry with me (a daily occurrence, multiple times), he grabbed Little J and threw him in the trash. A quiet kid pulled Little J back out and sat him in Jerrell's chair. Jerrell seized Little J again, crumpling him; without speaking, a different child rescued the paper boy and put him back in the chair.

Finally, Jerrell snatched Little J, ripped his head off, tore the trunk into bits, and stomped on the paper scraps. The class cried out in genuine horror. Once Jerrell was calm again, he began making a new version of Little J, reusing the original torn arms and legs and making a new head and torso.

My students heaped love onto Jerrell, via Little J. They complimented Little J's shirt that was identical to Jerrell's, down to the pocket. They made room for Little J to sit next to them during class meetings. They invited Jerrell and Little J to play with them at recess. They asked if Little J could have lunch in the cafeteria so they could show him off to other classes.

Late one afternoon, two of my students who attended the after-school program popped in to say hi. As they helped me move Jerrell's art studio to a different location in the room, Carmela said, "Hey, where's Little J? I want to sit him in the chair, so when Jerrell comes tomorrow, he'll be surprised."

Miguel said, "Yeah, I think Jerrell would like that."

I looked at these two young children. Where does such sweetness come from?

"You're both so kindhearted," I said. "What do you think helps you to be so kind to Jerrell?" I didn't add, "because I know he doesn't always make it easy."

Miguel looked quizzically at me, as if it were obvious.

"Because I think he's lonely."

* * *

Certainly, there's plenty I did wrong with Jerrell. If I'd been a different teacher, maybe I could have enticed him to do more schoolwork, or been successful at convincing his mother to allow an assessment for her child. He likely would have qualified for extra help. Part of being a teacher is forgiving yourself for the myriad ways you fall short.

I'm proud of everything I poured into being a teacher—creativity, passion, integrity, and commitment. But I'm as proud of my efforts to teach empathy and other social-emotional skills as I am of anything else I did during all those years. I wasn't alone; for nearly twenty years, all adults at my school were trained in and committed to an antibullying program that was grounded in compassion, communication, and conflict resolution skills. We practiced building empathy with kids, and I think that's a big part of what helped my students want to connect with Jerrell instead of exclude him for being different.

It's a powerful thing to ponder.

Because helping young children broaden their perspective, consider others, stretch themselves to see that another might be in need, understand what someone else might be feeling—that's *everything.* It's hard to imagine something that could have a greater healing impact on a child, a classroom community, a world.

* * *

"So what made you decide to meet with me?" I asked Quinn, a teacher who is transgender.

"Because I have a lot of privilege."

I blinked in surprise.

"I'm white," she continued. "I live in a fairly safe location. I have a good job, and I'm comfortable. The people with privilege are the ones with the ability to do activism most easily. Yes, it makes me feel a little vulnerable, but I have the power to do it. So I feel like I should."

Quinn transitioned several years ago, remaining in the position she'd held for many years. A major reason she decided to transition was because of her own kids.

"What message does that send to my kids—'Hold off being your authentic self for other people'?"

She had a rough road for a while but says she can now start to breathe and just focus on having a regular life. She made it clear, though, that "much happier" doesn't mean "easy."

"If you're straight and cisgender, the pandemic created a lot of anxiety. But most of us trans and gender-nonconforming people are dealing with that level of anxiety every day. It's like the pandemic never stopped for us because it went from the pandemic to *this.* We went from people starting to affirm trans identities, to backsliding into overt hostility and discrimination that's becoming normalized. It's really dangerous.

"So yeah, I have to use my voice."

* * *

Quinn serves on her district's LGBTQ+ advisory committee, where district teachers and staff discuss issues relevant to LGBTQ+ students and employees. The committee primarily focuses on students and was instrumental in creating a county-wide Pride prom.

"It was *beautiful*," she said. "Good stuff is happening here, too."

Despite the good stuff, the fact that the LGBTQ+ committee is headed by a straight, white, cisgender man, a high-level administrator, is problematic for Quinn.

"It's not that he's bad," she explained. "He's an ally in spirit, but a very ignorant ally. When we bring in issues that are affecting the LGBTQ community, there are lots of microaggressions. He'll say things like, 'Well, I WAS in a good mood before this meeting.'"

Ouch.

If the high-level administrator had a transgender child and knew the cumulative pain caused by microaggressions, would he still joke that the *real* problem is queer people raising issues?

At one advisory committee meeting, a parent was invited as a guest speaker. She talked about her neurodivergent child, who went through a period of expressing the opposite gender.

"The mother spent a great deal of time setting herself up as this really caring, progressive, open-minded person. So I was already on guard, because usually when somebody is talking themselves up that much, I wonder why they feel the need to make themselves have such impeccable character."

After the mother laid the groundwork establishing that character, she used her allotted thirty minutes to assert that the medical establishment pressured her to help her child transition. She presented "research" filled with debunked theories, statistics untethered to credible studies, and claims with no citations backing them.

"She said things like, '80 percent of gay and lesbian people at some point think they're trans.' I have no idea where she got that from."

The mother wrapped up by saying schools need to inform parents when queer kids come out to them. Then she referred everyone to the website of an anti-trans organization, one that uses pseudoscience to make its case.

"It was a long time for me to sit there," said Quinn. "I was biting my tongue, trying to be polite. Before I could say anything, the [high-level administrator] said, 'Wow, that's so interesting! I'm really glad you shared. I'm definitely going to check out these resources. . . . Would you be interested in joining the committee?'

"This was on Zoom, and I sent a chat to [the administrator], saying, 'Absolutely NO. If this woman joins, I'm leaving. She has no business on this committee.'"

After the administrator finished praising the woman, Quinn began speaking. Courteous yet assertive, she acknowledged the difficulty of the woman's journey with her child. Then she pointed out that resources the woman recommended were anti-trans.

"She used intellectual dishonesty to make it sound like lots of people detransition," Quinn told me. "Most people who *do* detransition do it because it's really hard to go through all that labor and still be treated like a second- or third-class citizen. Mostly, transitioners who have lots of dissatisfaction have it *not* because they're trans, but because people treat us like garbage."

Nobody on the committee chimed in to support Quinn's points. Afterward, a few members emailed, saying they were glad she'd spoken up, but a few others wrote to say, "Well, we need to hear all sides."

Quinn's response is, "Would you have a flat-earther come talk about environmental policy at our school? If someone's being intellectually dishonest and making shit up, they have no place on this committee."

The committee now felt unsafe to her, especially after no members had come to her defense. Later on, though, people eventually agreed that the guest speaker's presentation had been inappropriate.

"And it also led to recognition that we need to be more careful about who we have come in and speak."

It seems so *obvious*. It has to be exhausting for those who must remain constantly on guard, forever enlightening others about how the world looks from where they stand. I remember the Black parent who agreed to talk with me about blatant racism in her child's school district. Then I heard nothing until she sent this message: "I'm really over talking to people about what's happening. Or trying to convince people that no one has a right to deny another person's humanity. Good luck."

I didn't attempt to change her mind. I'm glad she was so blunt. Sometimes "blunt" is the way things are absorbed and remain forever.

* * *

The fact that an anti-trans person could be welcomed into the safe space of the LGBTQ+ advisory had a deep impact on Quinn. But she also recognizes positive developments. When her union secured legal protections for gender expression in the contract, it enabled her to transition; without the protections, transitioning might have meant losing her job. For the most part, colleagues and students have been "super supportive." The successful Pride prom helped her bond with the more understanding committee members. Since a few years ago, when racist incidents in her district led to a grand jury report, things have been "pretty good at this district, overall."

"But we have people like this in our community who are emboldened to do things they would not have done five years ago. And now they have all the narratives to use from these politicians."

Even in a relatively liberal region of a relatively liberal state, it's difficult for some people to just blend with the background and live their quiet lives.

"I'm really glad I transitioned," Quinn said. "I knew there would be a lot of new issues to deal with, but most of those are because we live in a transphobic, homophobic society, not because I'm unhappy with who I am.

"I think that's my biggest point I wish people understood. Yeah, trans people still have mental health issues. But it's because of minority stress. It's not because we're mentally damaged or fragile. We're really, really strong. I wish there was more focus on that rather than that there's something 'wrong' with us. There's nothing wrong with us, other than that people don't like us because of who we are.

"We're just part of the human experience, like ADHD or autism or other types of neurodivergence and sexualities other than what hetero people think of as 'normal.' All of these are normal, just not *common*. But show me a person who's not unusual in some way."

The broader our experience, the fuzzier the idea of "normal" becomes. "Normal" compared with whom? Who determines who is normal and abnormal? Does only the majority get to rest in the comfort of being normal? How far beyond the majority's edge can a person lean before they become "other"?

As Quinn implied, aren't we all somehow "other" to somebody?

"Other" is a lonely place to be. But when we come to understand the needs of people different from ourselves, we can cross the bridge from "other" to "connected." And after thirty-two years in the classroom, I know that developing kids' capacity for empathy is what builds that bridge.

* * *

Nestled among rolling hills is the peaceful town of Paso Robles, not far inland from California's central coast. The gentle countryside is dotted with magnificent coast live oaks, for which "El Paso de Robles"—the Pass of the Oaks—was named. The oaks' gnarled branches spread wide into giant umbrellas that offer shade from bright summer sun. Those same knobby limbs rain acorns in the fall, acorns the Native Salinan people once pounded into flour. Their ancient bedrock mortars remain—on hillsides of golden grass, slabs of stone with worn cup-shaped holes, littered with soil and bits of plant debris.

In Paso Robles—which locals anglicize to rhyme with "nobles"—the story once again starts with the school board.

* * *

Joshua is a longtime Paso Robles teacher, and when we first met in his classroom, I was charmed by his ease with students. As kids milled about during the passing period, Joshua's jokey banter and patient answers to questions made it clear he enjoys high schoolers. A quiet student asked to continue a project in an adjacent workroom, and Joshua gently nodded approval. He was casual and calm, but I glimpsed a feistiness when he popped over to his computer.

"It'll just take a second—I'm working on this email to an administrator who just doesn't get it."

I smiled. Easygoing and friendly, yet spirited. My kind of person.

When we met up later, Joshua spoke of the makeup of recent school boards.

"In 2021, that board was one of vitriol. Every time they met, they were making the newspapers with contentious issues."

It was hardly an exaggeration.

In late 2020, when trustee Chris Arend assumed the president's chair on the Paso Robles school board, members of the board received two letters. Arend, who, as we saw in an earlier chapter, would be hired two years later as the CRT expert for distant Temecula Valley Unified School District, was slammed by the letter writers for his lengthy, published treatise denying the existence of systemic racism. In the summer of 2021, with Arend as board president, Paso Robles became one of the first districts in California to ban CRT.

An opinion piece in the local paper criticized Arend for saying that a study of "gangster sub-culture, broken families, fatherless homes" could help explain high arrest rates of Black people.

"It's easy to understand why Mr. Arend might not be cognizant of any of this," continued the writer. "It's likely that he or his family has never suffered from the consequences of redlining, endured the racist epithets schoolchildren heard on their way to class, or experienced housing discrimination."[1]

A Paso Robles teacher spoke with the *Los Angeles Times* about teaching ethnic studies in the new climate. "It's difficult to teach a class that's so much under the microscope. I have community members who've asked that there be cameras placed in the classroom. . . . Parents and board members have been asking for detailed descriptions of assignments, and that's never happened before."[2]

An English teacher spoke to me about starting *To Kill a Mockingbird* with her students.

"I opened up the unit discussing Jim Crow laws and what was going on in the Jim Crow South—segregation, discrimination, etc. A parent got mad, and called and said, 'We need to meet because you're teaching my son critical race theory.'

"I met with my administrator and the parent. The administrator said, 'Can you define what critical race theory is?' The man couldn't.

The English teacher told the dad, "It's very important that when we read from a different time period, we know the historical context. Jim Crow and segregation *happened*. That's history. I'm not framing it in any certain way. I'm presenting the facts of history."

She told me that she was about to start that book again this year.

"The fact is that anytime you teach about race at *all* now, it's 'critical race theory.' The parents freak out. I'm sure there will be issues again this year."

I sighed on her behalf. She was probably right.

And I bet this year's complaining parents won't be able to define CRT either.

* * *

President Arend published his paper disputing systemic racism in late 2020. The board passed their ban on CRT in mid-2021.

With those two occurrences still fresh, a defining event for the town took place.

A month after the board banned CRT, a student entered a teacher's room between classes. He was speaking with a friend, then jumped up and yanked a large Pride flag from the wall. He, with others, took off running. When the shocked teacher went after them, one student returned. But the leader raced to the bathroom, where he tried to flush the three-by-five-foot banner down the toilet. When that didn't work, some kids defecated on it and tried to flush it again.

As if that weren't enough, the students took *video* of their efforts and posted the whole thing on social media. Word of the incident spread widely and rapidly.

Teacher Joshua told me, "I don't think it was about targeting the teacher. It was about targeting the *flag*. All the kids knew it was wrong, and akin to a hate crime."

The student body recognized the wrong, but the district leadership remained silent. Teenagers waited for the district response to the public targeting of the LGBTQ+ community.

They waited.

A week passed.

Two weeks.

Finally, the district released a statement condemning the hateful acts. But it simultaneously announced that classroom Pride flags were now limited to a two-by-two-foot maximum size. Standard indoor flags are two by three feet, so teachers currently displaying Pride flags in their rooms would exceed the new maximum. They'd have to take them down.

The end result: Pride flags were removed after the act of hate. The subtext: Display of a Pride flag was to blame for the incident.

"It felt like an attack on student identities," wrote one student in the school's newsmagazine. "Rather than protecting them after a hate crime, the district was censoring them."[3]

The Equity Club students were astounded both by the district's lengthy silence and by the weak response. They were also furious, claiming that a disparity in the district's discipline system had been exposed.

The students had waited long enough for the adults. It was time for action.

* * *

> This movement—this fight—may have started with a hate crime, but it will end with [an] improved future for queer students on this campus, through the efforts of students wanting change for the next generation.
>
> Student editor in chief, Paso Robles High
> *Crimson* newsmagazine, November 2021[4]

The title of the student newsmagazine's next issue read, "Coming Out Against Hate." The cover showed an unidentified student from behind, with arms outstretched, wearing a rainbow flag like a cape. Shown in mid-stride, the student is running, or maybe dancing. The rainbow is the only splash of color in the picture.

Filling the pages of the issue were *nine* articles about the flag incident's effect on LGBTQ+ students. In the words of one student writer,

> The Pride flag is an indicator of a safe space. On a campus where the students' identities are seen as a punchline, acceptance is a rarity when it should be the norm. . . .
>
> Forced to advocate for themselves, students ranging from freshmen to seniors have spearheaded the call for awareness with the 'Coming Out

> Against Hate' event . . . in hopes of initiating changes that could ripple across generations of classes to come.[5]

The student outcry was a long time coming, explained one teen journalist.

"It was simply the tipping point," she wrote, "after years of insufficient support, administrative inaction, and steadily increasing disrespect and hate."[6]

After teachers were directed to remove regular-sized Pride flags from classroom walls, students grabbed markers and paint and made colorful signs on letter-sized paper. Messages reading "Love over hate" and "You're valid" were taped up around campus.

LGBTQ+ student leaders then decided to hold a public forum. It would be an educational event, they said, enlightening others about the impacts of homophobia and transphobia that queer students face at school. Students would share their stories, show a short film on the challenges of high school for queer kids, and end with a Q&A.

As the student editor in chief wrote, "LGBTQIA+ students would come out again, but this time, it wouldn't be to define themselves. It would be to defend themselves—to come out against hate."[7]

Students were both excited and nervous.

"I'm really proud of the fact that so many people are brave enough to come up against the adversity that is very obvious here," said a senior. "We might get a ton of hate for this. We might get hate-crimed ourselves. But we can't let this continue."[8]

A letter from Paso Robles high schoolers published in the *San Luis Obispo Tribune* read,

> When you are a high school student in the LGBTQ community, you walk into every classroom and school bathroom not knowing if you've entered a safe space. You endure angry stares, hurtful comments, and relentless assaults of microaggressions that erode our mental health and self-confidence. It is exhausting. It is oppressive. It is unacceptable.
>
> And so we're coming out against hate.[9]

On October 20, 2021, the student-organized "Coming Out Against Hate" forum was held in the evening, in the high school's performing arts center. About 360 parents, grandparents, current and former students, siblings, friends, administrators, and faculty members crammed into the 250-seat theater. Overflow audience members leaned against walls, sat on the floor, or jammed folding chairs into pockets of available space.

"This was right in the middle of COVID, so everyone wore masks," said Joshua. "The community flooded in to support these kids. I provided a rainbow mask for every person there, and it was a beautiful sight to see. That theater was one big rainbow from the audience to the stage."

Kids stood before peers and told their stories. As reported in the school newsmagazine, one queer student told the crowd that she came out to her whole family before the event so she could speak freely. She wanted to stand up so that future generations of students could feel safe on campus. An anonymous student asked a surrogate to read their story to the crowd, a speech about the fear of coming out, and the lingering emotional impact of the event that caused her to come out. Four students and their teacher danced to Lady Gaga's "Born This Way."

A senior explained why kids from homophobic homes need to find a welcoming place at school. A freshman shared a poem about alienation and refusing to be silenced, while a sophomore stressed that LGBTQIA+ people need to be seen as human. After a student named Eve declared that "knowledge is power only when we *act* on that knowledge," she presented a list of demands to the district.[10] One was that a public apology be issued for the district leadership's feeble response.

As the Q&A drew to a close, the crowd stood and cheered for the students. Members of the school's Floral Club later presented flowers to each of the fourteen high school speakers, two of whom were proxy readers for students who wished to remain anonymous.

The drama teacher, who helped run the event, was quoted in the school's newsmagazine: "It was very emotional seeing the community come together. I am hoping this will create some momentum for change."[11]

After the event, Eve shared some reflections. Though only a sophomore, she was president of the Equity Club, and a driving force behind the forum. She'd also been an emcee.

"It's a very scary experience," said Eve. "It's not knowing if you're going to be outed to unsupportive family members. It's not knowing if someone's going to jump you on the way home because you wore a pride pin to class. . . . It's being scared to voice your opinions or come out."[12]

"LGBT isn't a category," she asserted. "It isn't something vulgar or gross. It isn't something you need to hide from your kids. . . . We aren't a belief. We aren't a political idea. We're not something controversial. We are a group of people."

A group of people.

Just—*people.*

* * *

I remember what Joshua told me about coming to better understand the needs of queer kids.

"This experience has helped me get around my preconceived notions about transgender students and nonbinary students. Now I'm like, 'Why wouldn't anybody else get it?'

"[Because] when you really meet real people and realize they're just like me, they're *people*—then you're not threatened anymore. It's made me a better person."

* * *

After sophomore Eve delivered the students' demands, the district demonstrated their intent to do better. Two days after the event, the superintendent met with the forum's twelve speakers whose names were known. They identified eight target areas for policy change, education, or training. Three weeks after the forum, the superintendent and assistants released a "Next Steps" action plan.

Thanks to the students, a district LGBTQ+ task force was formed. Once a month, LGBTQ+ kids and allies would meet with teachers, site administrators, and district administration to discuss issues on campus. Another of the kids' demands was about safety for transgender students. Joshua said, "PE is a nightmare for transgender or nonbinary kids. We need a gender-neutral changing area in the locker rooms."

Teacher training also made the list of "next steps," as did antibullying training for students. There would be education for all on the rights of LGBTQ+ students at school, and improved discipline and enforcement around actions of hate.

Students expressed dismay about the health education they'd received in middle and high school, saying, "We don't see ourselves represented there at all." Joshua said the district realized that its sex-ed curriculum was fifteen years out of date and immediately adopted a new, up-to-date curriculum with an LGBTQ+ component.

"That came *straight* out of the kids' task force meeting," he said.

* * *

Two days before the forum, the district upped the size of permissible indoor flags to two by three feet. Students still wanted the larger three-by-five-foot size of the defiled flag, but the district wouldn't allow it. However, an anonymous source was inspired by the forum to donate money for purchasing two-by-three-foot Pride flags for any teacher who wanted one. According to the student newsmagazine, about fifty teachers now post a rainbow flag in their classroom.

John Laird, the first openly gay California state senator, represents the area encompassing Paso Robles. Laird met with the twelve nonanonymous student speakers a month after the forum.

A statement from Laird reads, in part, "In recognition of [the students'] bravery, their efforts were acknowledged on the Senate floor. . . . Witnessing these young folks realize their own power was a truly inspiring experience. It was an important reminder for myself just as much as them on what a collective voice can accomplish in the face of what seems like daunting odds."[13]

In September 2023, two years after the forum, California's governor signed Senate Bill 857, authored by Senator Laird. The law requires the state superintendent of public instruction to convene an LGBTQ+ advisory task force, to identify the needs of LGBTQ+ students and make recommendations for creating a supportive learning environment. The law places students at the center of the discussion.

Laird's statement ends, "It is high time that we ensure California's students have a rightful place at the table when it comes to matters of equity and inclusion. They should not have to demand a seat only after a distressing incident occurs and makes headlines."[14]

* * *

There's still work to be done. Doug, an attorney whose focus is inclusivity in schools, spoke of those who would burn books.

"What they said is, 'We don't want you to just remove all the LGBTQ books from the high school library, because we know if you just remove them, they'll go in the superintendent's garage. And a few months later, he'll sneak them back in. We want to see them burned.'"

The idea was proposed by a parent, and a few board members supported it. That parent is now seated on the school board.

So there's that.

Moms for Liberty is active in the region. Two Moms for Liberty members are on the neighboring school board, and one teacher said the Paso Robles board members are being "fed" by the Moms. Attorney Doug said there is talk of the Moms establishing a new headquarters in the county.

Despite the progress sparked by teen activism, the board tried in 2022 to change district policy and remove antibullying language geared toward protecting LGBTQ+ students.

Again, the community rose in outrage. After the outcry, the board dropped the idea, though they passed a resolution requiring the district to not replace "traditional gender-specific names," such as "mother" and "father." A move to replace terms like that had never been on the table.

The county's Teacher of the Year was Paso Robles's ethnic studies teacher. In a local publication, he said,

> I don't think that the school board . . . is sensitive to issues of bullying against LGBTQ students, or racism that exists on campus, or the many forms of bullying and bigotry that take place. . . .
>
> I think the school board right now is much more interested in fighting imaginary culture wars than in actually strengthening the educational programs and resources at the high school and throughout the district. The school board right now needs to listen to students.[15]

Listen.

The school board should know better. "Listen" is a word teachers say constantly to kids.

* * *

For now, many agree that the power of the student-district LGBTQ+ task force has been diluted. It was changed from a "task force" to a "committee," and since "committees" are public, school board members can now attend. A few on the board are vehemently anti-trans. Students don't want to show up where they no longer feel safe.

Joshua said, "It changed the whole tenor. . . . It's a very uncomfortable committee now."

A "committee" formed to listen to kids. And now those kids are afraid to come.

But as younger students step into spaces that older students created for them in late 2021, perhaps they'll insist on grabbing the microphone, on forcing adults to listen.

They know what to do. They've seen how it's done.

* * *

Attorney Doug made me laugh when he said, "The ACLU is on my speed dial." An energetic, fiery advocate for students, Doug is still hopeful about the future of schools in Paso Robles, and beyond.

"The silver lining is that it woke people up," he told me. "And people said, 'NO!'"

He says lesbian and gay teachers who weren't out before felt they had to come out to support the kids.

"That was really important. It was very emotional for them," he said. "And the librarian, who isn't LGBTQ, was adamant about putting queer-friendly books in spots with more visibility."

This was *after* the push to ban and then burn books.

"I do see movement. . . . The new president of the board is saying, 'Let's treat everybody with civility.' What I'm trying to tell you is the teachers and parents have finally stepped up. . . . We now have leaders."

Teacher Joshua also feels hope, despite the changes in the task-force-now-committee.

"Four of those 2021 school board members were up in the next election, and all four got replaced. The community came out. . . . The teachers, the kids—everybody rallied to get rid of these toxic board members. We managed to get four intelligent, invested . . . nonextremist people on the board who have kids in the system, who are not out to try and hurt any kids.

"If I was going to give any message, it would be to tell people that . . . we all should have the same rights. . . . And that in order to protect the children, we have to keep an eye on our school boards. There's some dangerous ideology that's trying to force itself into our public education system and erase history."

* * *

In one city I visited, I was invited to be a guest speaker at a high school's Rainbow Club meeting. I didn't want to speak, though—I wanted to listen. I told the teenagers about this writing project and asked what they thought I should make sure to include. I was unprepared for their vulnerability, and for their eagerness to help me see their world.

A senior spoke of history I'd never known, of Berlin's Eldorado nightclub during Adolf Hitler's rise to power. The student recommended a documentary about the Eldorado—a gathering place for gay and trans people—and Germany's history of burning queer-related books. Another student urged me to remember that some people don't have romantic feelings or sexual feelings. There are many ways to be queer, the student said.

Many kids spoke of stereotypes, and about social pressure. When one teen realized he was part of the LGBTQ+ community, he said he felt like he was supposed to act *very* queer—to come out to everyone, to look and act "queer enough" to be accepted by LGBTQ+ peers, and to be believed by straight kids.

"A phrase I hear a lot . . . is, 'You don't look queer,'" he said. "Hearing these things can be very detrimental to queer people . . . who are just discovering themselves. . . . They lose their sense of self because they feel that being queer must become their whole personality, rather than a *part* of their identity."

The complexities of figuring out how to live authentically.

"When characters in a show have one queer friend, it's a stereotype. It reduces them to one-dimensional characters," said one student.

"Don't just talk about 'queer books' or 'queer movies,'" said another. "It's just *regular life*."

A refrain I heard was, "I don't want to be reduced to only queerness." One student expressed it as, "Think of being LGBTQ as a character *trait*. It's not the whole character."

Many heads nodded, and someone murmured, "It's not the most interesting thing about me."

Afterward, one student said he wanted teachers to know that small things matter. He said that a teacher who'd always shown him respect accidentally used the wrong pronouns once, in front of the class. The student was barely fazed, but after class, the teacher approached the boy and apologized. It meant the world to him.

"I will always feel safe and appreciated in his classroom."

It's what every student deserves.

And isn't it all that any of us wants?

* * *

On a Friday night in January 2023, I ducked into the Paso Robles High Performing Arts Center and sat near the side wall. Though it was a public gathering and the ethnic studies teacher had specifically invited me, I felt like an interloper. No one here knew me, and young people would be sharing very personal stories.

It had been a little more than a year since the flag incident, and queer Paso Robles students were this time holding a gathering called "Stories of Pride." The Equity Club president contrasted the purpose of this event with that of the previous year's forum.

"We are not here because of tragedy," she said. "We are here because of *legacy*."[16]

A recent survey from the Trevor Project included the finding that over half of queer youth surveyed had seriously considered suicide. That thought was never far from my mind as I looked at the kids on the stage, gearing up to share their struggles, but also to celebrate their identity.

This time, students were joined on the stage by adult community members and a couple of teachers. There were rainbows, sequins, banners, pearls, and a corset. I listened, waving the tiny rainbow flag I'd been handed by a trans junior in a satiny green gown. It was about the size of my hand—too small to represent the big feelings inside. I waved it energetically to compensate.

A middle-aged gay man touched his string of pearls, which had once been his grandma's. He remembered falling apart in front of her as a young person, sobbing, "Why can't I be *normal*? Why can't I just be *normal*?" Her response changed him forever.

"Why the f would you want to be normal when you can be marvelous?" She'd given him permission to be himself.

A twenty-eight-year-old teacher, her rainbow-sequined jacket twinkling and flashing under the bright lights, read a letter she'd written to her twelve-year-old self.

"You will know who you are, and have the chance to be that queer adult living a beautifully colorful life you wish you could have seen back when you were twelve. The good times are just over the rainbow. Just you wait."

A recent alum wore a black shirt proclaiming "Support Indigenous resistance." They said, "I mourn the loss of not getting to know myself as an out and supported queer trans teenager. But my journey isn't over, and neither is our collective struggle. . . . I came here tonight to say 'thank you' to all of you queer and trans relatives, from the depths of my big, gay heart."

There were stories of loss, and of triumph. There was pain, self-discovery, fear, and solidarity. During the Q&A, one question especially pierced:

"How can I learn to love myself?"

How does *any* of us learn to love ourselves?

* * *

Partly, I think, it's when we are lucky enough to see ourselves reflected in the love that others have for us. The love of others sometimes can help us believe we might merit that love. But when some of us are met with disdain, grimaces, and insults and can't see love reflected back, it's the job of the community to fill that gap, to offer the care and acceptance that each of us deserves.

I felt it that night, in that theater of strangers who somehow felt familiar. We cheered, whooped, and waved our tiny flags. I wasn't the only one who cried.

We listened.

We learned.

Young people stood before us, telling us of their lives. Many of the feelings were painful, and as we listened and gasped, empathy grew. We imagined what their futures would be.

What they *could* be.

Some people experience empathy spontaneously, unprompted. They simply know how another might feel.

But most of us need some help. We need people to share their stories, to give us hints of what is inside. When we listen, we can stretch ourselves to understand, to offer support. And to remind them they deserve love.

Especially with kids. Kids need to know there is a place for them, that they belong in this world, that they deserve to stand tall, to be appreciated exactly as they are.

Those Paso Robles kids were able to extend beyond themselves, despite knowing full well that the world beyond themselves is often not kind.

They stepped forward, outside safe circles, and invited others to join them.

The wonder of that still sends me soaring.

* * *

Storms had raged for weeks. When I drove out of town the morning after "Stories of Pride," I saw flooded riverbanks, places where the channel could no longer contain what coursed through it.

It was exactly how I felt.

The "Stories of Pride" were too big to be contained. Wonder, promise, mystery, beauty—the greatness of young people, and of those who nurture them. It all spilled over.

Hope overflowed as I remembered words, faces, cheers, community. There was brightness everywhere—brilliant blue sky, rich green that carpeted soft hills, and winter sunlight that made everything sparkle.

I opened the windows of my Prius, and the bite of that January morning stung my cheeks, whipped my hair, filled my lungs. I felt so *alive.*

Overwhelmed by such beauty. Such brightness.

And hope.

I felt such *hope.*

AFTERWORD

I was nearly four hundred miles from home in early 2024, in Los Angeles to celebrate a colleague who had won a state human rights award. As some teacher friends and I stood chatting during the meet-and-greet before the awards dinner, I noticed someone watching me from across the circle. My award-winning colleague was talking to the person, and both were smiling at me.

So I crossed the circle and asked, "Do we know each other?"

When I got an even bigger smile as my answer, I glanced at the name tag. The name was vaguely familiar.

Suddenly I gasped and cried out, "WHAT?! It's YOU?!" Then we threw our arms around each other as I exclaimed over and over, "I can't *believe* this!"

It was our first time meeting. I'd learned Olive's name a year earlier, when I read an article about the hundreds of people who'd shown up to a school board meeting clamoring for this nonbinary teacher to be fired. The reason? *The New York Times* had quoted them as saying, "Sometimes [queer kids] need protection from their own parents."

After reading the article, I had immediately jumped on social media to find Olive and message my support. I said that if they wanted to talk with me for this project, I'd welcome it, but that I was mostly writing just to say that I was in solidarity from afar.

Olive responded appreciatively but said that they couldn't speak to a reporter again, since they were too traumatized from the death threats after the article in the *Times*. There was certainly no point in explaining that I wasn't a reporter.

I checked in with Olive a few times over the next months to say I hoped things were going better. Over the course of the next year, I often thought about Olive, trying to imagine how a person who had experienced death threats and an enflamed hometown community might be faring. It felt too intrusive to keep contacting someone I didn't know to ask how they were doing, especially one who'd experienced such turmoil. So instead, I just wondered and hoped.

But even my wildest hopes fell far short of the reality I saw a year later in Los Angeles. Here was Olive—face lit up, filled with life and energy, with a demeanor that exuded power, grace, and light. I learned that Olive was in Los Angeles because they, too, had won a state human rights award in social justice, for "persistently [fighting] to eliminate stereotyping, discrimination, harassment, and hate-motivated violence directed toward LGBTQ+ students, fellow educators, and others."[1] Even in the hardest days after the *Times* article, Olive had never left the classroom. They had even continued leading the GSA.

The educators I met during this project had different ways of coping with their trauma. Some told me they might leave teaching, but I never equated potential "leaving" with "failure." Turning away from any traumatizing setting can be a way of reclaiming power, setting boundaries, or protecting well-being, and for some, leaving is an expression of strength. For others, the path to healing is to remain. Olive's path was to stay in the classroom and in the position of leadership of the GSA. Withdrawing from the public eye for a time had been necessary, a deliberate act of care and self-protection. But Olive was never defeated. As they explained, "That strength never left. It simply took a form that wasn't visible from the outside."

As I was still dazed from this shocking surprise encounter, Olive told me that because of all the fallout from the *Times* article, they had entered a doctoral program in educational leadership, with a focus on the experiences of queer educators.

* * *

Recently, Olive agreed to an interview. Here, from the vantage point of two and a half years later, is what Olive had to say after the events that had altered their life forever:

The backlash made something painfully clear: what happened to me wasn't even about me. It was about the systems that try to silence LGBTQ+ educators and youth, especially those who are Indigenous, queer, and outspoken. Starting a doctoral program gave me a way to understand that harm, name it, and work toward changing it. I didn't want to just recover; I wanted to research the very conditions that made the backlash possible and understand how and why educators sometimes are able to thrive despite these conditions.

I'm still teaching. I'm still here. The strength to keep going came from my family and my students—especially my queer and trans students. My students told everyone around them about the transformative power of a great teacher. I had days when I couldn't imagine walking into a boardroom ever again, and I also had days where laughter with my students was the only thing keeping me grounded at work. This incident galvanized my family's support for me and made it clear who my real friends were. I also channeled my energy into union work with CTA that felt deeply impactful. I leaned on radical community care, therapy, and storytelling. This incident was not one event either. I've been continuously targeted by alt-right news outlets since then.

Olive thinks they'll always be a teacher but might not stay forever in a traditional high school classroom.

There's nothing like building trust with students and watching them grow into their own voices. But I also feel pulled to do systems work: to mentor other educators, to shape curriculum, to push policy that actually protects queer youth and teachers. I want to keep building spaces where people can thrive.

Living here [in the Central Valley] feels different now. I'm more visible, but also more careful. I don't move through public spaces the same way I used to. Still, I've found new pockets of community—people who show up with quiet solidarity. There were folks I didn't know who were watching and reached out to say, "You're not alone." The board meeting revealed some of the ugliest parts of this place, but it also showed me who was willing to fight for something better. We are everywhere.

A lot of good came from this triggering experience. I built connections with educators and activists across the country—people who reached out not out of pity, but out of shared experience and collective vision. I deepened my own understanding of narrative, policy, and power. And most of all, I found clarity. I used to doubt whether I was doing enough to make radical change in my community. Now I know; I'm exactly where I need to be, doing work that matters.

* * *

When we say that public education is the cornerstone of our democracy, it's more than a cliché.

Learning for Justice's T. Jameson Brewer says,

> For our society to function and for citizens to engage in the democratic process, basic educational needs must be met, including, but not limited to, literacy and critical thinking. An educated workforce offers advantages to employers and furthers innovation and societal benefits for all. But schools are not merely places for workforce preparation.
>
> Schools are sites for exploration of ideas across a range of subject areas—math, science and technology, literature, social sciences, physical education and more—in the quest to facilitate individuals becoming the best they can and living fulfilling lives. And beyond individual self-actualization and upward mobility, education offers collective growth and progress for entire communities.[2]

When education is prioritized and available for everyone, regardless of income level, gender, race, orientation, ethnicity, ability, and immigration status, the entire *community* makes progress.

Public education is at the heart of our democracy.

* * *

It's surreal to think of all that has happened in public education since I began this project at the end of 2022. On the one hand, teachers in Temecula, California, are once again able to teach about Jim Crow and true history, thanks to a ruling by the California Court of Appeals. After an Oklahoma court ruled that it was unconstitutional to grant a public charter to a religious school, the U.S. Supreme Court's four-to-four deadlock failed to overturn the decision. Donald Trump has threatened to cut federal funding for public schools with diversity, equity, and inclusion programs, but a federal judge blocked those directives in April 2025.

And yet—

Trump has vowed to close the Department of Education, which oversees the federal funds used for extra support for low-income students. The department also funds resources and staffing for children with disabilities, so that they can receive the "free and appropriate public education" guaranteed them by the Individuals with Disabilities Education Act.

Trump's mission to deport millions of immigrants led some graduates and their families to stay home from graduation, fearful of being targeted by ICE. One of Trump's executive orders forbids K–12 schools from using federal money to "indoctrinate" children with "radical gender ideology and critical race theory."

Christian nationalists continue to rack up victories; two hours before I wrote the foregoing paragraph, the U.S. Supreme Court released its ruling blocking school officials in Maryland's Montgomery County from requiring young students to participate in lessons with books that conflict with their parents' religious beliefs. In other words, parents who don't want their young children to ever listen to a book that is LGBTQ+-inclusive can withdraw their child from those *public school* lessons.

Today, "religious beliefs" that LGBTQ+ people are an abomination can be honored in *public* schools. What stories will "religious beliefs" be allowed to block next? Books with heroic Black characters? Books with strong independent women? Books about Muslims? About true history? About the Holocaust? About people with disabilities? About immigrants?

About any one of us?

* * *

I think of Olive's words: "[It] revealed some of the ugliest parts of this place, but it also showed me who was willing to fight for something better. We are everywhere."

We are everywhere.

It's not easy to have hope right now. But if a teacher who was doxed and threatened with death sees brave fighters "everywhere," then maybe the rest of us can see them, too.

My last question for Olive was if, after everything, they had hope for the future of public education. This was their answer:

> Yes. I have real, grounded hope. Not because the system is working, but because I see students who are more awake and more powerful than I ever was at their age. I see educators resisting, dreaming, organizing. I see queer, Native, Black, brown, and trans youth refusing to be erased.
>
> Hope, for me, doesn't mean pretending things are okay. It means believing that we can still build something better and that we are building it, right now, in classrooms, in communities, in stories. That's where my hope lives.

In classrooms, in communities, in *stories.*

May our hope live there as well.

AUTHOR'S NOTE

In relating these stories, I supplemented teachers' narratives with countless hours of research. Interviewees' actual words comprise the dialogue, and there are no composite characters or events.

To protect educators' anonymity, I occasionally (though rarely) modified a minor personal detail, and almost always obscured precise locales. I changed all interviewees' names, except for those few who insisted I use their real names.

Regarding terminology and usage choices:

Black and **white** (for people)—I've capitalized "Black" but not "white." As explained by Marc Lacey, *The New York Times*' National editor in 2020, "For many people the capitalization of that one letter is the difference between a color and a culture. . . . They consider Black like Latino and Asian and Native American, all of which are capitalized."[1] In contrast, "white" doesn't connote a shared history and culture as Black does. It's also sometimes capitalized by hate groups. So I do not capitalize "white."

LGBTQ vs. **LGBTQ+** vs. **queer**—When quoting people, I used the term they use. When not directly quoting someone, I used "LGBTQ+" or "queer." In my research and in the conversations with educators, there was great variation in terms people used. Once a slur, "queer" is now "preferred by some LGBTQ+ people for its expansive and fluid nature, though others reject the word because of how it was used in the past."[2] It's "a word that describes sexual and gender identities other than straight and

> cisgender . . . sometimes used to express that sexuality and gender can be complicated, change over time, and might not fit neatly into either/or identities, like male or female, gay or straight."[3]
>
> Many of the young people I encountered, as well as some of the LGBTQ+ adults I met, favored the word "queer," so I asked if it was acceptable for me, a straight cisgender woman, to use the word. The consensus was that using "queer" was okay if the person being discussed self-identifies as queer, so I use both in the book.

I think of this book as a wartime love letter to public school educators and their students. My role in the narrative is not solely that of interviewer; I also serve as interpreter, translating the world of public education for non-teachers by weaving in my own classroom stories for context.

ACKNOWLEDGMENTS

Each person I interviewed is present in this book, whether each individual's story is typed into this final iteration or not. Every person I met, every perspective shared, and every story told shaped me into the person who wrote the book. I still marvel that these educators (plus a few community members and young adult students) entrusted me with their experiences and vulnerabilities. I hope they feel I've represented them faithfully. My forever-gratitude goes to Carina, Theresa, Lorena, Dana, Andy Hook, S. K., Adrienne Anila, Jenny H., Susan Noble, Damon, K. G., Michelle, H. T., Midwest Gina, Renee, Nancy Young, Steve Schwartz, Doug Heumann, Lance Mack, Clementine Morales, Quinn, Betsy, S. M.-W., Deon Hairston, Elisa, A. L., Rachel Cohen, Joshua Gwiazda, Deanna, Julie Geary, Geoffrey Land, Deb Sica, Olive Garrison, Danielle, and Andrea.

Working with a publisher like The New Press is the stuff of dreams. Their "About Us" page speaks of social justice, a more equitable world, defending democratic values, racial justice, inclusiveness, and the greater good; partnering with people who share these values has been an injection of hope in these demoralizing times. I'm so grateful to Nia Abram, who saw merit in my proposal and moved it forward. To my editor, Ben Woodward, endless thanks for your patience, your insight, your wisdom, and your good humor. My sincere gratitude goes to Melody Negron, mind-melding copyeditor Ashley Moore, and all the others associated with The New Press who work "to change the world, book by book."

Thank you to Evelyn Duffy at Open Boat Editing for coaching me into believing that I could tackle this topic. I'm grateful to author N. West Moss for her editing skills and good-natured guidance. Jane Friedman's course on writing a nonfiction book proposal and Deborah Davis's skill in editing were both invaluable; their knowledge made my proposal sparkle, which led The New Press to my manuscript. I'm so thankful for the generosity and expertise of each of these professionals. And Dave Eggers—I am so grateful to you.

To Briseis Sablan and to Oliver: Amazingly, you shared your thoughts, feelings, and advice with me long ago, when you were pretty young. Thank you for trusting me, and for helping me grow. To the young people I met as I traveled around California: I am grateful for your willingness to express yourselves with honesty, openness, and patience. (I'm still proud that I kept up with the *Heartstopper* conversation despite being a straight cisgender woman in her sixties.) Many thanks to Sandra Cox, MD, for allowing me to use her powerful words, and to Eve Barajas and the high school journalists from Paso Robles who so thoroughly covered the aftermath of the flag event in their student newsmagazine. You inspire me!

My world burst into color when I began writing for real in my early fifties. Writing Salon instructors Jenny Pritchett, Kathleen McClung, Elaine Beale, and Alison Luterman launched me as a writer, while Eileen Malone and Kathleen, through the Soul-Making Keats Literary Competition, nurtured the beginnings of my writerly self-confidence. Shizue Seigel of Write Now! SF Bay invited me to share my stories of teaching in the diverse Bay Area. At the Mendocino Coast Writers Conference, Susan Bono was sparked by my work and welcomed me as a legitimate member of the writers' community beyond the Bay Area. It was at the MCWC that I worked with authors Reyna Grande and Elizabeth Rosner. Learning from each of them has been a treasured life experience. To every one of these people, I extend deep gratitude.

Sarah Marxer, dear friend and brilliant writing partner, planted the seeds from which this project grew. Her countless hours of listening, encouraging, brainstorming, reading, and critiquing built the very foundation of this book. Sarah, you led the way for me with your genius writing on many of these same themes. I still can't believe we found each other in this world of writing; I am forever grateful, and can't wait until your book is finished and I'm holding it in my hands.

Blaze Farrar and Chivvis Moore, thank you for helping to shape sections of the narrative and for years of friendship, shared writing, and laughter. To my other Fort Mason writing buddies, including Sejal Patel, Barbara Ridley, Diane Simkin Demeter, Kim Steutermann Rogers, Devi Laskar, and especially JoAnne Tompkins: Thank you for your enthusiastic support and encouragement along the way. JoAnne, special thanks for your lovely words about this book. Lori Ostlund, thank you for reading my manuscript; your generosity toward fellow writers and to our world knows no bounds. To Kristi Hirst of Our Schools USA, I so appreciate your remarkable work and your willingness to read my manuscript. Michael Nguyen and Shannon Tom, thank you for connecting me with people I hoped to speak with. Kyle—thank you. You know why.

Deanna! You lived with me in college and somehow volunteered to do it again for this project. You and Paul repeatedly drove me long distances. You cooked vegetarian meals (so sorry, Paul), set me up in cozy guest quarters, talked with me about teaching, provided entertainment, and presented TWO dogs for my petting pleasure. "Thank you" doesn't touch it. I'm endlessly grateful to you for your support for this project, and for a lifetime of friendship and laughter.

Karen Boyden, you taught me how to be a teacher, which has been the source of great joy and purpose in my life. What miracle placed us together? Jen Vecchitto and Lori De St. Aubin, I *still* sometimes get teary when I remember how we staggered through distance teaching together as true companions. We are forever bonded as a triangle. Tracy Vernon, thank you for sharing many heart- and humor-filled vignettes of the teacher life with me. Marva Wilkins, thank you for helping me understand more about how things look from where you stand. Susan Marks, your alter-ego must have been a cheerleader in high school; a more enthusiastic and faithful supporter has never existed. Huge thanks for reading and giving feedback on so much of the manuscript, and for your continual encouragement. To "Principal John" Shimko—you've rescued me, inspired me, and shown me what true leadership and constant support look like. The time you cried out, *"And I'm not fucking around!"* on your first (still summer) day at our school remains one of my all-time favorite stories. You are forever my hero. To each of these educators: I treasure our friendship, and the opportunity to have worked alongside you.

My life is rich in people, and so many have extended themselves to support this endeavor. Steve, it meant so much to me that you asked to read the whole manuscript! Andy Alabran, thank you for sharing the importance of having laundry detergent commercials with men folding clothes; it pierced me in that moment, and I haven't been the same since. Mike Forte, Bobbie Webb, and Susan McDonough, thank you for your sincere and steady encouragement, along with Kathy Hallock, Patsy Paul, Pat Cull, Alexa Eurich, Lisa Rasler, and Diana Lopez. Don Norwalk, thank you for your support, and for being my Catholic consultant. Thank you to all my educator friends who responded on social media when I asked for teaching anecdotes.

As someone raised very Catholic, I shudder with anticipatory guilt, fearing that I've neglected to mention someone who deserves my thanks. Please know that I appreciate every word of encouragement from every person along the way.

Gail Marie Forte was my first reader when I started writing in mid-life. How can it be that she's no longer in this world where the book lives? I am forever grateful for our decades of friendship. I miss her every day.

My parents fostered in me a love of reading, and my elementary school teachers—especially Sister de Chantal (Sister Olive) and Sister Gemma—nurtured my love of the written word. This love has been the gift of a lifetime.

To each student who once sat in my classroom—I *loved* being your teacher. You live in my heart.

And, finally, to my husband, John—trusted reader, patient sounding board, recipient of endless chatter, steady encourager, cheerful voice of reason, and my personal stand-up comic—your immeasurable help in myriad ways enabled this book to reach completion. Of all the people roaming our planet, I somehow found you. I'm grateful every day.

NOTES

1. Under Pressure

1. Jaclyn Diaz, "Florida's Governor Signs Controversial Law Opponents Dubbed 'Don't Say Gay'," NPR, March 28, 2022, https://www.npr.org/2022/03/28/1089221657/dont-say-gay-florida-desantis.

2. Michelle Castillo, "What Texas' Classroom Censorship Law Means for Students & Schools," *Texas SB 3 Guide*, n.d., https://www.idra.org/wp-content/uploads/2022/02/What-Texas-Classroom-Censorship-Law-Means-for-Students-and-Schools-IDRA-2022.pdf#:~:text=Texas'%20classroom%20censorship%20law%2C%20Senate%20Bill%203,conversations%20about%20race%2C%20gender%20and%20systemi.

2. The Others

1. Hannah Natanson and Moriah Balingit, "Caught in the Culture Wars, Teachers Are Being Forced from Their Jobs," *Washington Post*, June 16, 2022.

3. A Low Bar

1. Phil Gloudemans, "BC Researcher Examines Impact of GSA Clubs," Lynch School News, Boston College, March 30, 2023, https://www.bc.edu/bc-web/schools/lynch-school/lynch-news/2023-news-archive/BC-researcher-examines-impact-of-GSA-clubs.html.

2. "Facts About Suicide Among LGBTQ+ Young People," Trevor Project, December 15, 2021, https://www.thetrevorproject.org/resources/article/facts-about-lgbtq-youth-suicide/.

4. The Hole That Remains

1. "New Survey Finds Major Barriers for Building and Sustaining Teaching Profession in CA," UCLA School of Education and Information Studies, September 28, 2022, https://seis.ucla.edu/news/as-california-grapples-with-teacher-shortage-statewide/.

5. Uncomfortable Truth

1. "About," Drag Story Hour, https://www.dragstoryhour.org/about.

2. "Press," Drag Queen Story Hour NYC, https://www.dshnyc.org/press.

3. Bob Braun, "Braun: Advocates of Privatized Education Want to End Public Schools," *Star-Ledger*, July 11, 2011, http://blog.nj.com/njv_bob_braun/2011/07/braun_goal_of_education_privit.html.

4. Barbara Miner, "Why the Right Hates Public Education," Rethinking Schools, June 2002. https://rethinkingschools.org/special-collections/why-the-right-hates-public-education/.

5. Maurice Cunningham, "Foot Soldiers for Ron DeSantis: The Right-Wing Money and Influence Behind Moms for Liberty," AlterNet, October 5, 2022, https://www.alternet.org/2022/10/foot-soldiers-for-ron-desantis.

6. Donald J. Trump, "Ending Radical Indoctrination in K–12 Schooling," The White House Presidential Actions, January 29, 2025, https://www.whitehouse.gov/presidential-actions/2025/01/ending-radical-indoctrination-in-k-12-schooling/.

7. Linda Darling-Hammond, "Evaluating 'No Child Left Behind,'" *The Nation*, May 2, 2007. https://www.thenation.com/article/archive/evaluating-no-child-left-behind/.

8. "Tinker v. Des Moines—Landmark Supreme Court Ruling on Behalf of Student Expression," American Civil Liberties Union, February 22, 2019, https://www.aclu.org/documents/tinker-v-des-moines-landmark-supreme-court-ruling-behalf-student-expression.

9. Attorney General Rob Bonta, State Superintendent of Public Instruction Tony Thurmond, and Governor of California Gavin Newsom, "Educational Rights and Requests to Remove Instructional Materials," June 1, 2023, https://oag.ca.gov/system/files/attachments/press-docs/Educational%20Rights%20and%20Requests%20to%20Remove%20Instructional%20Materials.pdf.

10. "The Freedom to Read Statement," American Library Association, https://www.ala.org/advocacy/intfreedom/freedomreadstatement (emphasis in the original).

6. Root for the Kings

1. Christina Buttons, "New Lawsuit Accuses California School District of Constitutional Violation for 'Parental Secrecy Policy' of Gender Transition," Daily Wire, January 12, 2023, https://www.dailywire.com/news/new-lawsuit-accuses-california-school-district-of-constitutional-violation-for-parental-secrecy-policy-of-gender-transition.

2. Katie J. M. Baker, "When Students Change Gender Identity, and Parents Don't Know," *New York Times*, January 22, 2023.

3. "The Trump Effect: The Impact of the 2016 Presidential Election on Our Nation's Schools," Southern Poverty Law Center, November 28, 2016, https://www.splcenter.org/resources/reports/trump-effect-impact-2016-presidential-election-our-nations-schools/.

4. Laura Meckler et al., "In States with Laws Targeting LGBTQ Issues, School Hate Crimes Quadrupled," *Washington Post*, March 13, 2024.

7. Kindergarten Dream

1. "Critical Race Theory: Frequently Asked Questions," NAACP Legal Defense Fund, https://www.naacpldf.org/critical-race-theory-faq.

2. Hannah Natanson, "Trust in Teachers Is Plunging Amid a Culture War in Education," *Washington Post*, September 6, 2022.

3. Tim Walker, "What Teachers Want the Public to Know," *NEA Today*, April 12, 2024, https://www.nea.org/nea-today/all-news-articles/what-teachers-want-public-know; Niraj Chokshi, "94 Percent of U.S. Teachers Spend Their Own Money on School Supplies, Survey Finds," *New York Times*, May 16, 2018; National Education Association, "2025 Reports Educator Pay in America," April 29, 2025, https://www.nea.org/resource-library/educator-pay-and-student-spending-how-does-your-state-rank#:~:text=Even%20with%20record%2Dlevel%20increases,$3%2C728%20below%202008%2D2009%20levels; Dana Braga, Kiley Hurst, Shannon Greenwood, Nick Zanetti, and John Carlo Mandapat, "What Public K–12 Teachers Want Americans to Know About Teaching," Pew Research Center, April 4, 2024, https://www.pewresearch.org/social-trends/2024/04/04/what-public-k-12-teachers-want-americans-to-know-about-teaching/#:~:text=The%20study%20surveyed%202%2C531%20teachers%20from%20October,third%20say%20most%20Americans%20trust%20teachers%20some.

4. "Fox's Greg Gutfeld Calls Teachers 'the KKK with Summers Off,'" Media Matters for America, July 7, 2022, https://www.mediamatters.org/fox-news/foxs-greg-gutfeld-calls-teachers-kkk-summers.

5. "Fox's Jesse Watters Accuses Teachers of Acting Like They Want to 'Groom Children to Exploit Them for Sexual Purposes,'" Media Matters for America, August 2, 2022, https://www.mediamatters.org/jesse-watters/foxs-jesse-watters-accuses-teachers-acting-they-want-groom-children-exploit-them; "Fox Host Says Teachers Deserve Low Wages Because They 'Work 20% Less,'" Media Matters for America, August 17, 2022, https://www.mediamatters.org/fox-news/fox-host-says-teachers-deserve-low-wages-because-they-work-20-less.

6. Chris Williams, "Trump Signs Executive Order Aiming to Cut Federal Funding for 'Woke' Schools," Live Now Fox, January 29, 2025, https://www.livenowfox.com/news/trump-executive-order-schools-dei.

7. Hannah Natanson, "'Never Seen It This Bad': America Faces Catastrophic Teacher Shortage," *Washington Post*, August 4, 2022.

8. Rainbows at the Sea

1. Jeff Horseman, "Why Conservative Christians Want to Take Over Southwest Riverside County School Boards," *Press-Enterprise*, March 31, 2022, https://www.pressenterprise.com/2022/03/27/why-conservative-christians-want-to-take-over-southwest-riverside-county-school-boards/.

2. "Taking Back the Public Square," Inland Empire Family PAC, https://iefamilypac.org/.

3. Temecula Valley Unified School District, "Resolution of the Board of Trustees Condemning the Teaching of Critical Race Theory, Resolution No. 2022–23/21," December 13, 2022, https://drive.google.com/file/d/1A-til-5o_wUtYhQGuzl7rxneZB-iPwR7/view?usp=sharing.

4. Temecula Valley Unified School District, "Resolution Condemning Racism, Resolution No. 2022–23/20," December 13, 2022, https://drive.google.com/file/d/1p4AhcZm1wQLj2yxkaGXcJTeSO1K85OhA/view?usp=sharing.

9. The Thing About Discomfort

1. "About PEN America," PEN America, https://pen.org/about-us/.

2. NEA, "Educator Pay Data: Teacher Pay and Per Student Spending," *National Education Association*, April, 2025, https://www.nea.org/resource-library/educator-pay-and-student-spending-how-does-your-state-rank/teacher.

3. Living Wage Institute, "MIT Living Wage Calculator," Massachusetts Institute of Technology, February 10, 2025, https://livingwage.mit.edu/states/06/locations.

4. "When Book Bans Came to Small-Town New Jersey," *The Daily* (podcast), *New York Times*, December 7, 2022, https://www.nytimes.com/2022/12/07/podcasts/the-daily/book-ban-high-school-libraries.html.

10. Journey to Misfit Island

1. "Question & Answer Guide on California's Parental Opt-Out Statutes: Parents' and Schools' Legal Rights and Responsibilities Regarding Public School Curricula," California Safe Schools Coalition, https://casafeschools.org/OptOutQA.pdf.

2. Elaine Povich, "Controversial PragerU Videos Gain Educational Foothold in a Handful of States," *Missouri Independent*, November 3, 2023, https://missouriindependent.com/2023/11/03/controversial-prageru-videos-gain-educational-foothold-in-a-handful-of-states/.

3. PragerU Kids, "Los Angeles: Mateo Backs the Blue," posted April 26, 2023, YouTube video, 8:24, https://www.youtube.com/watch?v=Dz3iOepQ5Sk.

4. PragerU Kids, "Aldo Buttazzoni Breaks Down the Truth with Jill Simonian," posted June 8, 2023, Facebook video, 33:48, https://www.facebook.com/watch/live/?ref=watch_permalink&v=784127243356643.

5. "Southern Poverty Law Center," University of Georgia School of Law, n.d., https://www.law.uga.edu/placement/southern-poverty-law-center.

6. Jessi Cruickshank, "Talking to Kids About Pride Month," CBC Life, June 2, 2018, YouTube video, 2:44, https://www.youtube.com/watch?v=9IMKpe5bmaw.

7. PragerU Kids, "Aldo Buttazzoni."

11. Past, Present, Future

1. Colleen Shalby, "Anti-Mask Politician Compares Herself to Civil Rights Icon Rosa Parks, Sparking Anger and Support," *Los Angeles Times*, April 29, 2021.

2. Mara Marques Cavallaro, "How Black Moms in Temecula Are Fighting the School Board's Right-Wing Takeover," *Nation*, October 31, 2023.

3. Terry Gross, "From Slavery to Socialism, New Legislation Restricts What Teachers Can Discuss," National Public Radio, February 3, 2022, https://www.npr.org/2022/02/03/1077878538/legislation-restricts-what-teachers-can-discuss.

4. Temecula Valley Unified School District, "Resolution of the Board of Trustees Condemning the Teaching of Critical Race Theory, Resolution No. 2022-23/21," December 13, 2022, https://drive.google.com/file/d/1A-til-5o_wUtYhQGuzl7rxneZB-iPwR7/view?usp=sharing.

5. Michael Shawn Tucker, "When Law Enforcement Killed My Brother, There Was No Video," *Washington Post*, June 15, 2020.

6. Mara Marques Cavallaro, "How Black Moms in Temecula Are Fighting the School Board's Right-Wing Takeover," *The Nation*, October 31, 2023, https://www.thenation.com/article/society/temecula-california-school-board-recall-election/.

7. "Improving Student Outcomes Through Restorative Practices," Learning Policy Institute, October 18, 2023, https://learningpolicyinstitute.org/product/restorative-practices-factsheet.

8. Diana Lambert, "Temecula Valley Unified CRT Ban Has Created a Hostile School Environment, Lawsuit Says," EdSource, August 2, 2023, https://edsource.org/2023/temecula-valley-unified-crt-ban-has-created-a-hostile-school-environment-lawsuit-says/695080.

9. Lambert, "Temecula Valley."

10. Lambert, "Temecula Valley."

11. Lambert, "Temecula Valley."

12. Jeff Horseman, "ACLU, Temecula Schools Settle Lawsuit over Ejecting People from Board Meetings," *Press-Enterprise*, April 16, 2024, https://www.pressenterprise.com/2024/04/16/aclu-temecula-schools-settle-lawsuit-over-ejecting-people-from-board-meetings/.

13. Bob Egelko, "California Court Blocks School District's Ban on Critical Race Theory," *San Francisco Chronicle*, May 19, 2025.

12. Just People

1. Albert Qian et al., "School Board Member Should Resign for Denial of Systemic Racism," *Paso Robles Daily News*, September 10, 2020, https://pasoroblesdailynews.com/opinion-school-board-member-should-resign-for-denial-of-systemic-racism/114065/.

2. Tyrone Beason, "This California Wine Country Town Is Multicultural. So Why Do So Many Feel Invisible?," *Los Angeles Times*, March 20, 2022.

3. Malia Gaviola, "Coming Out Against Hate," *Crimson Newsmagazine*, November, 2021, 16, https://crimsonnewsmagazine.org/flipbook/november-2021-issue-coming-out-against-hate/#16.

4. Malia Gaviola, "Coming Out Against Hate," *Crimson*, November 2021, 16. https://issuu.com/crimsonchronicle/docs/2021_11_comingoutagainsthate_1-36#google_vignette.

5. Maicah Cabello, "Doing Bare Minimum Isn't Enough," *Crimson*, November, 2021, 6, https://issuu.com/crimsonchronicle/docs/2021_11_comingoutagainsthate_1-36.

6. Cabello, "Doing Bare Minimum Isn't Enough."

7. Gaviola, "Coming Out Against Hate," *Crimson*.

8. Mackenzie Shuman, "Someone Defecated on a Pride Flag at Paso Robles High. Now LGBTQ Students Are Speaking Out," *San Luis Obispo Tribune*, October 8, 2021, https://www.sanluisobispo.com/news/local/education/article254792747.html.

9. Ava Hughes et al., "Students Say Paso High's New Restrictions on Pride Flag Mean the Haters Win," *San Luis Obispo Tribune*, October 11, 2021, https://www.sanluisobispo.com/article254867217.html.

10. Asusena Uribe and Jocelyn Lopez, "A Forum for Change," *Crimson*, November 2021, 18.

11. Uribe and Lopez, "Forum for Change," 19.

12. Maicah Cabello, "President of the Equality Club and Voice of the Movement; Eve Barajas," *Crimson*, November 2021, 20.

13. John Laird, "A Voice for LGBTQ+ Students: Governor Signs SB 857," press release, September 23, 2023, https://sd17.senate.ca.gov/news/voice-lgbtq-students-governor-signs-sb-857-senator-laird.

14. Laird, "Voice for LGBTQ+ Students."

15. Shwetha Sundarrajan, "Paso Teacher Butts Heads with School Board, Selected County Teacher of the Year," *New Times*, September 8, 2022, https://www.newtimesslo.com/news/paso-teacher-butts-heads-with-school-board-selected-county-teacher-of-the-year-12914947.

16. Kalani Gaviola and Michelle Rosas, "PRHS Equity Club Hosts First Ever 'Stories of Pride' Event," *Crimson*, January 29, 2023, https://crimsonnewsmagazine.org/60755/news-2/prhs-equity-club-hosts-first-ever-stories-of-pride-event/.

Afterword

1. "Human Rights Award Winner: Olive Garrison," California Teachers Association, April 11, 2024, https://www.cta.org/educator/posts/human-rights-award-winner-olive-garrison.

2. T. Jameson Brewer, "Why Public Schools Matter," Learning for Justice, June 2, 2025, https://www.learningforjustice.org/magazine/why-public-schools-matter.

Author's Note

1. Nancy Coleman, "Why We're Capitalizing Black," *New York Times*, July 5, 2020.

2. Scottie Andrew, "What It Means to Be Queer," CNN, June 11, 2024, https://www.cnn.com/us/queer-meaning-lgbtq-cec.

3. "What Does Queer Mean?," Planned Parenthood, n.d., https://www.plannedparenthood.org/learn/teens/sexual-orientation/what-does-queer-mean.

ABOUT THE AUTHOR

Sue Granzella is a writer and a longtime public-school teacher in the East Bay of San Francisco's Bay Area. Her writing has been recognized as Notable in *Best American Essays* and has won numerous awards, including runner-up for *Teachers and Writers'* Bechtel Prize. Her essays have appeared in over forty journals and anthologies, including *The Masters Review*, *McSweeney's*, *Full Grown People*, *Hippocampus*, and many others. *Pushed to the Edge* is her first book.

PUBLISHING IN THE PUBLIC INTEREST

Thank you for reading this book published by The New Press; we hope you enjoyed it. New Press books and authors play a crucial role in sparking conversations about the key political and social issues of our day.

We hope that you will stay in touch with us. To keep up to date with our books, events, and the issues we cover, follow us on social media and sign up for our newsletter at thenewpress.org.

Please consider buying New Press books not only for yourself, but also for friends and family and to donate to schools, libraries, community centers, prison libraries, and other organizations involved with the issues our authors write about.

The New Press is a 501(c)(3) nonprofit organization; if you wish to support our work with a tax-deductible gift please visit https://thenewpress.org/donate/ or use the QR code below.